CARD TRICKS
WITHOUT SKILL

Paul Clive

CARD TRICKS

WITHOUT

SKILL

FABER AND FABER

3 Queen Square

London

First published by the author in 1946
First published in this edition 1968
by Faber and Faber Limited
3 Queen Square, London W.C.1.
Reprinted 1971
Printed in Great Britain by
Latimer Trend & Co Ltd Whitstable
All rights reserved

© Third edition, Paul Clive 1959

ISBN 0 571 08929 1

TO MY WIFE

CONTENTS

♥ ♣ ♦ ♠ ♥ ♣ ♦ ♠ ♥ ♣ ♦ ♠ ♥ ♣ ♦ ♠ ♥ ♣ ♦ ♠

INTRODUCTION

♥ ♣ ♦ ♠ ♥ ♣ ♦ ♠ ♥ ♣ ♦ ♠ ♥ ♣ ♦ ♠ ♥ ♣ ♦ ♠

More than a decade has gone by since the first edition of this book was published. With the passing of the years new procedures and new effects have come into being.

In order to keep up to date, this whole edition has been revised and a fair, representative selection of new material added. In this connection, I should like to express my thanks to Mr. Harry Baron for his much-appreciated suggestions and observations.

The object of this revision has been to furnish opportunity for many productive hours of practising and perfecting; and, I trust, of pleasant reading.

I would like to refer here to a matter which is still a point of contention among magicians. Quite a few claim that I *have* included sleight-of-hand in this book, but I am still convinced that no true sleights are used. The nearest approach to a sleight, as I stated in that first edition, is the 'Double Lift'. Yet even here I hesitate to admit that I have overstepped the limit. The useful dodge of crimping the bottom left-hand corner of the lower card takes the sting right out of the Double Lift, and, I think, justifies its inclusion.

I do sincerely urge the beginner, however anxious to learn sleight-of-hand, to give non-sleight-of-hand magic a try *as well*. It will certainly give him a sense of advance, more satisfaction, and a greater tolerance of the necessary practising of sleights.

The title of this book is short for *Card Tricks without Skill in Sleight-of-hand*. Instead, another kind of skill is called for—a skill involving a certain ability to use subtleties not imagined by the spectator. There are many excellent books on sleight-of-hand with cards, to which I will refer at a later stage, but the discoveries of recent years have been so important and have had such a great influence on card magic, that it is now doubtful whether the beginner should **approach** this fascinating subject by the acquisition of card sleights. I am convinced, in fact, that many sleights are used unnecessarily, and however cleverly sleights are concealed, there is always a danger of something being seen. The tendency of recent years is to make wonderful things happen to a pack of cards with no apparent digital skill whatever. In fact if it appears that the performer does not handle the cards at all, so much the better.

It will be found that each trick is taken in two parts; first, the **Effect**; second, the **Method**. The Effect is written in the third person. I am describing to the reader what the trick looks like to the spectator.

In the **Method**, I take the reader into my confidence and talk as I would if actually showing and explaining the working in his presence. Therefore, the **Method** is written in the first person.

This does not apply in Chapter 8 where, generally, the actual scripts of the contributors have been used. This gives a break, too, in the style which runs through the rest of the book.

There is no need for a beginner to feel anxious about the tricks he does—for nobody else knows how the effect is brought about: also, the audience do not know what is coming, until the trick is over.

It is an axiom among magicians never to perform a trick more than **once** on **any one occasion**.

Adequate patter should be introduced during the performance of the various tricks, but it is a mistake to attempt making this very humorous unless this humour trips easily off the tongue. The development of patter and natural style comes only with experience. Style fits into the picture as time brings ability. It is not pre-determined.

My work has brought me into close contact with magicians and would-be magicians of all kinds; these contacts are so widespread that I have been able to feel the pulse of those interested in card magic. Many approaches have been made to me by beginners for works on card magic, but I have hesitated to recommend the many excellent books that abound on sleight-of-hand, well knowing that a full knowledge of all the sleights in these books of instruction would not only involve unessential work, but would give no clue to the riches that are now available in the field of non-sleight-of-hand work with cards.

For a moment let me address the advanced reader. Imagine a beginner conscientiously acquiring ability in the 'Pass' in all its variations, second dealing, bottom dealing and the rest, being confronted with a card trick involving the rough and smooth principle. Would he not feel discouraged? My feeling is that he should graduate from the simpler subtleties to the more complicated and more difficult sleight-of-hand, rather than from the digitally difficult to the easier subtleties.

All illustrations but one were especially drawn for this book by Wilfrid Jonson, an eminent authority on magic and a sleight-of-hand expert. His ready knowledge has resulted in illustrations both accurate and informative.

So in this book which I now offer, I have endeavoured to collate all the best material that does not involve skill in sleight-of-hand. It is a new approach to card magic for the beginner and, to my knowledge, the first of its kind to be written. To the advanced performer, it is hoped that the material collected between these covers will be of value and that these pages may become a useful work of reference.

CHAPTER 1

CONJURERS' TERMS AND ARTIFICES

♥ ♣ ♦ ♠ ♥ ♣ ♦ ♠ ♥ ♣ ♦ ♠ ♥ ♣ ♦ ♠ ♥ ♣ ♦ ♠

Although this book contains only tricks not calling for the employment of sleight-of-hand, there are numerous methods involved in which certain secret movements or preparations are featured. Here is a complete list of such, together with recognized terms in the profession. A full description and explanation of what they mean and how they are effected is appended in each instance.

Any term or 'move' with which you are not yet conversant will be explained in this chapter, all being alphabetically arranged. When following any 'move' it will be an advantage to have a pack of cards handy so that you can try it out at the time of reading it.

Box. To have a number of cards facing the rest of the pack. This is also known as 'facing'.

Break. To keep the pack open at a particular place, although to the eyes of the audience, the pack is closed, and properly squared-

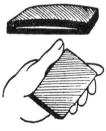

Fig. I   Fig. 2

up. This is usually done by inserting the tip of a finger—generally the left-hand little finger—or the fleshy part of the hand at the base of the thumb. (Fig. 1)

Bridge. A visible break in the pack, made by bending the top portion convex (or the lower portion concave). This bend is easily put into the cards when cutting for the return of a chosen card. The break or opening is readily perceptible along the sides of the pack but is completely masked from the audience by the fingers at one side and the thumb—which rests lengthwise along the edges of the cards—at the other. You can cut at the bridge at any time by the sense of touch alone. (Fig. 2)

Conjurers' Choice. A spectator is asked to choose a card, or pile of cards, from among a number, and, while that person is left with the impression that the choice was entirely free, it is, in fact, a **forced** 'choice'. In other words the card, or heap 'selected' is that desired by you.

Let us take the three most common examples:

1. Two cards are on the table and the right-hand card is to be forced. You say: 'Will you indicate one of these cards, please?' Suppose the card chosen is the left-hand—the **wrong** card. You pick this up and without showing it, push it into the pack, at the same time continuing: 'Thank you. That, then, leaves one card in view,' and your force is complete.

Note that you do not ask the person to take the card, but to indicate a choice. Also, the subsequent wording creates the impression that you were intending to put the selected card in the pack in order to leave 'one card in view'. Had the choice fallen on the right card the ensuing comment would then have been something like this: 'We shan't need this one, then,' and the other card would have been put in the pack. Generally the card nearest the selector is chosen.

2. Three cards in a row. In this instance the 'force' card is in the middle. It is extremely unlikely that either end card will be selected if you ask: 'Which card would you like?' You do **not** say: 'Take one of these.' Your request suggests a **verbal** reply, so that, even if working at very close quarters, there is no likelihood of

any card being taken. If the choice **should** be an end card, push it to one side, and spacing out the two remaining cards, turn to another person and ask: 'Which would you like?' The choice normally falls on the nearer card—a point to bear in mind when spacing out these two. If successful here, **you** are left with the force card, 'That leaves one card for me.' You take it and proceed in the normal manner, the other two cards being left where they are, or put back in the pack first.

If the second person chooses the 'force' card, you take the third, and picking up the first card selected, put these two in the pack —'We shall only require one card of course.'

3. Four cards, again in a row. A very simple but, I might almost say, never-failing expedient is resorted to here. The 'force' card is in the third position, as seen from the audience's view-point. You are behind the table, facing audience. With the request: 'Will somebody give me a number between 1 and 4?', you **must** have either the reply 'Three'—by far the more likely call—or 'Two'. If the former, you count 'One, two, three', finishing at the 'force' card. If two, you count from the **opposite** end of the row, and still finish at the card of **your** choice.

The request 'a number **between** 1 and 4' actually excludes both 1 and 4, so the selection is really confined to 2 or 3, although not one person in millions ever realizes this subtlety.

Whether you are dealing with single cards or heaps of cards in the foregoing examples makes no difference, naturally.

Conjurer's Wax. A specially-prepared wax which, while having a firmly adhesive propensity, leaves no trace when scraped off a surface (card, etc.). This removal is easily effected by means of a finger- or thumb-nail. It is messy to make up, and for a few coppers a supply sufficient to last for many months can be obtained from any Magical dealers. It is obtainable in several colours: black, brown, red, yellow, etc.

Crimp. *See* Locators and Key Cards.

Cut. This term is common knowledge among card players, and means the removal of a number of cards, usually about half the pack, from the top, thus making two piles of cards. To complete the 'cut' the original lower pile is placed on top of the original top pile, thus reversing their order. Cards may be 'cut' as often as desired, **but it does not alter the sequence of the cards at all**: a point of great importance in many card tricks. In card-playing, the card which is the 'cut' card, is the one at the **bottom** of the original top pile, but in conjuring it is the **top** card of the **lower** portion, and the 'cut' is often not completed, the top section being replaced after spectator has looked at the 'cut' card.

Double-Back Card. To all intents and purposes this is an ordinary card when looking at the back, but the 'face' of it is also a back. To make one of these, soak two cards in water and, while still quite wet, peel the fronts from the backs, then place the two backs together, blank sides facing, square them carefully, and leave to dry in a folded piece of blotting paper under pressure. (Two or three heavy books on top will answer the purpose admirably.) This is a most valuable adjunct in card deception and some very fine feats are performed with its aid.

Double-Face Card. As its name suggests, this is a card with a face on each side, say the 7 of clubs on one side, 3 of hearts on the other. It is made in identical manner to the double-back card and is almost indispensable at times in effecting a magical result, normally unobtainable by any means except sleight-of-hand.

Double-lift. This is the act of lifting two cards off the top of the pack, the audience believing only one card is taken. Although not difficult to accomplish, it needs to be done casually—just as the ordinary removal of a card would be. Of the many moves described in this work, this is the nearest approach to a sleight, yet I still would not describe it as one.

To perform, hold the pack, back towards the audience, in the left hand, the first phalanx of thumb midway along one side, the second, third and little fingers at the other. The first finger is curled and rests against the face of the bottom card. The right hand squares the pack; then, with a riffling movement at the near end, the right thumb pulls up slightly the two top cards at the corner (i.e. the corner of pack below the left thumb). Gripping these cards **firmly** between the thumb on face, and the first and second fingers on the back, the cards are lifted clear and immediately turned face-up. Usually they are replaced, still face-up, on top of the pack, but this depends on the particular needs of the effect in question. (Fig. 3)

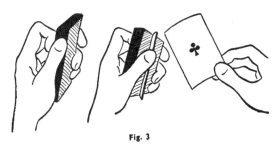

Fig. 3

It should be noted that the two fingers are pressed quite firmly at the corner of the lifted cards, thereby curving them somewhat concave on the face side.

Drop. In the following pages I have referred to the dropping of cards from one hand to the other, as in the over-hand shuffle, etc., as a 'drop'. Each little packet of cards so released by the one hand I have called one drop. The usual term is 'throw', but I have adhered to the word 'drop' as it seems to me a better expression. (Fig. 4)

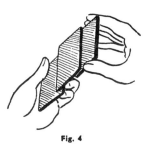

Fig. 4

FALSE CUTS

When it is necessary to cut the pack, yet leave certain cards at the top or bottom; a false cut achieves this object.

In the following methods you should have no difficulty if you follow the descriptions with a pack in your hands.

Keeping Top or Bottom Cards Intact. Apart from the slipping of one card to the middle of the pack, with this cut, the entire pack is in exactly the same order at the finish as at the beginning. It is an ideal cut for preserving either the top or the bottom stack. In the event of your requiring the top half intact, add an indifferent card to the top of stack before making the cut. The pack is held, resting on its side in the left hand, back of the cards towards the audience. The thumb is at the top side, near the corner. The first

Fig. 5

finger rests against the end of the pack (acting as a stopper) and the second, third and little fingers support the pack from the lower side (these fingers are held together near the first-finger corner). The right hand now takes the top half of the pack—but excluding the top card—and draws this section out by gripping at the sides, at near end, between the thumb at one side and the first and second fingers at the other. The two hands move away from each other, the left-hand fingers and thumb immediately closing over the cards held, thereby drawing them down into the hand. The right-hand packet is then brought back and thrown on the left-hand heap. (Fig. 5)

Keeping Whole Pack Intact. 1. The last method can be varied slightly so as to leave the entire pack in the same order. The cards are held as above, but instead of removing cards near the top, the right hand takes the **lower** half of the pack and, swinging the cards upwards a little, drops them on the table. The other half-pack is next taken in the right hand and placed on the cards on the table. (Fig. 6)

2. This is rather similar to No. 1, but the cards rest face-down on the table at the beginning. The pack is held at the ends, each hand gripping the cards between the first finger and the thumb. The right hand holds the upper half-pack, the left the lower half. The left draws its packet clear and, with a slight upward swing,

drops the cards about nine inches forward and rather to the right (or, in other words, nine inches half-right).

Immediately the left-hand pack was removed, the right-hand heap was allowed to fall on to the table (the right hand itself, of course, remaining stationary). This portion is now taken and dropped on the first heap. This may not sound convincing, but try it out a few times on an audience, acting without flurry or fear, and you will soon appreciate its genuine value.

3. Hold the pack in the left hand and bring the right hand over, as though to riffle the cards. As soon as it is hidden by the back of the right hand, 'break' the pack about the middle and insert the tip of the left little finger. With second and third fingers at one end

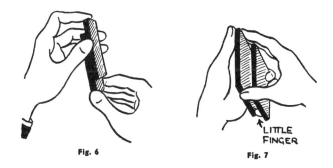

Fig. 6   Fig. 7

and thumb at the other, the right hand lifts all the cards below the break clear of the left hand and, moving to the left, drops them on the table. The removal of this packet is aided by the left little finger-tip pressing the upper packet slightly to the right, thus en-suring a clear passage. The left thumb is also moved clear during the passage of this first half of the pack, and closed in again immediately afterwards.

The heap in the left hand is now taken in the right and dropped on the first heap. From the audience's point of view, this is a very clean and natural-looking cut, but to cover the brief moment of securing a break either it should be made as an apparent after-thought or you must fill in with a few words of suitable patter. You should stand with your table a little to the left; this supplies adequate reason for reaching half-left to put the cards down. (Fig. 7)

4. Think of the pack as being in three sections—the top, part 1; the middle, 2; and the bottom, 3.

Hold the pack in the left hand, face-down, and lift off section 1, which you drop on the table. Take the remainder in the right hand and drop 3 on 1, but leaving it overlapping on the end nearest to the spectators. Drop section 2 at the side; pick up 1 and 3, pressing the end of 3 down a little. This will raise the inner end, making a break which is easily held by the thumb. Drop 1 on 2, place 3 at the side, drop 1 and 2 on 3.

(Try this out, using the whole pack, but first dividing it into the three sections, with an Ace a 2 and a 3, face-up on the respective heaps, the Ace being at the top.) (Fig. 8)

5. It is sometimes desirable to drop the cards into several piles, then gather them up, still keeping the whole pack intact, although you have apparently given a more thorough cut than the normal two-fold cut. Here is an extremely simple yet convincing method.

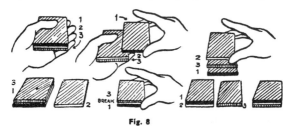

Fig. 8

With the cards held in the right hand, drop about a third of them (at 1). Move about six inches to the right and drop another packet (2). Drop the remainder between these two heaps (3). You now have these three piles in this order on the table: 1, 3, 2; No. 3 being the last or top portion. To gather up, take pile No. (2) and drop on (1); then take No. (3) and drop on the others—in other

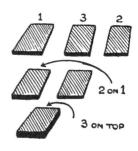

Fig. 9

words, when the three heaps are laid out, you drop the right-hand heap on the left-hand heap; then the remaining right-hand heap on the left-hand heap. (Fig. 9)

Under-cut. This is, as its name suggests, the cutting of a pack by removing a section of cards from the **bottom**, instead of the **top** of the pack, the spectators generally believing the cards to be taken from the top. This, at times, is a most useful subterfuge, perhaps for making a known bottom card into a locator when the pack is (under-) cut for the return of a chosen card, or when a prepared (rough, etc.) top or bottom card is to be brought into juxtaposition with a selected card.

Hold the cards in the left hand as though ready for an ordinary overhand shuffle, but with cards facing the thumb. Right hand takes the bottom portion of pack at opposite ends and lift them up and away, clear of the top portion. Both hands should be raised as the action takes place, the right hand, of course, rising more smartly, and farther, than the left.

If a card is to be replaced, it goes on the left-hand heap, the right-hand cards being placed on top.

The 'cut' may be somewhat simplified by previously breaking the pack with the left little finger which, by pressing top heap against left finger-tips, keeps the upper heap quite intact during the operation.

FALSE SHUFFLES

False Shuffle, or 'Blind Shuffle'. As the title suggests, this is **apparently** a genuine shuffle, but is, in reality, a make-believe. There are numerous False Shuffles, some designed to keep one, or a small number of cards, in a certain order, or at a particular part of the pack; others to maintain the entire pack in its existing sequence.

Box-False-Riffle-Shuffle. First method: Swing to the left, with the audience on your right. Hold the pack, backs towards the palm, in the right hand, the second and third fingers over one short end, the thumb over the other. The first and little fingers rest against the opposite (long) sides. With the back of the right hand towards the spectators, cut with the left hand, which is held palm towards the right, by drawing those cards (at near end) back with the left thumb, the left second finger pressing against the opposite end, near the top corner—just over the right second finger, and the fore-finger curled up on the face of the cards.

While making this cut, hold the pack just over the bended knee; now turn the left-hand palm downwards and bring the third finger over the end of the cards, alongside the second, and the little finger near the top of the long side. Tap the cards in the left hand against the face of those in the right to square them up. As you lower the left-hand packet to rest it on the knee, turn the right-hand packet face-down and bring them alongside, ready for a dovetail shuffle. You now have the cards in the left hand face-up, while those in the right hand are face-down. False-shuffle and then slide the right-hand packet on top of the left-hand heap, and you have your pack boxed in the middle. The right hand has completely hidden the move from the view of your audience, who will naturally believe you have given the pack a good, genuine shuffle. (Fig. 10)

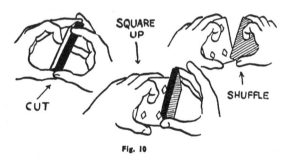

SQUARE UP

CUT

SHUFFLE

Fig. 10

Second Method. This is rather simpler, and yet just as convinc-ing. Separate the pack into two halves and genuinely dovetail-shuffle the corners together; then slightly raise the right-hand packet, bringing the back of the hand sloping towards the specta-tors and tilting the cards; at the same time turning the left-hand heap, face on to the right-hand portion. Square up the entire pack.

This will automatically disengage the riffled corners and pack will be crimped at the facing cards, ready for the subsequent separation. (Fig. 11)

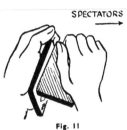

SPECTATORS

Fig. 11

In trying out either of these methods it is as well to have the pack of cards in your hands while you are reading the description, for although by no means a complicated move, its description is rather difficult.

This box-false-riffle-shuffle is an original idea of mine, but you will find on some occasions it is extremely useful, and it does work.

Hindu Shuffle. This shuffle, described under the heading of ordinary shuffles, lends itself readily to a false shuffle. If you have a chosen card, or a number of cards, at the top of the pack, you remove these as your first packet in your Hindu Shuffle. These cards (now in the left hand) are picked up between the tips of the right thumb and second finger as the second portion of cards is removed from the top of the pack.

A natural break will keep the original top cards slightly separated at the near, or wrist, end. The shuffle proceeds along the orthodox lines until it is complete, the 'stolen' packet going last on the rest of the cards; thus the original top cards are still on top at the conclusion of the shuffle.

Over and Under. This is a delightfully simple, yet most confusing, false-shuffle. In spite of having the appearance of being genuine, it looks a most careless, even clumsy, shuffle.

Hold the cards in the left hand, in a dealing position. The right hand comes over to the pack and a small number of cards are taken from the top. These cards are held between the right thumb, above, and fingers underneath. The left hand then brings the pack under the cards in the right hand, and a few more cards **from the top of the pack** are added to the **bottom** of the first packet. A few more **from the bottom of the pack** are next added to the **top** of the right-hand heap.

This process is continued until all the pack has been transferred to the right hand in small batches, to the top and bottom alternately. The two hands should share the movements as the cards are transferred, these movements blending into one continuous flow of cards from the left hand to the right. (Fig. 12)

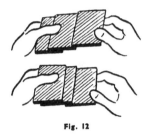

Fig. 12

Remember you transfer from the top of left-hand cards to the bottom of right-hand heap, and from bottom of left-hand heap to the top of right. The passing of the cards is aided by the fingers or thumb of the left hand, pushing the required cards into the right, the fingers and thumb of the right hand drawing the cards in.

At the conclusion the pack will be in the same order as at first, but will be cut. If you wish to leave the pack exactly as at first, you must in-jog the second packet or crimp the top or bottom cards, or use the bridge. After the shuffle a cut is a most natural move and you have your pack just as you wish.

Overhand False-Shuffle. To convert the ordinary overhand shuffle into an easy, convincing, False-shuffle, we have recourse to one of several methods:

(1) Entire Pack Intact. When the right hand lowers the pack into the left hand for the second 'drop', the first packet is picked up in the right again, by pressure of third and little fingers (which are raised slightly for this purpose), at one end, and the thumb at the other. These 'lifted' cards are now just under, and screened by, the pack in the right hand. A natural 'break' will keep these cards apart from the rest of pack. Now, when the right hand is raised again, only the second 'drop' remains in the left hand, although the audience are, naturally, unaware of this.

The right hand is lowered for the third 'drop'. The cards **below** the break (that is, the original, or first, 'drop') are allowed to fall on to those in left hand, the right hand rising clear again immediately afterwards.

Once again the right hand dips into the left, and this time leaves **all** the cards it holds in the left hand, at the same time picking up (by the same method as the earlier 'steal') all the cards hitherto held in the left hand.

In this, the fourth, 'drop' the cards should be momentarily tilted against the left thumb. The thumb tips them over against the fingers as soon as the right hand lifts the other cards clear.

Now all the cards in the right hand (that is, those just gathered up) are dropped on those in the left, and the entire pack is still in its original order! (Fig. 13)

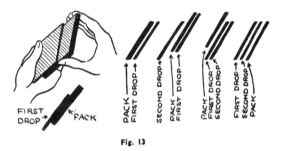

Fig. 13

Needless to say, this 'shuffling' should be done with the backs of the cards to your audience, as you stand with audience on your left. In this way, they have no idea how many cards are dropped, and they cannot see any tell-tale end-view of pack.

While making this shuffle, keep the cards in left hand standing fairly upright on their sides. Do not make any particular show or mention of shuffling; just do it casually, and repeat it when you feel occasion demands, and talk during the process.

(2) Entire Pack. (The various sections, or 'drops' are referred to numerically.) Hold for overhand shuffling and drop a small number (about ten, or a little less) into the left hand: this is No. 1 'drop'. Raise the rest of the pack and lower it into the left hand, leaving No. 2 'drop'.

As you lift the right hand away, take also No. 1 section, by gripping between the thumb and third and little fingers, carrying this off with the rest.

Once more lower the right hand and let No. 1 fall on top of No. 2.

When the two hands again separate tilt the left-hand cards against the thumb then lower the right hand and drop No. 3 in front of No. 2.

As the right hand clears the left, tip the cards over against the fingers, lower the right hand and **simulate** the dropping of a further packet on the top of the other cards.

Again raise right hand, tilt the left-hand cards against the thumb, and drop all the remaining cards on the face.

This false shuffle needs to be done fairly quickly, when the illusion is perfect. The audience are situated on your left.

The stealing of the first drop is completely covered.

(3) **Top Cards Intact.** As you make the second 'drop', pick up the first 'drop' as above and shuffle off all above these 'stolen' cards. When you come to the end of the pack proper, drop this little packet on top.

Though Jean Hugard attributes this false shuffle to Jules, the magician, a New York performer, I had been using it for quite a number of years before I read Hugard's *Card Manipulations*. Which just shows you!

(4) **Top Cards Intact.** Commence in overhand shuffling manner by dropping about a third of the cards from the top of the pack into the left hand. In-jog the next card—one card only is drawn from the pack at this second drop—then shuffle off the remainder. Conclude by cutting at the in-jog (but not including that card) and drop these cards on top.

(5) **Bottom Cards Intact.** Overhand shuffle until about one-third of the pack remains (more or less, according to the particular needs). In-jog one card and drop the balance on top. Cut at the in-jog (including same) and shuffle off.

Riffle-Shuffle. The genuine riffle-shuffle lends itself particularly to a superb false-shuffle. At the completion of the riffling (corner method) turn the open ends of the 'V' together—this apparently to push the interleaved cards in flush, at the same time bringing all four fingers over the ends of each section. As the two halves are turned level (or in other words, as the 'V' closes) pull the far end of the right-hand packet upwards a little; this closing and upward pressure will draw the interleaved ends quite free. The right-hand packet you now slide on top of the left-hand portion. (Fig. 14)

To the audience it will appear that you have merely pushed the riffled halves into each other, for the entire manœuvre is beautifully hidden by the fingers in a perfectly natural manner. (When riffling the ends together, allow only a small section of the corners to interlock. This will facilitate the subsequent separating process.)

THE INTERLEAVED V

THE RIGHT HAND HALF
GOES ON TOP

Fig. 14

Note. In the above explanation it is assumed the top half of the pack is held in the right hand. Should you take the top in the left hand you would, of course, return that section to the top. In this manner the pack is left at the conclusion of the shuffle in exactly the same state and order as it was before.

Two or Three Cards at Top or Bottom. When you desire to keep just a few cards at the top or bottom, a straightforward riffle-shuffle will suffice. If the cards are at the bottom, release these first in the riffling; if at the top, retain these to the last.

Fanning. Holding the pack fan shaped, that is, with the lower ends close in together, and the tops ribbed out, semi-circular fashion, like the hub and spokes of a wheel (or half a wheel). This is 'fanning a pack'. 'Card fanning' is quite different and is, in fact, an expert's process, in which the performer displays various fans with a pack of cards, these 'fans'

Fig. 15A

being of differing sizes and designs. This process, however, does not call for more than a passing reference in this work. (Fig. 15a)

Fanning Powder. After a certain amount of use any pack develops a tendency to 'stick'—that is to say that the cards do not separate freely and easily. This fault may even occur with a new pack of cards. It is, of course, essential that a pack should have ease of movement, especially when it is desired to 'fan' the pack, or spread the cards evenly for choice of card by the audience. Zinc stearate powder is considered ideal for the treatment of playing cards that stick. Good alternatives are talcum or good-class soap powders of fine texture.

To apply the powder use a small pad of cotton wool. Rub a little powder on both sides of the cards. After each card has been treated, riffle the whole pack and the surplus powder will be dispersed. If, after use, the cards seem to require a further application of powder, the process may be repeated. Should superfluous powder remain on the cards small black spots may appear as time goes on, for the specks of powder attract dust. These spots may be removed by a flick of your cotton-wool pad.

An excellent and easy method of applying the powder to each side of each card is to make a small gadget consisting of two pads. Each card is pushed between and through the pads. On emerging, the card will be correctly powdered on each side. Each of the pads

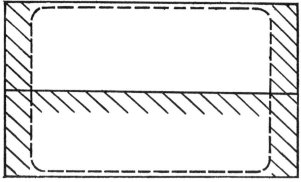

Fig. 15B

is made as follows. Take a few disused cards, about ten in number, and a strip of felt or similar material a little wider than the cards' longest measurement. Wrap the felt around the disused cards as shown in Fig. 15b. The size of the felt should allow for a slight overlap at each end and also at the top. These overlaps, which are shaded in Fig. 15b, should be glued together. The felt can also be glued to the top card of the ten or so wrapped in the felt. The second pad is made in the same way. Powder is applied to the smooth (i.e. non-glued) face of each pad and these powdered sides are placed face to face, this sandwich being held together by rubber bands placed at about a third-of-an-inch from each end of the felt-covered cards. The playing cards to be powdered are then pushed one at a time endwise between and through the two pads. On emerging, the card will have received sufficient powder. The two pads may be squeezed together with a gentle pressure, as the cards are passing through, to ensure an even distribution of powder. The pads should be re-powdered from time to time.

FORCING

When a card is being 'chosen' it is often necessary that this be a particular card. This is 'forced' on the unsuspecting selector by one of many methods available (*see also* 'Conjurer's Choice', *supra*.).

Forcing Pack. There are two types of Forcing Pack: one is a pack in which all the cards are identical; for instance, all 7 of spades. With the pack face-down, any card can be chosen from any part of the pack, and naturally it is bound to be the 7 of spades.

Such packs are known as Single Forcing Packs, because there is only the one denomination and suit to force.

There is another type, known as 'Forcing Threes', or 'Treble' or 'Triple Forcing Pack'. In this instance the pack has sixteen or seventeen cards of each of three denominations. As an example, a Treble Forcing Pack could consist of seventeen cards each of the 2 of hearts, the 8 of spades and the queen of clubs. The three sets are segregated, with the card you wish to force in the second or middle section. With this pack, of course, you can force one of each denomination: at times a very useful advantage.

Of the two types of Forcing Pack, the 'Threes' is the more popular; certainly no skill is required to force a card with either of these packs. They are obtainable at any conjuring depot; it is advisable also to obtain an ordinary pack to match, so that you can switch the one for the other.

Hindu Shuffle. This is a very easy force. While executing a regular Hindu Shuffle, ask a spectator to call 'stop' at any time. When this is done you simply turn up the right-hand packet and show the bottom card—the original bottom card. This is, of course, your force. Although so obvious to yourself, an audience will never realize that they have not had a completely free choice.

Knife-Blade Force. A key-card (short, etc.) is your Force Card. Request a spectator to insert the point of a knife anywhere in the end of the pack as you riffle the cards. You have already located your key at the near end and you hold a break there with your right thumb.

Riffle the end (near spectator) with right fingers and see that the knife is pushed in at some point below the key. (The key-card should be about a third of the way down in the pack.) As soon as the blade is well in among the cards, dip the far end of the pack downwards, taking the knife with it, and invite your assistant to release the knife, by saying 'Thank you'.

Slide the top cards, down to and including the key, forward about three-quarters of an inch and, pressing the whole pack, with the knife, firmly together with the left hand, transfer the

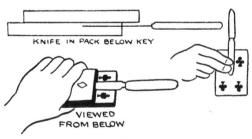

KNIFE IN PACK BELOW KEY

VIEWED FROM BELOW

Fig. 16

right-hand hold to the exposed end of the top cards, the hand also gripping the knife. Draw these down and away, withdrawing the knife from its actual point of insertion, then hold up, exposing the key-card with the knife-blade resting on its face. This will appear to be the selected card. (Fig. 16)

Short Force. Although you may doubt the efficacy of this force it is surprisingly accurate and can be very conveniently used as a mental-selection force.

With a known card over the short, square the pack and riffle the cards in a steady stream before the spectator's eyes, asking him to 'just think of a card as I flick them before you'. Using a steady, flowing riffle, a perceptible break occurs at the short, just giving your assistant that little extra glimpse of the card above the short. (Fig. 17)

Fig. 17

This is one of the many excellent examples given in Anneman's *Two Hundred and Two Methods of Forcing*.

Slip Force. This force, although less acceptable in a conjuring sense, is often preferred by beginners, as it cannot fail.

Hold the pack in left hand in readiness for the 'riffle'. The card to be forced is on top. Ask a person to insert the blade of a pen-knife (or a finger will do) anywhere in the pack as you riffle the cards. When the knife-blade is inserted, open the pack a little at

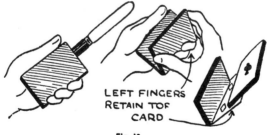

LEFT FINGERS RETAIN TOP CARD

Fig. 18

that particular spot, by tilting the cards above the blade against the left-hand fingers, and, blending the action of drawing the pack away from the knife, with the movement of raising the cards above the 'cut', press gently with left fingers on top card, **retaining** it when the other cards are lifted clear. (Fig. 18)

This (the apparently top card of the lower part of pack) is the one 'chosen'. (*See also* 'Slip (Top)' under 'Locator' *heading*.)

'Take a Card' Force. The card to be 'forced' is somewhat near the middle of the pack, and its position located by the little-finger break. Holding the pack forward between the hands the cards are fanned slightly and, starting about a third of

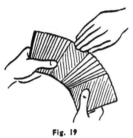

Fig. 19

the way down the pack, each card below this position is pushed singly with the left thumb into the right hand—of course, under those already there—this pushing of the cards being a continuous and natural process. Just as the hand of the selector comes forward to take a card, the cards above the 'break' are pushed to the right, not in a bunch, but continuing (apparently) the normal 'offering' process, and retaining the fanned-out appearance: the 'force' card is, with a slight space on either side, the middle 'card of the fan and, consequently, the natural one to be chosen! The 'force' card should not be standing out too obviously from the rest, but should, as far as the spectator is aware, be the card which just happens to come under his, or her, fingers at the time, for you (obligingly?) move the pack forward a little and the force card is, although not put into the hand, 'just there on time'. (Fig. 19)

Should you get to the break before the 'choice' is made, close the pack up and, with some remark, such as 'Don't let me see the card you choose', try again. If you fail to 'force' the right card you must be prepared to do another trick with the card that is chosen. You then proceed to 'force' your card on a more adaptable person.

Until quite certain of your ability to force in this way on anybody, choose as your selector the easygoing type of person, who will readily take the card of **your** choice. Women, particularly those not-too-young, are (generally speaking) better for that purpose than men.

This is an excellent force, and should not be shirked because of its apparently difficult nature, for it is simple to 'put over' and is most natural in effect.

Glide. Where a card, or cards, are being dealt from the bottom of a pile, or pack, it often happens that a certain card must be dealt at a certain number. This is accomplished by slipping or 'gliding' this card back a little from the squared ends of the rest of the cards.

With the card to be 'glided' at the bottom, place a pack on the table, face-down. Now pick it up with the left hand, the four fingers at one of the longer sides, the thumb at the other. Have about a quarter-inch of pack projecting beyond the little finger—fingers are held together.

With the aid of the right hand, square up the pack and bring left fingers over the edge of pack—still on longer side—the first phalanx of second, third and little fingers resting on the face of bottom card.

Now, with audience on your right, turn the back of left hand towards them. In this position, the forearm slopes downwards, and away from you, and the pack projects **below** the hand (on thumb side).

The first finger and thumb grip the sides of pack firmly, and the

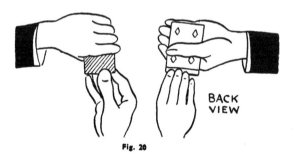

Fig. 20

little finger, pressing on the face of the bottom card pushes, or rather, **pulls,** this card upwards nearly half an inch.

The right hand now comes up to the lower end of pack and draws off what appears to be the bottom card, but in reality the next card. This is repeated for the following cards until it is desired to remove the actual bottom card, when the right fingers reach up a little higher, and draw that card away, with an identical movement to that which achieved the previous 'removals'. In this way, your audience can have no suspicion that each card was not drawn from the bottom in proper rotation. (Fig. 20)

The glide itself can be effected as the hand is lowered for the counting off. The tips of the second and third fingers are momentarily raised slightly from the face card as the glide takes place.

This is a most valuable move in certain circumstances and is very easy of accomplishment.

In-Jog. *See* Locators and Key Cards.

Jog. *As* In-jog.

LOCATORS, AND KEY CARDS

Locator. A card, or cards, specially made, altered, or treated to enable the performer to find that card, or cards, quickly and surely at any time while handling the pack.

Key Card. A key card is a master locator card. A pack may contain several locators but the key card is the most important of them all. Below are a number of key cards, each of which is particularly useful under certain conditions.

Crimp. In the following pages you will find in many instances I have made use of the crimp principle. This is one of the most useful impromptu indicators in the whole realm of card magic.

The card is very speedily crimped at any time during a performance, right under the very noses of your audience, yet without anyone having **any** suspicion that the slightest move has taken place.

Centre Crimp. As the pack is cut the cards in the right hand are bent backwards somewhat. When these are replaced they form a concave arch on the lower, straight, portion. If the end of the cards nearest the audience are held flat you have a convenient break at the near end where these two sections meet. (Fig. 21)

Corner Crimp. A small section of the corner of the card is bent down or up, either beforehand as an indicator or during a performance, at the time **that** particular card is inserted in the pack. If the card is being replaced by a spectator, you hold the pack forward, flicking the end of the cards nearest spectator, and ask that the chosen card be put back 'anywhere you like!'.

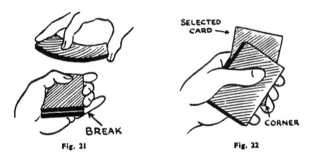

SELECTED CARD →

BREAK

CORNER

Fig. 21   **Fig. 22**

As the card is pushed into the pack, grip fairly firmly, and give a slight turn to the right. This will cause the lower right-hand corner of the selected card to protrude at the finger side of the pack. This protruding corner is pressed down firmly against the cards beneath, by a finger of the left hand. Immediately the pressure on the whole pack is relaxed, and the card pushed in flush with all the rest. The pack may be thoroughly shuffled, yet this crimped corner makes a readily perceptible break which you can locate in a fraction of a second. (Fig. 22)

End Crimp. This is imparted to a card as it is being pushed back into the pack, by a side pressure from the first and little fingers of the right hand, which squeeze downwards while the second and third fingers pull slightly upwards. (Fig. 23)

Another type of end crimp is obtained by drawing a card back over the end of the pack and pressing downwards, then pushing it back flush with the pack. This end crimp can also be applied instead of the previous end crimp when pushing a chosen card back into the pack. (Fig. 24)

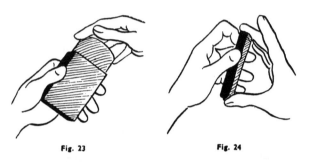

Fig. 23   Fig. 24

Lengthwise Crimp. This is a bend running down the middle of the pack and is easily effected at the time the cards are cut for the return of one selected, by holding the lower part of the pack in the left hand, between the thumb at one side and the second finger at the other, and as these are pressed together the forefinger presses upwards against the middle of the pack. (Fig. 25)

To cut a pack crimped in this way at the line of demarcation just hold the pack close together with the fingers of the left hand; the pack will open out at the required spot on the thumb side.

Jog. This is a card which projects beyond the end of the rest of the pack. In overhand shuffling, when you need to keep track of a certain card, the jog-card is an invaluable aid; for instance, it frequently happens that a chosen card is on top of the pack and you desire to keep it there, although you shuffle the pack. This is easily effected by the use of the jog. Hold the pack by the ends in the right hand, ready for an ordinary overhand shuffle. Drop about a third of the pack into the left hand; raise the right hand clear, and as you lower it again for the second 'drop', move the cards of the right hand slightly beyond one end of those in the left. With the thumb of the left hand, draw off the top card only (this card will project beyond the first 'drop') and is your jog-card. The remainder of the pack is now shuffled off. Finally cut at the jogged-card, taking away all those **below** it, and replacing them above as with one cut. Your chosen card is now on top, although to your audience you have thoroughly shuffled the pack.

In-Jog. This is a jogged card which projects on the inside, or little-finger side, of the pack. (Fig. 26)

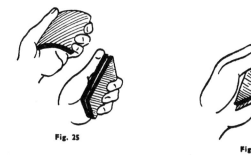

Fig. 25

IN –JOG

Fig. 26

Out-Jog. This projects from the end of the pack, away from the body. Although not so popular as the in-jog, owing mainly to its being on the side near the audience, it is at times more suitable for certain effects.

Odd and Even. Separate the odd cards from the even; Jack and King are odd, Queen, valued 12, is even. In this case, of course, you pay no attention to suits or colours—simply the value of the denominations. A pack arranged like this can be fanned to allow your audience to see the cards, yet they will not suspect any arrangement. In both this and the Red and Black location, a card removed from one section and returned to the other is naturally very easy to discover.

Pricked Card. A pin-point pressed through a card from the back at a position which the fingers would normally cover in dealing the cards off is another very useful locator. If you take an 8 of any

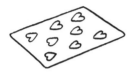

Fig. 27

suit, and mark at the side of one of the centre pips you will have about the right position. A needle-point, of course, will give a somewhat finer 'hump'. (Fig 27)

Red and Black. 1. Get about half a dozen cards of one colour to the bottom of the pack, or you can glance through the pack until you come to a spot where there are a number together of the one colour, and cut the pack there, bringing them to the bottom. Pass these cards in a fan into the right hand, then bring the rest of the pack in front and run them off singly into the right hand, passing the original coloured cards on the faces of those spread out, and the other colour in front. The cards fanned at the back thus mask the operation of splitting the other cards as you run through them. Your apparent object in doing all this is to locate and remove the Joker.

2. Run the cards singly into the right hand, one colour protruding well above the hand, the other being about three-quarters of an inch lower in the hand. Whatever the colour of the first card, that is the colour of the protruding half-pack.

The right thumb adjusts the position of each card in taking it from the left, either pushing it up a little, or drawing it down. When all the cards have been run through, you turn to one side, at the same time swivelling the two halves apart, in a sort of scissors action. Patter while you do this, then false riffle-shuffle on the knees. (When separating the two interleaved colours they must be firmly held between the hands at opposite ends, thumb at one corner, second finger at the other.)

Reversed Card. This is an excellent key or locator card. Either reverse the bottom card, or draw the top card down on to the bottom by means of the fingers of the left hand, turning the card in the process. A card placed on the top of the pack, then the pack cut, will, of course, bring this reversed card immediately over the one chosen. In shuffling the cards you can either keep this reversed card concealed or 'blame' yourself for having turned one card whilst shuffling. (Fig. 28)

Short Card. An excellent Locator or Key Card. This card is slightly shorter than the rest, having about a sixteenth of an inch (or the equivalent thickness of a sixpence) cut off one end. This should be done with a very sharp instrument, otherwise a burred

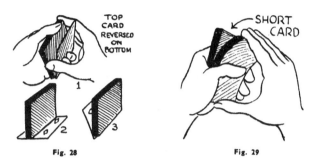

Fig. 28   Fig. 29

edge may result. The two corners must be rounded off again afterwards. Such a card is undetectable to an audience but very quickly discernible to the fingers of the performer, when the pack is riffled. (Fig. 29)

Sighting. *See same.*

Slick Card. *See same*

Slip (Top). The top-slip is the removal of a known card from the top of a pack in the act of cutting, or as a prelude to a force —this slipped card being the force card.

Hold the pack in the left hand, thumb along one side (**not on** the cards), fingers curled up over the other, long side. The right hand takes the cards at each end, and, cutting about the middle, rapidly lifts off all that portion except the top card, which is retained by left fingers. The retained card immediately falls on top of the cards still in left hand. The right hand completely masks the whole operation. At this stage the card can be used either as a force card or locator. If a force, the right-hand cards are clamped down on the left, a break being held at the inner end, and the card forced by the usual fanning method. When used in this way, the

raising and lowering again of the right-hand packet is so rapid
that no one realizes the cards were even cut. To perform this neatly
needs considerable practice, and I should definitely classify it as a
sleight. It is indeed, in capable hands, a most useful sleight, and
its possibilities are appreciated only by a select few. My reason for
including this sleight is that, as already explained, the Top Slip is
a good locator. Proceed as already shown, up to the separating
of the two portions of the pack, and the slipping of the card. Now
offer this lower portion for the chosen card to be replaced, then
drop the right-hand packet on top, and hand the cards for shuffling. An ordinary overhand-shuffle will not separate the two cards
and when you want to discover the selected card, you find it
immediately over the force card. (*See also* Slip-Force; a simple
adaptation of the slip, and force.) (Fig. 29A)

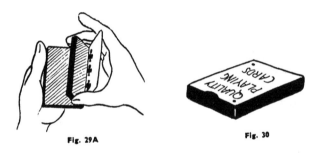

Fig. 29A

Fig. 30

Tanned. You will often find if you open two or three packs of
cards with identical backs, that the shading of the printing varies
a little, so if you remove a card from one pack and insert its
duplicate from another pack you can easily pick out this one in
fanning the cards or passing them from hand to hand. It will be
found that certain inks exposed to bright sunlight for long periods
will lose some of their strength. An ingenious adaptation of this
is to put the pack in its case, first puncturing the packet in the top
left-hand corner and in the right-hand bottom corner, making a
hole sufficiently large for the sun's rays to leave a perceptible faded
spot for subsequent identification. Of course, only really strong
sunlight will help. (Fig 30)

Another method is to wipe the back of the card lightly with a wad of cotton wool which has been dipped in **weak** tea. This, of course, will cover the whole card instead of just the pattern, unless you take care to leave the white border free.

Thick Card. This is an ordinary pip card with one centre pip thicker than the rest. This extra thickness is obtained by soaking a playing card in water, then peeling the back off the front, and allowing the face part to dry under pressure. (Place flat in a folded sheet of blotting paper and rest a heavy book on top.) When dry cut one pip out of this face section and paste it on a middle pip of the corresponding suit. When this card is inserted in the pack it is found immediately by cutting or breaking, and yet can be handled by a spectator without fear of detection. (Fig. 31)

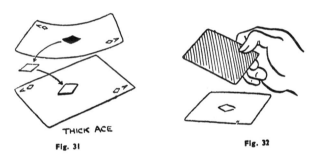

THICK ACE

Fig. 31

Fig. 32

The best cards for this additional pip are the Aces of diamonds, hearts and clubs. You can, however, safely use them with a 3, a 5 or a 9 of any suit.

Thumb Nail. Hold a card in the ordinary dealing position in the right hand, press firmly with the thumb nail and this will leave a slight, embossed, ridge on the under, or face, side. This, again, is a very helpful ruse in locating, and has the added advantage of being entirely impromptu—a decided asset when working with a borrowed pack. Both this and the last method are of particular use in effects where you deal to the selected card. (Fig. 32)

Under-Cut. *See* False Cuts.

Up and Down. There are twenty-two pip cards in the pack with more pips pointing to one end of the card than in the opposite direction. These twenty-two cards are the Ace, 3, 5, 6, 7, 8, 9 of clubs, hearts and spades and the 7 of diamonds. If you have these twenty-two cards at the bottom, with the other thirty cards above, you have a very fine locating system. You need not, of course, arrange the pips of the twenty-two cards in any one way, as you know just which cards they are.

Misdirection. Drawing the spectators' attention away from the pack at the moment a 'move' is made.

This most valuable aid to a performer comes mainly with experience, but can be cultivated, as indeed it should, from the very beginning of conjuring.

A most important point to bear in mind in this direction is that the audience will instinctively follow your glance (provided you let it rest a few moments). In misdirection you must trade on this valuable asset, or knowledge of probabilities.

Then, there is the value of the spoken word. A remark about something in view of your audience will draw their eyes in that direction. Speak to a person and all glances, at least momentarily, will focus on the individual addressed.

Indicating by hand is, of course, one of the simplest forms of misdirection, but this does not leave both hands free to make any necessary move with the cards.

Mock Pass. The 'Pass' is a most useful card sleight for bringing to the top (or, occasionally, from the top or bottom to the middle) of the pack a certain, or chosen, card. But, because it is a sleight —necessitating, in fact, considerable practice to achieve indetectably—it is not dealt with here.

The following, which I have dubbed the 'Mock Pass', I have never seen mentioned in print. Perhaps I should admit I have only seen it used by one other person; he was a street performer whom I used to watch on Tower Hill, in London, when I was a lad.

It is a cheeky, yet thoroughly deceptive, move which I have used many times, and still do on occasions.

A chosen card is being returned to the pack, and the performer, with one half of pack held forward in left hand, has the card placed on top. The cards in right hand are apparently placed on those in left, but are actually slipped under them!

The chosen card is thus conveniently left on top of the pack. The method of holding the cards is all-important: those in the left hand are held with the thumb at one side, near the top, the second, third and little fingers at the other, the first finger is bent so that the fingertip is resting against the face of the cards (the hand is held palm upwards). This is a perfectly natural way to hold the cards for the return of the chosen card.

The cards in the right hand, which is held to the right of, and above, those in the left, are held by the thumb at the lower end, with the second and third fingers at top end, the cards facing downwards. This is also a natural hold.

As the two hands come together those in the left are tilted, by the first finger pressing upwards and the thumb downwards, the lower end of cards coming under a grip from the ball of the thumb. The cards in the right hand are swivelled by the third finger pulling upwards (the second finger and the thumb remain rigid).

The right-hand cards are slipped under those in the left, then the whole pack is allowed to lie flat on left hand. (Figs. 33 and 34)

This may appear somewhat complicated to the reader, but follow the movements through with the pack in your hands and you will see it is quite straightforward. After very little practice the move is easily made without your having to glance at your hands.

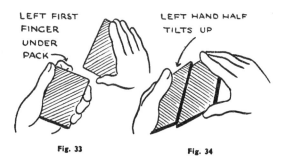

LEFT FIRST FINGER UNDER PACK

LEFT HAND HALF TILTS UP

Fig. 33   Fig. 34

At the same time as the Mock Pass is made turn to the right, also making some remark such as 'I hope you all know the card . . .'. In this way the movement will not be apparent to anyone.

You will doubtless think this is such a bare-faced move that nobody would be deceived by it. But get it right—and this is not difficult—then try it, and you will know how good it is.

In the original method the hands were just brought together and the lower half slipped on top of the previous top half, and I doubt if any member of the general public ever realized what had been done. I watched this performer (and he **was** a performer) many times and I never heard a murmur against this move of his. The idea of tilting the cards is my own, and I venture to suggest it is a definite improvement on the original method. Anyway, try both methods if you wish, and act according to your own judgment.

Move. The execution of a Sleight, or subterfuge, with the pack.

One-way Backs. Certain packs of cards have a back design which has some distinguishing mark or characteristic, differentiating one end from the other. For instance, the design may represent a view, with a windmill. If you place all the cards one way, with the view in proper perspective, then have one card chosen, turn the pack endwise, and have the selected card returned, you can locate this one card at any time you wish, for it is upside-down compared with the rest.

This is the basis of the one-way back—a principle which is responsible for some extremely clever tricks.

You would not, of course, use a pack with such a glaring difference. A pack with a slight variation is what you require, but in England this is not easy to obtain, as most packs have a simple, regular design.

However, you can make your own, without considerable trouble. The best type of pack is one in which the design is close, with frequent small markings. One of these markings, near the top left-hand corner, you enlarge enough for it to be instantly visible to you, but unnoticeable to anyone not specifically seeking it.

Naturally the alteration is made in a similar colour to the painted design; usually blue or red ink is suitable.

A more satisfactory method, though rather longer to effect, is to erase a small part in the design. It need only be a little larger than a pin-head, although you must see that it is sufficiently discernible for your eyesight. To erase, use a sharp penknife, rubbing near the point gently. When you have removed the print, burnish with a hard polished surface (often the butt of the penknife will do). This will restore the gloss to the spot from which the scraping had previously removed it. Treat all the cards in the same manner, erasing the identical section from each. (Fig. 35)

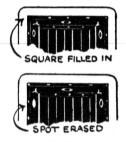

SQUARE FILLED IN

SPOT ERASED

Fig. 35

Out-Jog. *See* Jog *under heading* Locators and Key Cards

Reversing Bottom Card. In many effects it is necessary to have the bottom card of the pack reversed—that is, face-up when all the other cards are face-down.

To turn the bottom card is by no means a simple achievement. The actual turning is not so difficult, but the flick of the card is distinctly audible unless neatly executed.

A far simpler method is to transfer the top card to the bottom and turn it in the process by a 'slip' movement. Hold the pack at the ends, between the right thumb and the third finger, the back of the hand nearest the audience. The left hand takes the (long) sides, with the thumb at the top and the fingers curled round from below, on to the pack. The left fingers pull the top card downwards and round, close to the edges of the pack. When the card has been drawn down about three-quarters of an inch, the left forefinger is bent down behind and presses against the pack, while the left thumb pulls the upper side of pack down till it comes to rest against the root of the left forefinger, having swivelled between the right thumb and third finger.

The original top card is now face-up against the bottom card, but extending beyond the right edge. The left fingers draw this card in flush with the rest of the pack. Throughout this move your audience have seen only the back of the right hand, which has been motionless; consequently nothing can be suspected.

The easiest alternatives to reversing a card while the pack is held are, of course, to add a card which is already face-up. For instance, if you are on a level with your audience you can have a face-up card on the top of a tumbler. Provided the tumbler is at their eye level, no one can detect the presence of the card. All you have to do is to place the pack face-down on this card, which you pick up when you remove the pack. The invisibility of a card so placed on the top of a tumbler is a most useful secret and one which can be utilized in various ways.

If you are above the spectators' eye level you can have the card lying flat, face-up, on a table and you merely drop the pack on top. Again, if you are moving among them, you can precede the particular trick (in which you require the reversed card) with one of those where you have the pack in the pocket; in this case you turn the bottom card before removing the pack.

Ribbon-Spread. To spread the cards on the table in a continuous line, usually from left to right, and generally in a straight line. Each card overlaps its predecessor, so that there is no break between any cards.

Riffle. Hold the pack in the left hand, across the palm, thumb across the top, fingers curled up over the far side. With the right

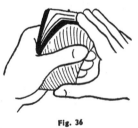

thumb at lower end of pack, place the second and third fingers over top end, and draw the cards back, then release them in a continuous, clicking stream. This is often useful when you desire to make your audience believe you are performing a sleight. When you declare, as on occasions you may wish to, that you are 'putting on the 'fluence', a Riffle will convince them that you have 'done something'. (Fig. 36)

Fig. 36

Rough and Smooth. This is the term applied to a pack of cards, or a lesser number of cards, in which certain cards are 'roughed' on their faces, and either others are (1) roughed on their **backs** (so that, when the rough-faced cards come in contact with the rough-backed ones, they adhere), or (2) the **faces** of the rough-free cards are 'slicked'. In this latter case, the roughed cards can be inserted separately anywhere in the pack, and they will move with the card below—it can hardly be said that they adhere, but there is so much less 'slip' about them that the two can be easily shown as one. The possibilities of a pack in which this ingenious principle is employed are tremendous. If you intend using this process much, 'slick' the faces of a complete pack, and roughen the faces of all the cards in another pack, using cards with a similar back design. You can then vary your force card from time to time. The 'slick' duplicate of the 'rough' card in use is, of course, removed from its pack, unless you are switching one for the other.

A simple alternative is to put a dab or two of conjurer's wax on the face of the card to be vanished. Just a very small spot on two of the pips is sufficient. A little squeezing of the cards, so pressing the wax firmly between the two surfaces, and the two cards appear as one. This pressure is often also necessary with the Rough and Smooth cards.

Roughing Fluid. A liquid which, applied to the back of one card, and the face of another, then these two treated surfaces placed together, causes the cards to adhere. Two such cards, properly squared up, can be freely handled as one card, yet, when it is necessary to separate them, a little sideways pressure will fan them out.

A simple and satisfactory formula for making this fluid is:

Spirit Gum, diluted with Methylated Spirit

The amount of meth. to be added to the gum will depend on the strength of the latter. A certain amount of experimenting is therefore advisable. Try a proportion of 50-50 in the first instance, then adjust if required. Once you have found the right consistency you will be able to mix the two very quickly. It is better always to obtain the same make, and you will have unvarying strength. Many chemists mix their own spirit gum. If you buy any in this way you may find a variation in consistency. Spirit gum is normally obtainable from theatrical depots. In this case you usually get a branded article. When mixing, shake the bottle to obtain a perfect mixture, and keep it tightly stoppered, away from heat. To apply, use cotton wool dipped in the solution and quickly wipe it across the card, using straight strokes. The methylated spirit evaporates very speedily, leaving a tacky surface, but let it dry for half an hour or more. If the solution is weak, a second application will be necessary.

If the solution is too 'gummy' and you only discover this after applying to a card, or cards, dab a **little** meth. on another wad of cotton wool, wipe the card with it, and it will take away the excess.

When the card is dry, a **slight** discoloration is perceptible, but if you use the right proportion, this is not sufficient to cause concern. If the solution has too much gum, the card has a definite brownish tinge when dry.

For best results with this formula the dried surface of a treated card should be a matt colour (dull). The film left on the card is of a slightly greyish colour, whereas if the mixture is thick enough to dry with a gloss the brownish tinge just referred to, is evident—and 'talks' (see p. 57).

A better formula, compounded, I believe, by E. A. Litzau, is as follows:

$\frac{1}{4}$ oz. Sandarac
$\frac{1}{4}$ oz. Gum Mastic
$\frac{1}{2}$ oz. Liquid Carbolic Acid
4 oz. Grain Alcohol (or Denatured Alcohol)

Put all in a 6-oz. bottle and shake. When the gums are quite dissolved strain the resulting liquid through a fine cloth.

This mixture is practically colourless when dry, and leaves the surface of card glossy.

A dab or two of conjurer's wax can, in most cases, take the place of the roughing and slicking of whole packs, so saving considerably in preparation. A spot on two or three pips is ample. Often one small dab in the middle of the card will do. It is applied to the surface to be concealed, or which is required to hide the contacting surface of a card next to it.

Shuffle Off. To shuffle, overhand fashion, the remainder of a pack (after the execution of a move, etc.).

SHUFFLES

Box-Riffle-Shuffle. This is a genuine dovetail shuffle, designed to 'undo' the boxing of a pack. You proceed as in the box-false-riffle-shuffle, but as the pack is **already** boxed, you cut at the facing cards. This is easily done in the first method by allowing the pack to 'break' while it is held in the right hand. The break always occurs at the facing cards and can be held at the 'short' ends by the right hand. The left hand then takes the cards below the break. In the second method the crimp imparted by the original shuffle will provide a natural break.

Fig. 37

With both heaps now face-down, dovetail-shuffle. Keep your right side towards the spectators until the separated heaps are face-down; you can then complete the shuffle, facing your audience if you wish—provided you imply a reason for facing them. (Fig. 37)

Dovetail Shuffle. Under the heading 'Riffle-Shuffle' two methods are explained—one where the complete ends of the cards interleave; the other where only the corners meet, the cards being held in a 'V'-like manner; this latter shuffle is in reality the dovetail shuffle; owing to this being so commonly called a riffle-shuffle today, it has been referred to frequently as such in the present work.

Hindu Shuffle. Hold the sides of the pack at one end in the right hand, between the thumb and second finger. The pack is face-down with the right hand back upwards.

The pack is brought over the left hand, which is held palm upwards, and grips a few top cards between the thumb and the second, third and little fingers. Withdrawing the right hand, these

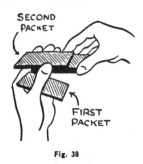

SECOND
PACKET

FIRST
PACKET

Fig. 38

few cards are drawn off the top and fall on to the left palm. The pack is brought over the cards in the left hand and a few more at the top of the pack are gripped as before and the pack withdrawn once more. These cards in the left hand then fall on the top of the first few. The shuffle continues in this manner (a small packet drawn from the top of right-hand pile being added to those in the left at each move) until the pack is exhausted. (Fig. 38)

Overhand. This is the normal method of shuffling (most common among English card players). Hold the pack in the left hand, the cards resting lengthwise on their sides across the base of the fingers, the face of cards towards the fingers. The right hand then grips the pack, fingers at one end, thumb at the other and, in raising the pack, allows a few cards (about eight or ten) to fall back into position in the left hand from the top of the pack. The rest are lifted clear, and those in left hand then rest against the fingertips. The right hand is lowered again, and a few more cards dropped from the top of the pack into the left hand, on top of those already there. This process is repeated until all the cards have been dropped, piecemeal, from the right hand into the left.

Riffle-Shuffle. This is a very popular shuffle among certain card players but is far less often seen in England than in America, although it seems to be gaining some popularity over here now. To execute the shuffle, cut the pack about the middle and hold in each hand, pulling upwards the inner ends by the thumbs. Then release cards from the thumb-grips so that they rapidly fall, each section interleaving with the cards from the other hand. The interleaving can be done from the ends meeting full-on, or from the corners. In the latter case the cards are held almost together, forming a sort of 'V', whereas in the previous case they interleave as in a long straight line. When the interleaving is complete, the cards are pushed in together and the pack squared up.

Many people have difficulty in making this shuffle while the cards are held in the hands, clear of the table. It is, however, quite simple to do this. The second and third fingers rest over the far ends of the cards, holding by the short sides, the second finger very near the corner; the little finger is curled against the long side; the thumb is held at the near short end. As the thumb draws upwards, the first finger presses down on the backs of the cards. Now, as the cards are released the first phalanges of the second, third and little fingers, which in the meantime have been projecting below the cards, are curled up against the faces, which they now grip. (Fig. 39)

If you follow the above instructions you should not have any difficulty in shuffling the cards, although you hold them well away from any support.

Sighting. (Also known as Glimpsing or, Peeking.) Obtaining sight, unknown to audience, of a certain card. This may be the bottom card; the one just above a break; or another at a specific place. When doing this, the glance should be casual, and **only a** glance. A sweep of the arm: an apparently natural gesticulation, emphasizing a point in speech, this 'sweep' bringing the pack across the line of vision—a good method of sighting, provided it is naturally executed.

When separating the pack for the return of a chosen card, you note the value of the **bottom** card of the **top** heap. (Fig. 40)

THE LEFT HAND

Fig. 39

Fig. 40

In overhand shuffling you can sight the top or bottom card; **the top** by pulling back with the left thumb (press on the back of the top card, with the curled forefinger to simplify this 'peep'); **bottom** by leaning the pack for a split-second against the left thumb. (Fig. 41)

A good method of sighting a particular card when fanning a number between the hands (cards facing audience) is to turn the lower left-hand corner back with the left thumb as the cards are opened out or passed into the right hand. This is simpler still if the first finger of the right hand rests at the back of the cards and the other three fingers on the face. The left-hand thumb crimps the corner upwards a little and the right thumb completes the move. The cards are held firmly between the fingers of the right hand. (Fig. 42)

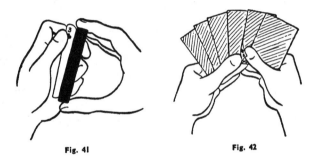

Fig. 41   **Fig. 42**

A riffle or dovetail shuffle lends itself very readily to sighting.

In overhand shuffling, a certain card at a known position can be glimpsed quite openly during the shuffle by having the cards facing the left thumb.

Sleight (pronounced 'Slite'). A secret, skilful, move by which a performer effects a magical change. Sleight-of-hand is often referred to rather loosely as applying to anything in conjuring in which the hands are used, but among conjurers it is regarded as a **change**, a false move, or a manipulation, depending on **skilful** handling of the article or articles concerned. Chambers's Dictionary gives the definition 'legerdemain'. The same dictionary defines legerdemain as 'sleight-of-hand'. Of 'sleight' it states 'cunning, dexterity; an artful trick', but I think all conjurers of experience will agree that **any** sleight requires skill, and consequently, considerable practice; otherwise it is not a sleight. There are many clever, cunning artifices detailed in this book, but I would not at any time classify them as sleights.

Slick Card. This is a card, generally an Ace, with a specially glossy face, which enables you to cut at this card, however much the pack may be shuffled.

The best method of preparing, is to apply 'Simoniz' (the car polish) to the face of the card (using a very small quantity) and polishing as directed for car use. A good quality wax floor polish will also do the trick, but several **daily** applications are needed, whereas with Simoniz one application will last for a number of performances. When using wax, apply with a small wad of cotton wool and allow to dry thoroughly. Then burnish with a circular and outward movement.

When the efficacy of the treated card begins to decrease, a further application will revive its 'slicking' propensity.

In use, you hold the pack in the left hand in the dealing position, but with the thumb pressed on top. By pressing the thumb forward towards the fingertips, the pack will automatically break at this 'slick' card, which will be at the top of the 'break'—the **bottom** card of the **top** section.

An Ace is suggested because Aces naturally have a tendency towards slipping as they have a smaller quantity of printer's ink on them than any of the other cards, and it is the printer's ink which retards the slipping of cards against each other. (Fig. 43)

SLICK
ACE

Fig. 43

Slip. *See* Slip (Top) *under heading* Locators and Key Cards, p. 41.

Stack. ('Set-up.') A number of cards, whether a full pack or less, in a certain, arranged order.

Steal. To secure, unknown to the audience, the possession of a card, or cards.

Switch. To change, unknown to the audience, a card, number of cards, or even a whole pack, for another card, or cards.

Here are three suggestions for a simple 'switch' (the pack in use up to the time of the 'switch' is referred to as the **used** pack, the other as the **new** pack).

1. A very simple and deceptive switch is this. A coat is hanging over a chair back, an open outside pocket, with the new pack upright in it, at the back.

The chair is apparently in your way, so you move it back a little. To do this, one hand grips the front of the chair and the other, holding the pack of cards, dips into the pocket, picks up the new pack, and drops the old, in the very act of assisting in the chair-moving!

It is not always reasonable to have a coat slung over a chair-back at a time when you are showing tricks. To meet this difficulty try the following 'switch'.

2. The new pack is on the table, hidden a little way behind a bunched-up handkerchief. The old pack is placed down, close up to handkerchief (actually between it and the new pack). The coat sleeves are pulled back, as though to prove 'there is nothing up my sleeves', and the new pack picked up. To the audience, you have simply put down the pack while you pulled back your sleeves, and then picked the pack up again.

3. The new pack is lying lengthways in an outside pocket of coat. Have a card selected from the old pack, returned, and bring the card to the top. Place this pack, upright, in the same pocket as the new pack and request a spectator to call a number, under ten. Remove a corresponding number of cards from the old pack —one at a time—placing each on table as produced. The last card is taken from the **top** of the pack, all the others from the **bottom.** Hold up the last card, showing it to be the one chosen, then gather together all those just counted and replace in pocket adding them to the old pack. Immediately take out the new pack, audience naturally thinking this is the pack which has been in use hither-to.

Talking. This is an expression among conjurers, denoting a sound made by an article or articles in use, the presence or use of which at the time is unknown to the audience. In the case of cards, the sound of a card being moved, or the flick when the performer is supposedly merely holding the pack, would be 'talking'. Embarrassing for the conjurer and something to be avoided at all costs.

Throw. *See* Drop.

Top Slip. *See* Slip (Top) *under* Locators and Key Cards, p. 41.

Turning a Pack Over. With one or more cards reversed at the bottom of the pack, it is often necessary to turn the whole pack over (for the return of a card, etc.). This move must be carried out secretly, speedily, and in the normal routine of the particular effect in which it is employed.

It must, therefore, be covered by natural movements.

Two simple methods are available:

1. Hold the pack in the left hand, in the normal dealing position. Lower the hand to the side while pattering. (If a card is in the possession of a spectator, you can urge that as many as possible shall know its value, etc.). Raising the pack for the card to be pushed in, you hold the left hand **back upwards**. In other words turn the hand, and the pack, over. This is a ridiculously easy turnover and one which you may think, is very obvious, but try it out, and you will find it always gets by without being discovered. (Fig. 44)

2. Hold the pack as in previous example, except that on the thumb side the cards rest against the second phalanx (instead of in the crook) and the first finger is bent down under the pack, pressing slightly upwards.

As the hand is lowered to the side, remove the thumb, and, **at the same time**, extend the first finger, maintaining pressure with the second, third and little finger. These movements result in the pack turning completely over. Immediately lower the thumb on to the (now) top card and hold the pack firmly—it is gripped at this stage between the **nails** of the second, third and little fingers **below**, and the thumb and first finger **above**. Transfer the first finger to

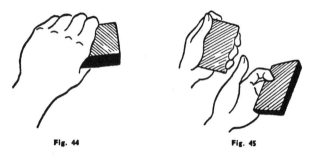

Fig. 44   Fig. 45

the underside of pack, and extend the other three fingers. If any cards have swivelled out of true at all, a little pressure against the leg will square everything up. (Fig. 45)

All this can be effected without once looking at what you are doing. Try it out with a pack in your hands while you read the directions, and you will find it all quite simple and straightforward.

Under-cut. *See* False Cuts.

CHAPTER 2

BEGINNERS' TRICKS

♥ ♣ ♦ ♠ ♥ ♣ ♦ ♠ ♥ ♣ ♦ ♠ ♥ ♣ ♦ ♠ ♥ ♣ ♦ ♠

The effects in this chapter are **not** amateurish, or evident to the spectators. They are all good mysteries, but are brought about by means so simple that an entirely new recruit to Card Wizardry can perform them successfully in the shortest conceivable time.

THREE ODD HEAPS. No. 1

Effect. The spectator deals three heaps of cards—the number of cards in each heap can vary if he so wishes. This done, he looks at the top card of each heap. The three piles are then assembled and the whole pack cut as often as required.

The magician now takes the pack and discovers the selected cards.

Method. Note the top three cards of the pack when concluding the previous trick, or under the pretext of removing the Joker, or again, as you finish shuffling. (Fig. 46)

Handing the pack to your assistant you ask him to deal the cards into three heaps. Stress the word 'deal' and he will automatically deal out the first three cards; that is, the cards you know. As he continues the deal mention that he can put as many cards in each pile as he wants. The number need not be the same in each heap. Also he can use part of the pack or all the pack, as he wishes.

Fig. 46

59

When he has satisfied himself by dealing as many cards as he wants, the balance of the pack, if any, place on one side, and he then looks at the top card of each heap. Or you can have three other people look at the top cards.

The three heaps are then assembled one above the other and cut a number of times. All you have to do to discover the cards, of course, is to find your three memorized cards and under each is one of the noted cards.

If you remember the order of the memorized cards, you can also state each person's particular card. The selected card on **first** heap will be that following the **third** memorized card, and so on.

YOU DO AS I DO. No. 2

Effect. Two packs of cards are introduced. The performer and spectator stand side by side, each with one pack in hand. Every move the performer makes with his pack, as detailed below, is copied by his assistant, step by step.

1. The pack is shuffled.
2. The packs are exchanged.
3. Shuffled again.
4. Exchanged again.
5. Any card is selected from the pack in hand, looked at and replaced on top of the pack, which is then cut.
6. The packs once again change hands.
7. Looking through the cards, the one just previously chosen from the other heap is removed and held face-down. (Up to now neither party has exposed or named any card.)
8. Stressing the possibility of 'influence by example', the magician asks his assistant to turn up his card. He does so. The conjurer then turns his, and both cards are identical.

Method. This effect swept the conjuring world by storm, when first introduced some years ago. For many months it was subjected to a myriad 'improvements' and variations, mostly under new names. On the whole, however, the improvements were more or less insignificant and the general effect was as before. The whole routine is a fine lesson in misdirection; the frequent interchanging of the packs completely misleads your audience and masks the simple secret.

There is no preparation or difficult move throughout. All you have to do is when you shuffle the spectator's pack to note the top or bottom card as you hand the pack back for him to choose one card. Cutting the pack brings the chosen card next above or below the sighted card, according to whether you noted the top or bottom card. (Fig. 47)

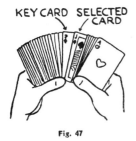

KEY CARD   SELECTED CARD

Fig. 47

When you again exchange packs to (apparently) remove the card just noted in the other pack, you look through till you find the key card and remove the next one to it—the card the spectator noted. The card you previously 'chose' you do not even trouble to remember.

THE CUCKOO MATES. No. 3

Effect. The pack is shuffled and cut into two heaps, one of which the spectator chooses. The other is handed to the performer. Each takes any card from one pile, looks at it, then replaces it on top. The performer's cards are now placed on top of those held by the assistant, who cuts the pack several times.

Both cards are named and the spectator, on going through the pack, discovers these two cards together.

Method. You name the bottom card, not the one you selected. That is the whole secret of this effect. Owing to its extreme simplicity, and the lack of effort required, the title 'cuckoo' has been chosen symbolically. This effect is one of the few in which you can claim that the spectator does it all himself and, on the face of it, this is so.

When your portion is placed on the cards held by the assistant, naturally the two chosen cards come together and all that remains is to reveal the cards at your convenience.

OVER THE PHONE. No. 4

Effect. The performer telephones a friend and requests that, having shuffled a pack, any card be chosen, looked at, and placed at the bottom. The pack is next cut into two heaps and both are turned face-upwards. However many pips are on the chosen card, that number of cards is dealt on to it from the other pile—all face-up. (Court cards count 11 for Jack, 12 for Queen and 13 for King.) The listener now reads out the names of cards from this pile until the performer says 'Stop'. The conjurer then succeeds in naming the selected card.

Method. Before you phone, arm yourself with a numbered list from one to fourteen or fifteen, putting the numbers under each other. With this list conveniently placed, and a pencil in hand, you phone your friend. You now proceed as described above until you come to the point where the cards are called over the phone to you. Don't take any note of the first card as this is in excess of the number you require. The second card called you place against the number 1, the third goes down to number 2, and so on. When you have your list complete, call 'stop' and glance down your list until you find the number agreeing with the value of the card. If there is only one such instance, that is the chosen card. If, however, there are two (you may even find three, but this is exceptional) you discover which, by the usual 'pumping' process. (Fig. 48)

Take the following example and you will see there are actually three cards where the values agree with the numbers at which they are called. These three are: 1, A.S., 7, 7-D., and 13, K.S. You would approach by saying 'You chose, I think, a black card' (as two are black and only one red the probability is that so far you would be right). If your listener confirms, you proceed, but should he not answer, say: 'That is so, isn't it?'

You will know now it is either the Ace or the King of Spades, so you continue: 'It is a high card. A picture card, I think?' and again 'fish' for the accuracy of this suggestion. In this way you whittle down, until you get to the right card. There is another point, and that is, as in the above example, that you would have a good idea whether or not it was the first

Fig. 48

or the thirteenth card because of the time taken while you were waiting for the cards to be counted.

1.	A.S.	6.	A.D.	11.	9.S.
2.	10.D.	7.	7.D.	12.	9.H.
3.	K.D.	8.	7.C.	13.	K.S.
4.	3.S.	9.	2.C.	14.	8.S.
5.	4.S.	10.	3.D.	15.	K.H.

I KNOW THAT ONE. No. 5

Effect. A spectator shuffles the pack, cuts, notes the card at the cut, replaces the top portion, and finally cuts again—several times if he wishes. The performer now deals the cards into six rows and, upon being told in which column the card is situated, he gathers them up and produces the selected card.

Method. This, at first sight to the layman, will perhaps look like one he already knows. For this reason it is best kept for use when the annoying 'I-can-tell-you-how-to-do-that' guy is in evidence.

In taking back the pack after shuffling, sight the bottom card and place the pack on the table. It is advisable to have the cut made by a second spectator, otherwise you have no excuse for taking the pack back. As an alternative, you can eliminate the sighting at this stage and, after the cut, take the pack, sight the bottom card and then cut the pack yourself.

When the first cut is made note the approximate number of cards taken off the top. This is more easily reckoned if you stand back a few feet and compare the relative sizes of the two portions of the pack. (If **very nearly level**, the lesser portion will probably contain about twenty-four cards, the larger twenty-eight—try this on your own a few times and you'll be amazed how accurate your judgment will speedily become, even after just two or three attempts.)

The cut completed, you know to a card or two just how many cards past your key (sighted) card is the chosen one. The pack may now be cut *ad lib*.

The cards are next dealt into six columns in the following sequence:

1	2	3	4	5	6
7	8	9	10	11	12
13	14	15	16	17	18
19	20	21	22	23	24
25	26	27	28	29	30
31	32	33	34	35	36
37	38	39	40	41	42
43	44	45	46	47	48
49	50	51	52		

The top card, pack held face-down, goes at position one, the second at two and so on, each card being turned face-up as placed on the table. There will thus, at the finish, be six vertical columns, the first four with nine cards in each, the last two with eight. The cards may overlap in their own particular column, but take care to keep each row reasonably in line.

Next, ask in which vertical column the chosen card is situated. As soon as you know this you will know the card, for in laying out the cards you naturally watched for your key card—and you knew approximately how many cards farther on the chosen card was. The exact column puts you in possession of all you need to know.

As an example, suppose your key card turns up at the fourth position on the second row; that is, the tenth card, and you estimated the number of cards cut to be twenty-two: if you were told the chosen card was in the fourth column, you would know it was the thirty-fourth card, i.e. four rows down from the key card. You would have misjudged the cut by two, the actual number cut being twenty-four. The card you had **expected** it to be would be the second card in the sixth (horizontal) row down; in other words, the real card was two farther on than you expected.

Naturally, when estimating how many rows down from your key card, is the chosen card, you just divide the estimated number by six.

It is at this stage, when you ask in which column the chosen card is, that the 'know-all' will probably pipe out 'I know that one'.

This is just what you've been leading up to, and you now admit that the trick is not original, but that you can't believe this person knows how it is done, even if he has seen it before. This challenge will undoubtedly draw him, and you settle the point by stating that you will finish the trick, then he can repeat it. If you feel so disposed, you can work it round to a wager basis.

If no claim has yet been made to knowing the trick, you can stress the difficulties (?) of this particular effect and, if that does not bring your man into the open, you can take it as certain that he does **not** know it (the old method). So you can proceed in comfort, and bring the effect to an entirely successful conclusion.

To conclude, you know the card. Gather the six columns up into three heaps, two columns to each heap. Keep the column with the chosen card **behind** its companion column, the cards still being face-up. Turn the three heaps face-down. Now, in the above example, the chosen card was the sixth down in the fourth column.

Have the three heaps in a line across the table, the heap with the chosen card in the middle. Ask someone to choose a heap. If the middle heap is not chosen, force it.

Take the heap in hand and announce: 'You chose the . . . of . . .' removing a card at each word and turning up the card at the last word—the chosen card.

The wording and number of cards removed must, of course, be adjusted to the needs of the trick on each occasion.

For instance, suppose the chosen card is only third down. You would then take the cards off as follows: 'You (1) chose (2) the (3) . . . and hold the third card face-down while you name it, then turn it up for verification.

It is as well, when asking your assistant to cut the cards, to suggest 'somewhere near the middle', for if he lifts off a big slice, or a very small one, the relative quantities are much harder to estimate. Should this, however, happen, you can either say: 'No, don't be greedy. Treat them both alike,' (or words after that effect) and replace the cut portion, with the request that your assistant try again. Or, alternatively, make your estimate, and proceed as above, until you lay the cards out, which you do in **eight** columns:

1	2	3	4	5	6	7	8
9	10	11	12	13	14	15	16
17	18	19	20	21	22	23	24
25	26	27	28	29	30	31	32
33	34	35	36	37	38	39	40
41	42	43	44	45	46	47	48
49	50	51	52				

This gives you a latitude of four either side of your estimated position; a latitude you should never fully need. Another point: if the last four cards break into your reckoning (between the key card and the chosen card), you can discard them on the plea that they will be 'odd cards'. Or, again, you can work backwards from the key.

Suppose the cut was—you reckon—twenty cards, then the number of cards **back** from the key to the chosen card would be thirty-one (fifty-two minus twenty-one).

When a spectator cuts much more than the half-pack, I always reckon back from the key card, as I consider this simpler.

FIVE IN HARMONY. No. 6

Theo. Annemann

Effect. Five cards are taken from a shuffled pack and laid in a row, face-down, on the table.

While the performer is out of the room, or turns his back, one of the cards is looked at. All five cards are then dropped into the conjurer's pocket and, after producing four, one by one, the chosen card is named, and the spectator takes the last card from the pocket—it is the very card just named.

Method. So typical of the late Theodore Annemann, subtlety, simplicity and finesse are the strong features of this delightful effect.

The chosen card is forced; very simply, too.

All the five cards on the table are of the same suit and denomination; for instance, the 8 of diamonds.

To prepare, the five 'force' cards are on the top of the pack, with an indifferent card—preferably of the red suits—between the second and third 'eights'.

A further five cards from the pack, including the 8 of diamonds, are in the inside breast pocket of coat, the 8 of diamonds being at the bottom. These cards are faces towards body.

You are now all set.

False-shuffle the pack, keeping the top half-dozen cards in position. Either deal off the five cards yourself or allow the spectator to do so. Next state that, while you are out of the room, or you turn your back, spectator is to turn up one card, look at it, then put it back. Warn him against turning the card by pulling up one corner, as this bends the corner, thereby leaving a tell-tale sign by which you could know the card. As you say this you show what you mean by turning up the corner of the middle card.

(This is, of course, the indifferent card.) Turn this card face-up and then, explaining that the card is to be put back, face-down, turn it over again. Hesitate, then, as though fearing this may be misinterpreted as an indication card, push this middle card somewhere into the pack, and place the next top card (the last of the 'force' cards) in its place.

Finally, instruct your assistant to move all the cards a little—show what you mean by slightly pushing them forward—so that you cannot have any idea which card was chosen.

Leave the room, or turn away, while the instructions are carried out.

Make a little heap of the five cards and, holding the bottom of coat-lapel with right hand, you appear to drop the cards into your inner breast-pocket with left hand. In reality you slip them into your top waistcoat pocket, at the same time holding the second, third and little fingers forward, and inserting them into the top of breast pocket, thereby making a little bulge which is visible to the audience, and is 'conclusive' evidence that the cards **did** go into that pocket (not that anyone has any reason to doubt such a fact).

As you withdraw the hand, you can hold the coat open wider and your audience can see the hand coming from the breast-pocket.

Recapitulate what has happened and ask your assistant to concentrate his thoughts on the chosen card. Now remove the first card—the one nearest the outside of coat—and hold it face-down. Then, remarking, 'Still think of your card, but don't name it yet', take out the second, then the third, cards. Next ask another assistant to put his hand in your pocket and take out one of the two cards still there. He will naturally take the one at the back (on the outside), but if you have any fears of his not doing so, turn the front card (the 8 of diamonds) on its side—the other card will be the first to hand, and the natural one to take.

CHOSEN CARD TAKEN FROM PERFORMERS POCKET

Now ask the first assistant to name his card. The second assistant turns his card over, and you, fanning the three, turn those also. The chosen card is not among the four. Asking the first assistant to take the last card from the pocket, hold the coat open, and the card is held up for all to see:

Fig. 49

yes, it is, **the chosen card**. (If only they knew how it was done.) (Fig. 49)

'TOPS' FOUR-ACES. No. 7

Effect. The pack is dropped into four piles. A few cards are counted, first from one pile on to another, then from a different pile again, and so on.

Finally, the conjurer turns up the top card of each heap; there are the four Aces.

Method. To commence, the four Aces are on top of the pack.

False-shuffle if you so desire, then
hand the pack to someone, with the
request that he drop the cards into
four heaps, allowing them to fall on
to the table from the bottom of the
pack. (Fig. 50.) The heaps do not
need to be of even depth.

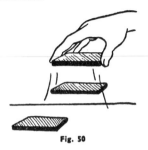

Fig. 50

This done, you suggest that one
heap, say the second, requires two
cards more on top. These are coun-
ted, SINGLY from another heap, which you indicate. Then you
have a small number moved again from one heap to another. Continue this a number of times (but not for too long), moving any
number from one to five cards—five is a reasonable limit, as your
audience must not find this phase in any way tedious.

All this while, of course, you are keeping a weather-eye on the
four Aces, which you are really guiding to the top of the four heaps.
When you have these in place you are set to declare them, and
turn them up.

I usually finish this number in this manner: 'If you were playing
a game of cards and, with a good cash balance to play for, you
had four cards left and four tricks to win, what cards would you
most like to hold?' The answer is usually 'The four Aces'. In which
case you say: 'The four Aces. The—four——Aces——' As you
make the slow repeat, turn up the four Aces, and—unusually
simple though the whole thing is—your audience will show
genuine amazement.

Some people, instead of replying 'The four Aces', answer 'Ace,
King, Queen and Jack'. To this you can come back with any one
of three good get-outs. First, you can state: 'Then you lose, for
I hold the four "Aces",' and you turn them up. Second, have an
extra Ace and the King, Queen and Jack of one suit in your
pocket. Take these and throw face-up on the table. 'There you are,
your hand. Now I'll show mine.' Turn up the Aces as before.
Third, stack the top **seven** cards, the bottom four of which are
Ace, King, Queen, Jack of one suit. Be sure these four are together
at the end of the moving of the top cards. If your assistant names
Ace to Jack, just take off the four cards from the particular heap,

turn them face-up and, as you place them back on top of their heap, name them: 'Jack, Queen, King, Ace.' This leaves the Ace exposed. You now suggest, as in the first instance, that you win—and you do, even if only appreciation.

And this is 'Tops' in four-Ace effects—in more senses than one.

SYMPATHETIC ACES. No. 8

Stewart James

Effect. The four Aces are dealt in a row, face-up. Three indifferent cards are then dealt, face-down, on each. The Aces are next turned face-down at the bottom of their respective piles and all dropped on remainder of pack. The top sixteen cards are again dealt into four piles, the fourth, naturally, being the pile of Aces. This heap is marked by turning the bottom Ace face-up. One of the heaps of indifferent cards is chosen and the bottom card of that heap also turned face-up.

Here the performer declares this effect to be a study in sympathy. The exposed Ace is transferred to the bottom of the indifferent cards and the other face-up card is inserted under the Ace heap.

Turning the two heaps face-up, all the Aces are found together, the original 'Ace' heap now consisting of indifferent cards.

Method. This is an ideal follow-up for the 'Tops' four-Ace number. As no preparation whatever is required, it is also a fine

item for the first of any number of impromptu tricks.

The course of dealing the cards, faithfully follows the description, up to the point where the cards are re-dealt. The first four cards are laid out and, taking the fifth card in hand, you remark that the last heap is the Ace-heap. Frequently, someone will suggest that 'It **should** be'. But, whether or not this doubt is ex-

Fig. 51

pressed, you replace the card you hold UNDERNEATH the pack in your hand, and immediately turn up the Ace, at the same time remarking: 'Of course it is.' Turn this card face-down again, and continue to deal until you have the four piles of four cards. (Fig. 51.) Three Aces are now at the top of the third heap, and one Ace at the bottom of the fourth.

Here force the third heap by the 'conjurer's choice', discard heaps one and two and conclude as already described under 'Effect'.

You need have no fears that anyone will notice you slip the fifth card under the pack. All thoughts are inevitably elsewhere, and no one ever realizes what you have done.

THE TEN HEAPS. No. 9

Effect. An assistant from the audience deals the pack into a number of heaps, the number being his own mental choice. One card is noted, all the cards assembled, and the pack cut. The performer discovers the chosen card.

Method. The pack is shuffled, then, taking it back, note the top two cards, in the act of further shuffling. Turn your back and hand the pack to the assistant with the request that he think of a number—not too high, say, under ten, then to deal to this number and look at the last card in the row. The rest of the cards are then dealt on the row, a card to each position in turn, until all are used up.

The assistant then collects the cards, starting with the last heap and placing it on the previous pile. These are dropped on the next pile. All these go on the next, and so on. Finally, the complete pack is cut.

Facing your audience again, take the pack and run through until you come to what had been the second card down in the pack. Now run on (to the right, cards facing you) till you reach the other noted (original top) card. The number of cards **separating** these two represents the position farther on of the chosen card. As an example, suppose the original top card was the Jack of diamonds and the next the 4 of spades. These two will be the bottom cards of the first two heaps. Now, if the spectator chose the number 7 and the seventh card was the 5 of hearts, when he collects the heaps together the pile with the 4 of spades at the bottom is dropped **on** the heap with the Jack of diamonds at the bottom (thereby reversing the original order of these two cards). Cutting the pack brings the chosen card under the Jack of diamonds. As the pack was dealt into seven heaps there will be eight cards in the Jack of diamonds pile and seven in the 5 of hearts heap. (52 divided by 7 equal 7 plus 3 remaining. These extra cards go one each on the first three heaps.) So, when you finally examine the pack, locate the 4 of spades; count forward (right) to the Jack of diamonds, and you find there are seven indifferent cards **between** them—that is, you **exclude** from the number counted your two key cards. So, you count seven forward from, but NOT including, the Jack of diamonds, and the seventh card is the chosen card; in this instance, the 5 of hearts. (Fig 52)

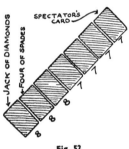

Fig. 52

(Similarly, if ten cards separated your key cards, then the tenth card **past** the lower of these would be the one chosen.)

Note. If the pack is dealt into two heaps, or four, the same number of cards will separate the key cards as separated the lower key card from the chosen card. The separating number in such case will be either twelve or twenty-five. You can bear these two numbers in mind, or avoid this possibility by suggesting a number be thought of 'not too low, in case you think afterwards the low number played into my hands'.

The method of 'discovering' the chosen card can be according to your own likes, but quite a good plan is to shuffle the pack, then deal the cards face-up, stopping at the one selected.

ONE AND TWO ARE . . . No. 10

Effect. The shuffled pack is dropped into three heaps and the performer turns up the first two cards, and, by adding the pip values together (or deducting, according to the needs of the moment) he names the value of the top card on the last heap. His forecast always proves correct. The effect may be repeated *ad lib.*

Method. This is quite a novel application of the fore-knowledge of the top card of the pack. The turning up of the first two cards entirely misleads even those who have some idea of this secret formula. (Fig. 53)

When the cards are shuffled and returned to you, hold them sideways on the fingers of the left hand, cards facing fingers. Appear to judge the exact thirds of the pack, which you proceed to cut and lay face-down, side by side. While cutting in this manner you have sighted the top card by drawing it back with the left thumb. All you need to do now, when you turn up the top cards of the first two piles is to add, deduct, multiply, or divide, in such manner that you come to the value of the known card, which you then turn up. For instance, suppose the card at the top of the third pile is the Queen of clubs. On the other two piles you turn up a 6 and a 10. You now say: 'Six and ten equal sixteen; deduct the ten. Multiply the six by two, gives twelve. The last card must be a Queen.' You then turn up the known card—and there you are!

Take another two or three examples: Suppose you turn up a 5 and King and you know the last heap is topped by an 8. Say: 'King, 13, minus 5 equals 8.' As you say this you turn up the last card. Again, you turn up, say, a 10 and a Queen, and you know the last card is a 4. Here you have to be somewhat accommodating, so you remark: 'Ten from twelve leaves two; there's two cards; two times two equals four.' And again you turn up the top card of the last heap.

One more example: You turn up an Ace and a Jack. 'One from eleven leaves ten; add the numbers of ten (1 and 0) equals one, and we have another Ace.'

Alternatively with this last number you could have said: 'Ace and Knave; the Knave's a rogue, so we want nothing to do with him; that leaves the Ace, and here we have another Ace.'

These few examples actually turned up as I was cutting the cards while writing the above description. From these you will see that, whatever you turn up, you can, by a certain amount of wangling, arrive at the value of the third card. The patter, and the showing of these first two cards, will puzzle your audience to a considerable extent, and you will find this particular effort more memorable than many which **you** know are on a higher plane.

TURN AGAIN, WHITTINGTON. No. 11

Effect. Several cards are laid face-up in a row and, while the performer's back is turned, one, or any number of the seven, is turned end for end. The performer then names the moved cards.

Method. The cards which are placed out are all 'pip' cards. By examining a number of 'pip' cards, particularly odd numbers, you will find that most of the pips on each card are pointing towards one end of the card, and this is the secret of the whole effect. (Fig. 54)

When you place the cards out, you have all of them with the majority of the pips pointing either away or towards you, remembering, of course, in which direction they are pointed. When the

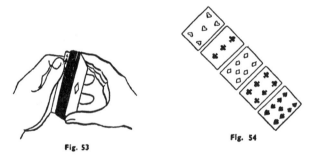

Fig. 53

Fig. 54

card, or cards, have been turned, and you return to the table, you have very little difficulty in stating which cards are not in their original positions. Before doing this, however, it is as well to look along the row, apparently seeking some tell-tale marking on the cards. You then push out of line those turned, then gather up the rest, and, pointing, declare that those alone were altered. You can then pick them up, and as you add them to the others, again turn them in the right direction, and you are ready to repeat the experiment.

Here are some of the cards which you can most easily detect: 3, 5, 6, 7, 8 and 9 of spades, clubs and hearts, and the 7 of diamonds.

THE MARK OF AGE. No. 12

Effect. A spectator shuffles the pack and removes any card. While the spectator holds one end of the card, the performer holds the other and also the free hand of the spectator. The spectator then returns the card to the pack, again shuffling. Without any questions the performer takes the pack and deals the cards into two heaps. Suddenly he stops and asks for the name of the card selected. Immediately this is stated he turns up the card in his hand; it is the very one just named.

Method. An old pack is required for this effect. If you examine an old pack of cards you will find every card has some identifying mark by which it is easily distinguishable. This, of course, applies to the back and the face. The mark may be a smudge, a crease, a spot of grime, or any other blemish which naturally results from the long use and wear of a pack. You will now realize why you have to hold one end of the card; it is **not** to obtain any mental telepathy but to give you the opportunity of looking unobtrusively at the back of the card.

Should you have any difficulty in readily distinguishing the mark you are seeking—and of course it may be on any part of the back, in the design, or round the edge— you can have recourse to another method: Have the spectator put the card on the table and just place the fingertips on the extreme end, you doing the same on your side. If you are both seated you will have ample opportunity of finding the mark while you are pattering about vi-

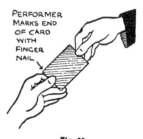

PERFORMER
MARKS END
OF CARD
WITH
FINGER
NAIL

Fig. 55

brations and sympathy. Still another alternative is to press your fingernail into the face of the card when you and the spectator hold it between you. In this event you must note, of course, whether the card is returned to the pack with the embossed nail-mark near you or towards the spectator and take note how the pack is situated when handed to you for dealing out. If you seek the nail bulge you will find this, of course, by feeling with the thumb in the act of dealing. If you are looking for the tell-tale mark, you naturally spot this with the eye. (Fig. 55)

CHAPTER 3

IMPROMPTU MYSTERIES — TRICKS WITH ANY PACK, AT ANY TIME

♥ ♣ ♦ ♣ ♥ ♣ ♦ ♣ ♥ ♣ ♦ ♣ ♥ ♣ ♦ ♣ ♥ ♣ ♦ ♣

FACE YOUR NEIGHBOUR. No. 13

Effect. One card is selected and returned to the pack. A second card is next taken and turned face-up and pushed into the pack while the performer's back is turned. The conjurer then remarks on the apparent impossibility of intentionally inserting the face-up card within a given number of the first card. It would be even more difficult, says the magician, to place the two cards next to each other. The pack is then spread out, face-down, and there, next to the face-up card, is the original chosen card.

Method. The first chosen card is brought to the top of the pack. (A simple method is by keeping a break when card is returned, then riffle-shuffling, thereby bringing the chosen card on top.)

You turn your back while the pack is left on the table, and ask another person to remove one card, turn it face up and insert it in any part he likes. When this is done you should again face the audience and, picking up the pack, you remark: 'You did place one card face-up?' As you say this you start removing the cards from the top of the pack, one at a time, into the other hand, but after doing this with about half a dozen cards, push the cards from the top of the pack into the other hand **without** altering their arrangement, until you come to the face-up card. (Fig. 56)

You then place all the cards just pushed off the pack on to the chosen card (the bottom card of this heap is now, of course, the first chosen card) and square up the pack, at the same time remarking: 'You must excuse my doubts, but the other day someone turned the whole pack over, and, naturally, that was not in the trick.' You place the pack down and, as already described, draw attention to the extreme doubt of being able to place the face-up card within a specified number of the first chosen card.

When the final examination of the pack is made, discovering the two cards together, allow this to be done by a member of the audience, and the effect will certainly be most gratifying.

THE OVERHAND SPELLER. No. 14

Effect. Any chosen card is shuffled back into the pack and is then spelt out one card for each letter. On the last letter, the chosen card is turned up.

Method. Of the vast array of spelling tricks this is undoubtedly the most straightforward of the impromptu versions.

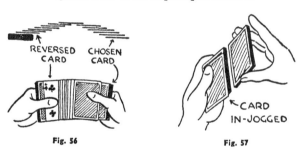

Fig. 56   Fig. 57

The chosen card is brought to the top of the pack and in overhand shuffling **mentally** spelt out as you shuffle the cards off one at a time. When you reach the end of the spelling, in-jog the next card, continue the shuffle without any pause and then cut immediately below the in-jog and you are ready to spell the name of the card aloud. (Fig. 57)

In this method, of course, you must know the chosen card and you must be able to bring it to the top. The first you accomplish by one of the methods described elsewhere in this book (by pre-arrangement, or sighting while shuffling, etc.). The second you bring about by crimping, bridging or mock-pass.

Before you begin the spelling ask spectator the name of the card, as it is inadvisable to let him know that you already know it; then proceed with the spelling.

A CUT IN THE DARK. No. 15

Effect. The spectator cuts a pack into two heaps and chooses one heap. Turning this heap face-up he selects one card and places it on top, all the cards still being face-up. The performer takes the other heap, which is face-down, putting this on top of the first pile. There is now, more or less, half the pack face-up, the rest face-down on top; in other words the pack is what is known as 'boxed'.

The performer states his intention of causing the chosen card to vanish from its present position. Flipping the cards, he then separates them but neither of the face cards is the one chosen. Turning all the cards face-down, the pack is now shuffled, then covered with a handkerchief. Under cover of the handkerchief, the spectator cuts the pack, actually cutting at the previously chosen card.

Method. After the cutting of the cards, when the spectator has taken his heap, you pick up the other, and while he is selecting his card you reverse the bottom card of your portion. His cards are now face-up, with his chosen card in full view. You place your stack on top and, after declaring your intention of causing his card to vanish from its position, you flip the pack, top and bottom, with your fingertip, turning the pack over in doing this, but remembering in which portion his card is now placed; then separate the cards at the point where they face each other and, showing both the face cards, turn the two sections face-down, place them on the table, side by side, then show the top cards. Push these top cards into their own heap and, once more showing the bottom cards, take these out and push them into their own heaps, being careful, of course, not to expose the next card of either heap.

Riffle-shuffle the two piles together, keeping the chosen card at the bottom. You now place the pack under a handkerchief and immediately it is out of sight turn the cards face-up. (An ordinary linen handkerchief is not thick enough as the card can be seen through. It is best to use a coloured handkerchief of some type.)

Now ask the spectator to cut the pack through the handkerchief. He does this, of course, by holding the pack from above and your hand is placed underneath, so that he leaves the lower part of the cut in your hand. As you bring these cards into view you turn them over so that they are face-down. (Fig. 58.) Again putting your hand under the handkerchief you take the rest of the pack and bring it forward, also face-down, then turning the chosen card to view.

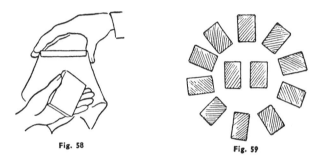

Fig. 58   Fig. 59

TEN STEPS TO FREEDOM. No. 16

Paul Clive

Effect. Two chosen cards are shuffled back into the pack. The performer now tells the story of 'A Famous Prison-Camp Breakout during the Last War'. In order to illustrate the story an assistant from the audience is given the pack to deal into ten heaps, making a small circle of the heaps. The two remaining cards are placed in the centre of the circle.

The story goes that the circle of cards represents a special prisoner-of-war compound, each pile being a small strongpoint, manned by a number of troops. (Fig. 59)

As is natural under the circumstances, all the prisoners have ideas of escape. Two such prisoners actually made the attempt and are represented here by the two cards in the middle. To all appearances they are just like any of the other prisoners—here the two cards are turned face-up and shown. Again putting them face-down the conjurer is about to continue his story when he suggests it might be better to use two cards which are not known to any-one. The assistant then collects two cards from anywhere round the circle, from the top, or inside, the heaps, and these are changed for the two just shown. (1)

'You may think there is a rather extraordinary number of guards,' says the performer. 'But then these were very special prisoners, whose escape must be prevented at all costs.' (2)

The performer continues his story: 'These prisoners decide to try and escape in a bold and novel manner. They dress themselves in the uniforms of their captors and, knowing that each evening several batches leave their strongpoints to go down into the town, they decide to mingle with them just prior to departure. They do this.' Here the two cards are placed in, or on, any two heaps by the spectator. (3.) Those two heaps are pushed outside the circle.

'No sooner has the escape succeeded than it is detected. Im-mediately, two further batches of troops are sent into the town to join their comrades, and all seek the missing men.' Here two other piles are pushed out of the circle, and the four so displaced are stacked into one heap. (4.) 'They don't succeed at first in capturing their quarry. As their search extends they gradually separate into search parties.' To illustrate this the cards are dealt into two heaps. (5)

Saying 'Have they found their men?' the conjurer turns up one pile (6), shows the cards to the audience and says 'No'. The remain-ing cards are again dealt into two piles, and again one is inspected. This process is repeated until only two cards remain. These prove to be the originally chosen cards.

Method. The effect sounds very lengthy but has been set out in full in order to acquaint you with the sequence of the events of the story and to facilitate the description of the working.

When the chosen cards are returned, keep a break at this point, then, separating the pack at the break, 'dovetail-shuffle' the two halves together, bringing the chosen cards to the top. Hand the pack to the assistant to deal out ten cards in a circle, then for him to continue dealing round until he has only two cards left.

The chosen cards are, of course, the first two dealt, and these two heaps you must bear in mind.

Now taking the bracketed numbers in the 'Effect' description as we come to them, we have:

(1) Ask the spectator to exchange the cards for any other two, either from the top, or any other part of the heaps.

(2) Here you take one of the heaps with the chosen card at the bottom and say: 'Let's see, how many cards are there at each strongpoint?' and, counting them out singly, you reverse their order, bringing the selected card to the top.

(3) Should your assistant put one on the heap you reversed, remark: 'You can bury it in the pile if you like,' and, suiting the action to the words, you take the card just placed on top, and shove it in lower down. It is usual for at least one of the heaps chosen to be a 'prisoner' heap. This is because, when dealing out the first ten cards, your helper will start just in front of himself and work the circle away. Also, he will normally take the piles closest to him when he has to select.

(4) Here look round as though wondering which two piles to take; then remove those with the selected cards. If, and this does happen, the two piles with the 'escaping prisoners' contain the **selected** cards, you can give your assistant the choice of indicating the second pair of piles to be removed from the circle. In assembling the heaps you place a five-card pile down first. On this goes the pile with the chosen card at the **bottom**; on this again, the other indifferent pile. The heap with the chosen card at **top** is placed on last. (The two chosen cards must rest sixth from the bottom, and at the very top. All, of course, are face-down.)

Should neither of the 'prisoner' heaps be a selected-card heap, take up the bottom-selected-card-heap first; pick up one 'prisoner' pile, leaving, as though by mistake, one card on the table. Drop the 'prisoner' pile on the other; then 'seeing' the card left behind, put this on top and continue as already outlined.

(5) Deal the second card to the right of the first; put the third on the first and so on, alternately, on the two piles.

(6) Turn up the right-hand pile. (The right-hand lot is always the discarded heap.) Continue in this manner, dealing each time into two heaps and turning the right-hand pile face-up, until you

have only two cards remaining in the left hand. These will be the chosen cards.

IN THE BACK. No. 17

Effect. A shuffled pack, from which a card is selected, is put into the performer's hands, which are held behind his back. The chosen card is then pushed into the pack, which is still held behind the back, and may be shuffled again. The conjurer then produces the chosen card.

Method. Although so very effective, the working is extremely simple. When the card is pushed into the pack you hold the cards firmly, with the result that the selected card does not go flush. Give a slight twist to the pack while the assistant is still pressing the card in, and one corner will project a little. This corner you crimp, either by the fingers or thumb, according to which way you turn the edges of the pack. The crimping is done in a split-second and is not detectable to your assistant be-cause it is hidden by the very fingers which do it. (Fig. 60)

CORNER OF CARD

Fig. 60

Relaxing the pressure you allow, and can even assist, the pack to be squared up. Although the pack may be further shuffled you have no diffi-culty in locating the card, which you withdraw and, as you hold it up, straighten out the crimp with the fin-ger tips.

Should you not feel happy about concluding the trick behind your back, bring the cards to the front and in an overhand shuffle locate the crimped card, in-jog and produce from behind the back or otherwise as you desire.

NEIGHBOURLY REVERSE. No. 18

Effect. A member of the audience shuffles the pack and cuts it into two heaps. One heap is then chosen. The performer takes the other. The spectator removes any card from his heap, looks at it and places it on top, while the conjurer turns his back. The conjurer's pile is then put on top of all.

The assistant now takes the pack and, holding this behind his back, he moves the top card and pushes it in near the bottom. The bottom card he inserts near the top. The (next) top card he reverses and pushes in somewhere near the middle. Examining the pack, he now discovers his selected card is right next to the reversed card.

Method. You reverse the bottom card and the second from the top when you turn away with your half-pack, while assistant chooses his card from the other half. When you replace your heap on his, your lower reversed card naturally comes next to his selected card. The other moves simply follow according to the effect already described, and the mystery is complete. (Fig. 61)

CHOSEN BOX NUMBER. No. 19

Effect. A member of the audience is asked to select mentally any card as the performer passes them in front of the eyes, and to note at what position this card lies. A second number is chosen by another person and, counting down, the selected card is turned up at the second number indicated.

Method. The pack is shuffled and the cards slowly passed from the top of the pack, which is held in the left hand, singly into the

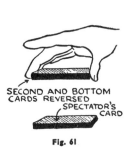

SECOND AND BOTTOM
CARDS REVERSED
SPECTATOR'S
CARD

Fig. 61

Fig. 62

right, without disturbing the order. Give your assistant plenty of
time to make a choice (without dragging out the effect) remembering to stress that the position occupied from the top of the pack
must also be noted. To prevent any doubt in this direction, count
the cards as you remove them, calling 'One, two, three, four', etc.,
as the cards are dealt off. (Fig. 62.) When you have counted off
about a dozen or so, ask if the card has yet been noted; if not,
the hint will be taken, and a choice made soon afterwards. When
you are satisfied the choice has been made, close up the pack, and
as you ask a second person to think of a number, which you suggest should be between twenty and thirty, turn with your right side
towards the audience, and, separating the pack roughly into two
halves, riffle-shuffle on your left knee in a similar manner to the
false riffle-shuffle, but instead of replacing the top portion, which
is in the right hand, **on** the lower, place the two 'halves' face to
face. If you stand in front of a mirror and try this over two or
three times, with your right side to the mirror, you will find it very
simple to box the cards in this manner without your audience
being able to see anything of the manœuvre. (*See* Box False Riffle-
Shuffle, p. 23.)

Now with the cards in the left hand, thumb one side, second,
third and little fingers extending well beyond the other, and the
first finger bent down underneath—drop the hand to the side and
turn the pack over by releasing the thumb as you extend the first
finger; then replace the thumb on this side and withdraw the first
finger, which now joins the remaining fingers underneath.

As you turn the pack, ask the first person the number at which
his card stood. Start to count this number, removing cards from
the (now) top of the pack as you count, and when you have reached
about number six, ask the second person: 'And what number did
you think of?' As you repeat the number they name, mentally
deduct the first from the second, and continue counting until you
have reached either the first person's number, or the difference,
whichever is the less. For instance: if the first person thought of
9 and the second number was 22—the difference, of course, is
13—you will count down to number nine, turn up that card and
say: 'Is that the card you thought of?' Naturally the reply is 'No'.
You count four more cards from this side, then pause for a

moment, and as you lower the hand once again to turn the pack over, make some remark such as 'I hope this turns out all right, but then it usually does'.

Then count off the further nine cards from the (original) top, continuing the count. This will bring you to the '22' and you turn up the original, chosen, card.

When counting out the cards after boxing them, be sure to hold them closed at the end nearest the audience as the riffle-shuffling will have bent the two halves back a bit. When you turn up the chosen card all eyes will naturally fall upon it. This gives you convenient opportunity for cutting the cards at the break, and another 'knee' riffle-shuffle will enable you to get rid of the boxing effect in the same way as you previously made it.

This effect is based on an item by Jean Hugard, in Volume 1 of his very excellent *Card Manipulations*. In that effect, instead of riffle-shuffling as suggested above, the boxing of the cards is done while they are held behind the back. Excuse for this is afforded by your looking intently into the eyes of the two spectators, requesting them to concentrate on the numbers they have thought of.

HAIR-RAISING. No. 20

Effect. A hair is 'sensitized' by drawing through the performer's fingers; a selected card is shuffled into the pack. The hair is now dangled over the pack, just touching the cards. As you gently draw the hair upwards, the selected card rises from the pack and is passed for examination.

Method. This is a good example of 'cod' conjuring. The 'magic' may or may not be regarded as real but in any case the effect is amusing entertainment.

To begin with, the hair is non-existent. You have any card chosen, then placed on top of the pack. Now ask 'any lady with strong hair' to spare you one strand. Look around expectantly, then glance at a gentleman near-by (choose your man with reasonable care) and say: 'Oh, thank you, sir, I'll have the loose hair on your coat. Gentlemen prefer blondes, but not always.' Apparently pick a hair off his shoulder and draw it between the hands, holding them about eight inches apart. 'Nice black hair, sir; very convenient—for this experiment I mean.' Hold the 'hair' up at arm's length in one hand and with the other take it between the first finger and thumb, briskly drawing this hand downwards, creating the impression you are pulling the hair between the finger and thumb. Repeat this movement a few times, then lay the hair down. Now with the same finger and thumb rub the back of the card, 'to sensitize the chosen card as well'. False-shuffle, retaining the selected card on top.

Lying sideways in the left hand, one end of the pack is held loosely in the crook of the thumb, and rests against the little finger, which is curved somewhat for this purpose. (The back of the hand is nearest the audience.)

The right hand takes up one end of the 'hair' and holds it above the pack, gradually lowering it until it 'touches' the side of the pack. Expressing success, raise the right hand a little, at the same time pushing the back card up slightly with the left thumb, which has been bent for the purpose, then letting it fall back. With an air of disappointment, you suggest it may work better from the end of the card. Shift the right hand to a position over the end of the pack (away from the thumb) and, with the thumb bent right down into the hand, draw the card upwards and inwards (a natural swivel, resulting from the straightening and raising of the thumb, which presses lightly against the chosen card). (Figs. 63 and 64)

With the card well raised, hold it steadily for a moment or two; then, with a lowering and circular movement, appear to twist the 'hair' round the first finger of the right hand. (Each time the finger

Fig. 63

Fig. 64

moves slightly to the right in this winding movement, lower the card—just a **very little**; then raise it again as the finger moves back to the left. It is a good plan to try this out a few times in the privacy of your own home, using a genuine hair, or length of cotton, and fixing it to the card with a dab of wax. This will show you the exact movements to simulate.)

When all the 'hair' except about a quarter-of-an-inch has been thus wound up, grip the corner of the card between the right forefinger and thumb and lift it clear of the pack, at the same time lowering the left thumb.

Ask if this is the chosen card and, dropping the pack on the table, pass out the card and secure a horse-hair previously placed just inside the trousers pocket or other convenient spot, and, walking towards the gentleman from whom you 'borrowed' the 'hair', pretend to unwind it from the finger, at the same moment drawing the length of horse-hair out and asking the gentleman if he would like it back.

The suggestion that horse-hair should be used is entirely on the assumption that you want to get the utmost humour out of this number, but you can, of course, delete this idea if you so desire.

Well-used cards are inclined to stick a little and sometimes when you raise the chosen card the next one will come up with it. Should you fear this is likely to happen, bend back the ends of the selected card at the conclusion of the false-shuffle, and it will rise on its own. Alternatively you can damp the left thumb, when the card will adhere sufficiently to enable you to do the rising effect.

SPECTATOR'S FOUR ACE. No. 21

H. Lloyd

Effect. A member of the audience shuffles the pack and takes out the four Aces, which are dealt into a row, face-down. On each Ace three more cards are dealt; then all are gathered up, placed on the top of the pack, and the pack is cut.

The spectator deals the cards into four piles again, and the Aces all appear at the top, middle or bottom of any heap, as desired by the assistant. The pack throughout has been handled by the assistant only, the performer not even touching any card.

Method. When the spectator is sorting out the Aces, you note the bottom card of the pack. The twelve cards dealt on to the Aces are naturally taken from the top of the pack. The four heaps of four cards each are placed on each other, then all on the top of the remainder of the pack. Request the assistant to deal the cards face-up from the top into four piles, one card to each pile, in rotation.

As soon as this is started, ask in which heap it is desired the Aces should appear. Whatever pile is selected, you know that the first card **following the key card** must be dealt on to the heap to the **right** of the **chosen** pile. For example: if the third heap is indicated for the Aces, the first card after the key must be put on the fourth pile. As soon as the key card is turned up, stop your assistant with some such remark as 'Just a moment. I didn't ask you whether you wanted the Aces at the top of the pile, near the middle or at the bottom, did I?' Naturally the reply is 'No'. You now give that choice.

Whatever the choice may be, you next ask him to continue dealing, but to deal the cards **face-down**. Also the first face-down card you indicate to be placed on the heap to the right of the 'Ace' pile.

If the Aces are wanted at the top of the pile, again request your assistant to deal the cards face-up as soon as the sixteen face-down cards have been dealt. (You don't, of course, tell him to deal face-up, until he has dealt these sixteen cards.)

If the Aces are to be at the bottom or near the middle, have all the remaining cards dealt face-down.

The Ace pile is now taken and if Aces are required:

    At the top—Have the face-down cards removed and put on top of the face-up cards, then turned over, one by one.

    In the middle—Have the whole pile gathered up, then turned completely over and spread out.

    At the bottom—The face-up cards are turned face-down and put on top of the other four.

The foregoing may sound complicated but is really quite simple.

In tabulated form, here are the steps progressively for the first part of the trick:

1. Note the bottom card.
2. When spectator starts dealing, ask in which heap the Aces are wanted.
3. Watch for the key card, then call 'Stop'.
4. Four cards face-down on **each** pile, in single rotation, the first card going on the heap to the right of the Ace pile. (If the Ace pile is the fourth heap, the first face-down card will go on the first heap.)

If you wish to dispense with the 'top, middle or bottom' idea, you can call the second 'stop' when the sixteen face-down cards are dealt, and request that these be turned face-up. Your excuse for first calling 'stop', when adopting this course, is to ask your helper not to deal too quickly, and 'perhaps we'll have a few face-down now'.

The routine as suggested above is rather an embellishment on the original of Mr. Lloyd's, in which case the cards were not dealt into four piles until you were ready to deal the Aces with their indifferent cards.

FOUR-DAY WEEK. No. 22

Effect. The performer displays four cards, one of which is mentally selected. Turning these cards with backs to the audience, they are mixed up, then three placed in the pack, the one remaining being put in the conjurer's pocket. Asking the name of the chosen card, the magician removes the one from his pocket; it is the mental-selection of the assistant!

THREE
CONCEALED
CARDS

Fig. 65

Method. You really have seven cards and when you fan the first four, the three extra ones are hidden behind the top, or left-hand card. (Fig. 65)

These three hidden cards should have one corner crimped—the three crimped as one. Closing the fan, turn the backs of the cards to the audience, and cut them a number of times, taking care not to spread the cards out too much. You complete the 'shuffle' by seeing that the three crimped cards are on top.

Now, holding the cards, backs to the audience, draw off the top card, and place face-down on the table, taking out the crimp as you do so; hesitate, and ask the person who made the choice to think a little harder; then remove the next card and finally the third. This apparently leaves one card in the hand, which you place in your pocket. The three cards on the table are now pushed separately into the pack, and you ask your assistant: 'You had a completely free choice, didn't you?' Upon receiving a reply, dip a hand in your pocket and ask for the name of the chosen card. Immediately you know which of the four in the pocket you must take out, but before doing so (and this gives you ample time to find the card) remark: 'And you are still convinced I didn't influence your choice?' Withdraw the card, and hold it up for all to see.

THE BANK ROBBERY. No. 23

Effect. Any Jack is selected by the audience, to represent a Bank robber. Two Kings—any two—are the policemen. The story goes that the pack represents a Bank, into which a burglar has somehow made his way. Here the performer asks a member of the audience to push the Jack into any part of the pack and to shuffle the pack.

The conjurer explains that somehow the warning goes round that a thief is in the Bank and, while watch is kept outside, two police enter—one from the back, one from the front. Here the two Kings are pushed into the pack.

The magician explains that after searching through the premises the police meet and come out, bringing between them the robber. The two Kings are withdrawn from the pack as one card, then fanned to show the Jack between. Everything may be thoroughly examined.

Method. This is just another little example of the extreme usefulness of the corner crimp. When the Jack is pushed into the pack it doesn't go into place very easily because you hold the cards tight enough to prevent this. Giving the pack a slight twist, so that the right-hand lower corner of the Jack projects from the side, you pull it down with the fingers of the left hand, which are curled up over the sides of the pack. You then release the pressure on the pack and allow the Jack to be pushed in flush with the rest of the cards.

Hand the pack for shuffling—you have no need to fear the crimp will be taken out. Take the pack and hold upright, facing the audience, with the crimp at the top. You take one King, which you bring up over the front of the cards, and slowly pass it over the tops of them until you come to the front of the crimped card. Then push the King part-way into the pack. The other King is brought up similarly from the back and is inserted immediately behind the crimp. With the two Kings part-way showing above the

Fig. 66

pack, take them firmly between the left finger and thumb and push them right down as far as they will go, still retaining the corner hold. Now draw the cards up a little bit and give a slight turn; this will bring up the Jack as well. The object of the turn is to rest the lower end of the Jack, which will now project, on the third finger of the right hand, and you push down the Kings again until all three cards are flush; then draw them out as one card and spread them out. Put down the pack; separate the three cards, at the same time taking the crimp out of the Jack, and everything may be thoroughly examined. (Fig. 66)

THE WISHING WELL. No. 24

Effect. One spectator chooses a card and replaces it in the pack, which is shuffled or cut. A second person thinks of a number and, placing his hand on the pack, and wishing that the chosen card will travel to the number thought of, counts the cards, reaches the number, and—it **isn't** the chosen card.

The performer explains: 'This is known as the wishing well trick. Evidently you didn't wish well enough. If you don't wish well . . . well! 'Now I'll show you how to do it.' And, repeating the second assistant's actions, the chosen card appears at the desired number.

Method. Delightfully simple, though none the less effective. While the chosen card is being shown, separate the pack at about centre for the return of the card, and bridge or crimp (a corner crimp is best) the bottom card of the top portion of cut. After the return of the card replace the top cut, then false-shuffle or cut several times, finally cutting at the crimp, bringing the chosen card to the top. (Fig. 67)

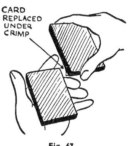

CARD REPLACED UNDER CRIMP

Fig. 67

The second person now thinks of a number; a number not exceeding twenty-five is best, and counts the cards out **one by one**, thereby bringing the chosen card to the bottom of the counted pile. On reaching the number and finding 'it hasn't worked', suggest one more card is tried. The next card is turned up: still wrong. You take over from your assistant here—for he has done the counting—and replace the counted cards on top of the pack, **including the extra card.**

False-shuffle or false-cut, keeping all cards, down as far as the one chosen, in the same order, at the top.

Emphasize the 'well-wishing' and, counting down to the number thought of, find the very card!

THIS IS YOUR CARD. No. 25

Jordan

Effect. A spectator names a number and counts down in the pack, noting the card at that position.

The pack is now cut as required and then dealt, face-down, into several heaps. The performer takes one heap, assistant another, and, without any questioning, or seeking for information, the conjurer produces the selected card.

Method. Note the position of the fourteenth card down in the pack. This can either be done when concluding the previous trick, or in looking through the pack to remove the Joker; 'he is not a suitable companion in this trick'.

False-shuffle, then ask your helper to 'give me a number, between ten and twenty'. Start to count down to the number, then suggest it would be better for the assistant to do this himself, and hand the pack to him, replacing the cards on top.

When the card at the named number has been looked at, and the counted-off cards replaced, have the pack cut, take it back, false-shuffle, or cut further, and, mentally deducting the smaller from the larger number, deal the cards into as many heaps as represented by the number in difference. For instance, if the number seventeen is called—and this is, curiously enough, the usual number—deduct fourteen; leaves three, so you deal into three heaps. If eighteen had been called, you would deal into four heaps (18 minus 14 equals 4). Similarly, if the number named was eleven (14 minus 11 equals 3) you still deal into three heaps. You know the card that was fourteenth, so, by dealing three heaps, the chosen card will be the one **above** the key card. The seventeenth card will be the next card below the key, as the heap lies, with cards face-down.

You, naturally, do not know which of the three heaps contains the chosen card. So you ask your assistant to take any heap he chooses and look through it, while you look through another. Emphasize that if he sees his card, the spectator is not to tell you, as **you** intend telling **him**. Look through the heap for the key card and if it is present, you know which card was chosen (the next one over it, or below, in above instances).

If the key card is not in evidence, just remark: 'I don't like this heap. This will be better,' and you pick up the remaining heap from the table and continue your search.

If still unlucky, say: 'I'm still not satisfied. Let us exchange heaps,' and you change with the assistant. This time you've got it.

This changing of the heaps in no way detracts from the effectiveness of this number. In fact, it rather enhances it, as spectators are wondering if the magician has been foiled.

For numbers twelve, thirteen, fifteen and sixteen, there is no need to deal the cards into heaps. Simply have the assistant cut several times, then cut the pack into two heaps and take one heap. You take the other.

Of course, this latter procedure **could** be utilized for any number. You merely count so many forward or backward from the key card.

An alternative method to knowing the fourteenth card is to sight the top card and, when the assistant counts down to his number, have him do this by counting the cards out singly on to the table ('so that everyone can see clearly just what is happening'). When he reaches one short of the number, instruct him to look at the next card, then replace it on top of the pack, finally returning the counted cards and cutting. You false-shuffle and hand to him to cut into two heaps.

By this means the chosen card lies next underneath the key card. If working this method, it is well to count with your assistant, thereby controlling the situation, and you will find no difficulty in having him replace the selected card on the pack, and the reversed (counted) cards on the top again.

The routine and variations suggested above are rather a wide departure from the original, but the basic idea still belongs to Mr. Jordan, and due credit is therefore given to him.

PREDICAMENT IN PREDICTION. No. 26

After Jordan

Effect. The pack is spread ribbonwise on the table and the performer writes something on a piece of paper, which he puts in the spectator's breast-pocket, this person then choosing a card.

Gathering the pack, the card is returned, and all are dealt into four face-down heaps. Here the conjurer remarks: 'Your card is in one of these four heaps, but as I cannot know either the heap, or the card, the odds are three to one against my selecting the right heap. But if I place one heap on another, so, and this third

heap on the fourth, making two piles, then I have an even opportunity of finding the right pile, although as there are twenty-six
cards in each pile now, my prospects of finding the right card are
still not very rosy. Still, it might give me confidence. And I might
do better than you expect, because I know Rosie.'

Taking one pile, he places it to his ear and, riffling, listens.
Explaining that he can't get any response ('maybe Rosie isn't in'),
the performer cuts the pack, riffles again, and still no luck. Hesitat-
ing, he glances at the half-pack still on the table, then slaps those
in his hand on the top. Now, with the whole pack, he riffles again
and beamingly exclaims his satisfaction. Shuffling the pack, he
hands it to his assistant to cut into two heaps and choose one.

Now he reads the message on the slip of paper; it proves to be
an instruction to count to a certain number in the selected heap.
When he does so, the chosen card is turned up!

Method. The cards may be shuffled before 'spreading'. As soon
as selection is made, gather the pack and crimp the lower (or near)

right-hand corner of top card. This is
easily done by pushing the card just
over the edge of the pack with the
thumb and pressing downwards with
the little-finger tip. (Fig. 68.) These
movements, done by the left hand, are
completely masked by the right hand,
which is on the top of the pack, ready
for cutting. When cutting the cards for
the return of the one chosen, draw the
top, crimped, card down on to the

CRIMPING
THE
CORNER

Fig. 68

lower half of the pack with the left-hand fingers, the right hand
lifting off the top portion.

The chosen card is thus replaced directly on top of the crimped
card.

The pack is dealt into four heaps, a card to each in turn. Watch
for the crimp, and note in which heap it falls. You then know the
chosen card is in the heap just before it (i.e. if crimped card is in
the third heap, the chosen card is in the second).

When pattering about the odds being three to one against you, pick up the heap containing the crimped card and drop it on the heap with the chosen card. The two remaining heaps are likewise made one. This gives you your 'odds and even' position. (Should the crimped card be in the first heap, take the second heap and drop it on the third, then the first on the fourth.)

As you hold up the cards to 'listen' when you riffle, note the position of the 'crimp' and cut there, completing the cut, and bringing the crimped card to the top. These twenty-six cards are dropped on the other half-pack and, when riffling for the last time, take the crimp out of the card. The chosen card is now the four-teenth down in the pack—thirteen cards below the 'crimp'—as is **always** the case.

Your prediction reads 'Count down in the heap to the fourteenth card'. You can, of course, make the number more, or less, than fourteen. In that case you count the difference in the number above, or below, the crimp before cutting.

Before having the prediction read out, false-shuffle, keeping the top stock in position, and ask the assistant to cut into two 'fairly equal heaps'. Ask him to put his hand on one heap. If that is the one you wish him to use, say: 'Very well. Now will you read the message on the paper I slipped in your pocket?' If his hand rests on the wrong heap, pick up the other, saying: 'Thank you.' When the prediction is read, hand him the cards you hold.

DUET FOR ONE. No. 27

Paul Clive

Effect. Any pack is thoroughly shuffled. The performer sits at a table opposite a spectator. The pack is dealt into two heaps, a card to each, in turn. One heap is in front of the spectator, one in front of the performer. Now, taking a pencil and paper, the con-jurer writes a short message and places it on the table, face-down.

The assistant next chooses one heap, the cards of which are dealt into two face-down piles as before—the remaining original heap is put on one side. It is also the assistant's choice as to who shall deal.

Whoever deals this (second) time puts his own heap on one side and his opposite number now deals his own heap. (Thus, if the performer takes the deal, he takes the heap of twenty-six cards and deals into two heaps of thirteen cards. The spectator next deals **his thirteen** cards.)

So, taking it in turn, the number of cards dealt is dwindled down until only two remain. These are finally dealt one to each of the 'players', and here the conjurer invites the spectator to read aloud the message which all this while has been face-down on the table beside him.

Fig. 69

It is a prediction of what his (the spectator's) last card will be. Turning up the solitary card in front of him, he finds the prediction correct. (Fig. 69)

Method. After the cards are shuffled by the audience, give a final shuffle yourself, sighting the third card from top of the pack.

Now deal into two heaps.

Before the cards are touched further, write your prediction, and place it face-down on the table near at hand.

Now say to your assistant: 'Will you take one heap, please?' or words to that effect. Do NOT say: 'Which heap shall we use?'

The sighted card is now next to the bottom of the heap dealt to your partner (cards face-down, of course). This, then, is the heap to be forced. If your helper is of the meeker type, he will choose the heap which lies just in front of him. If he is not that type, his choice will, in all probability, fall on your pile.

But it does not matter. If he takes his own heap, push yours to one side and proceed. If he takes yours, hand him the card-case as you remark: 'Will you slip them in there, out of the way, please?' and you pick up the other pile, ready for dealing. Again, you may prefer to pick up the card-case as you ask him to take a pile. If he takes his own, you pick up your pile, as you make your next remark, and drop the cards into the case. If he takes yours, you hand him the case, as already suggested. There is perfect cover in this force and no doubt can exist that your assistant had a free choice.

Whichever his choice, you now ask: 'Would you like to deal, or shall I?' In this he **has** a free choice, for it doesn't matter who deals. Each subsequent deal is taken in turn, until only two cards remain to be dealt. Here is all you have to remember: if the spectator deals these two cards out, one to each of you, he will automatically get the predicted card, but if it is your turn to deal them, the bottom card has to be slipped out and dealt to your partner. This is most easily effected by asking him, as you pick up the cards: 'Will you read out to everybody what I wrote on that paper when we started,' and, nodding, you indicate the slip with the prediction. Immediately, all eyes are diverted from you, and you place the bottom card in front of your partner, dropping the last card in your own place.

He reads the prediction, turns up his card, and 'All's well that ends well'.

As a point of interest, and it may on occasions be a serviceable knowledge, here, in table form, is the position occupied by the sighted card, right from the beginning to the end of the trick:

Before dealing:	Third (from top) of fifty-two.
After first deal:	Next to bottom of twenty-six.
After second deal:	Top of thirteen.
After third deal:	Bottom of seven.
After fourth deal:	Top of four.
After fifth deal:	Bottom of two.

The fact that the spectator has the choice (?) of heaps after first deal, and option of dealing, also that he handles the cards by dealing several times during the effect, completely convinces people that pre-arrangement is out of the question.

A non-card-player may give an awkward moment—or so it could seem. Card-players always deal to the other person first. Anyone not used to cards may deal the first card to himself. In such a case it is best to correct him. This can be done without difficulty or fear of causing suspicion. Just stop him, and say: 'I don't want anyone to think you're a confederate, or that you're trying to help me, so we'd better deal in the orthodox manner.

You deal to your opponent first. Not that we're opposed—just a little opposite.'

If preferred, the prediction can be made before you commence the initial deal.

'TELLING' FINGERTIPS. No. 28

Conrad Rheiner

Effect. The performer holds a shuffled pack behind his back. An assistant cuts the pack and looks at the next card, afterwards replacing his cards on top. Touching the assistant's fingertips, of the hand which held the chosen card, the conjurer succeeds in naming the card.

Method. When the assistant cuts the pack, you turn to him, asking: 'Have you cut yet?' As you swing round in this manner,

slip the bottom card, which you previously sighted, to the top. The rest is obvious—to you. (Fig. 70)

Note. In the above version a very definite snag is that the performer is at a distinct disadvantage if the audience is at all dispersed. A satisfactory alternative method in such a contingency would be to know the third card from the bottom of the pack, and, with the three last cards reversed—the known card thus becoming the bottom card face-up—when you turn (slightly) and ask if he has cut, turn the whole lot over in the hand. This is much simpler than drawing a card from underneath and placing it on top.

Fig. 70

When the force-card is 'chosen', ask your helper to 'Hold it up and let everyone see it'. As he does so you again turn the cards you hold (all eyes are on the card held up and none will detect the slight movement on your part, for a turn of the wrist is all that is necessary).

When the chosen card is replaced and the others dropped on

top, you can either step back while you turn the two bottom cards, or slip the pack in your pocket, then rub the fingertips of both hands together 'to effect increased sensitivity'. (In this case, turn the two bottom cards before taking the pack from pocket at conclusion.)

TAKES THE PIP. No. 29

Charles T. Jordan

Effect. A member of the audience shuffles the pack and cuts it into two heaps, then hands the performer one pile. Looking carefully through these cards he states his intention of performing an exceptional feat in memorizing.

The assistant now takes any card from the inspected heap, and the performer, on again going through these cards, names the one removed.

Method. Ask the spectator to cut the pack into two heaps, as nearly equal as possible. This done, one heap is handed to you, and you look carefully through the cards. Naturally, you do **not** memorize the cards. Instead, you first add together all the pips. This is really quite easy because each time your total exceeds ten you drop the ten. (For instance, say you have a 5 and an 8. This being thirteen you only carry the three in your mind.) Leave the Court cards till last, then add them on to your previous total, allowing one and a half for Jack, two and a half for Queen and three and a half for King. (If the halves give you any difficulty, include these at the very last; thus if you have a Queen and two Kings to go, with, say an outstanding balance of five from the 'pip' cards, you will complete your total like this: $5 + 2 + 3 + 3 = 13 - 10 = 3$ & $1\frac{1}{2} = 4\frac{1}{2}$. This final figure you bear in mind (see Note below). Now run through the cards again, adding the suits together. Allow one for each club, two for a diamond and three for hearts, ignoring the spades. As with the 'pip-adding', you only carry in your mind the excess over every ten.

You now have two totals, which you remember, as (for example) $4\frac{1}{2}$ and 6.

Now hand these cards to the helper, with the request that he shuffles them, and take away one that he fancies. He may afterwards shuffle again if he desires, then pass them back to you.

As before, you count through, totting the pips, then the suits. Deduct these new quantities from the old, and you know the card. Should the number to be deducted—of either 'pips' or suits—exceed the first number, you merely add ten to the smaller number, then deduct.

To facilitate the adding process it will be found an advantage if the cards are held in one complete fan, or arc, so that the index of each card is clearly visible.

If half a pack seems too much, have your assistant cut the pack into three heaps 'all of about the same number of cards'. One of these heaps is then handed to you, and you have only about sixteen cards to calculate, instead of twenty-six.

Note. If you find any difficulty in memorizing the first totals, you can mark the bottom card of the pile with your thumbnail. Imagine the two ends of the card as being divided into five sections, numbers 1 to 5 at the top end, 6 to 10 at the lower end. Use this for the 'pip' total. If there is an odd half in the total, mark two strokes instead of one. Similarly, use the long sides—divided in like manner, five each side—for the suit total. Then all you have to remember is the bottom card, and on which end of the card you marked your pip total (i.e. top or bottom). (Fig. 71)

When you get the cards back, look for the card you marked, cut it to the bottom—and go ahead. If that card is missing, you know the chosen card very quickly.

ON THE SIDE. No. 30

Effect. A spectator shuffles the pack, which the performer then hands to another spectator to cut, asking him also to count down to any mentally selected number, under twenty. He (spectator) then looks at the next card, replaces those counted off, finally replacing the balance on the top. The performer discovers the noted card.

Method. The principle employed here is both unusual and ingenious. After shuffling, the pack (which should, if possible, be fairly well-used) is handled by you for a moment or two when you take it from the first spectator to hand to the second. Choose the second assistant at some distance from the first. This will give you ample time, while walking from one to the other, to make the necessary move. This is a secret marking on the side of the pack, in the form of a sharp pressure from the left thumb-nail, diagonally across the sides of the entire pack. This results in an indentation, or scratch, clearly visible to the naked eye. The pack is cut, and the selected number counted off, one at a time, thereby reversing a section of the line. When these cards are replaced and the cut-off portion put on top the mark on the side shows itself in three sections, as shown in second illustration. The chosen card is the one at the bottom of the middle stroke. (Fig. 72)

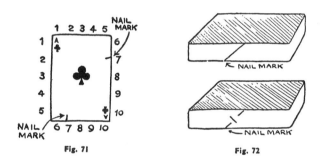

Fig. 71   Fig. 72

To discover this card, without **being** discovered, you need reasonable eyesight and an adequate excuse for turning the pack on its side. To this end, cut the pack into small heaps, apparently counting a certain number of cards each time. This will give ample time to spot the chosen card. Separate the pack at this point, before you 'count' down to it, and note its value when placing that little heap out. Finally, gather up the heaps, bridging the packet with the chosen card, and patter along these lines: 'I get the impression your card was a black card. I think—yes—it was, a spade. It was a low card—the 4 of spades.' Whilst saying this, cut the pack at the 'bridge' and as you say 'The 4 of spades' draw the card away and show.

Note. If you do not feel confident of detecting the indentation clearly, you can mark a pencil line across the pack, but this must be done beforehand, and does not allow of having the pack shuffled.

ACCOMMODATION SPELLING. No. 31

Ben Erens

Effect. A shuffled pack is cut into two heaps. A spectator chooses one, which he cuts again, and notes the card at the cut. The cards just cut are replaced, and the whole pile dropped on the other half-pack.

A further shuffle, and the performer spells out the chosen card, which turns up at the completion of the spelling.

Method. When the pack is first cut, ask your assistant to cut the pack 'somewhere near the middle'. The two packets are naturally laid side by side and you can estimate very closely how many cards are in each pile. Try this over on your own a few times, and you will be really surprised how quickly and accurately this estimate can be made.

Whichever heap is selected for the second cut, you know, very nearly, how many cards this contains.

Now say to your helper: 'I want you to cut your heap into two piles, like this' (cut the remaining heap—the one **not** selected—into two fairly equal stacks). 'Then look at the top card of the lower heap, replace it, and finally put the other portion back on top.' When the card is being looked at, it is a simple matter to estimate how many cards are cut off. When these are replaced on the inspected card the whole half-pack is placed on the top of the other half. False-shuffle, retaining the top fifteen to twenty cards in existing order and position.

The number cut from above the chosen card will almost certainly be between ten and sixteen. By the use of a little accommodating wording you can spell any card out within this limit. For instance, if you estimate there are fourteen cards in the cut, thus making the chosen card the fifteenth, and the chosen card is the 5 of clubs, you would say 'The five of clubs', spelling one card for each letter, and turning each card face-up as spelt. If the card does not turn up by the time you reach the 'clubs' continue 'five of——' and throw the next card. If this is still not the noted card, turn the next, at the same time calling 'clubs'. Should you still draw a blank, turn up the following card, remarking 'So'.

Supposing the card had been estimated at, say, eleventh. Well, in that case you would have spelt 'Five of clubs', the 's' being the turn-up.

Taking an extreme case, Queen of diamonds at the, say, tenth card, you would 'spell' **one card only** for the word 'Queen' and another for 'of'; then, if the card should turn up at the second 'd' you would stop there, as though that was already known to you.

(If you prefer to have, say, two more cards above the chosen card, give an overhand false-shuffle, first dropping off nearly twenty cards from the top into the left hand, then 'shuffling off two singles on to the first 'drop', lift all these up in the following 'drop', shuffle off the remainder of the pack and lastly, put the original 'drop'—with the two extra cards—on top of all.) (Fig. 73)

THE TORN CARD OBLIGES. No. 32

Effect. A chosen card is shuffled into the pack, the pack then being torn completely in halves. Holding one half-pack in his hands, the performer asks the spectator to call a number. Counting down to that number, one piece of the chosen card is discovered. Taking the second torn half-pack, another number is called, and the other half of the card is found at that position.

Method. Any card is selected, and after return to the pack, is brought to the top. The pack is then torn in two halves as described on page 122; one half-pack is laid on the table and the other held upright in the left hand, the torn section being hidden by the fingers. The top card is then drawn down an inch or so, and it is the following cards which you count out. When you reach the

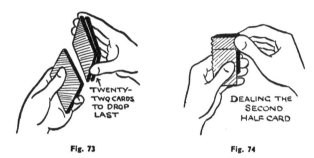

Fig. 73   **Fig. 74**

final number, the right thumb draws this rear card to the top, then counts this off as though it is the naturally succeeding card. The same procedure is adopted in finding its counterpart. (Fig. 74)

A SLICE OF LUCK. No. 33

Paul Rosini

Effect. A chosen card is shuffled back into the pack, and an indifferent card handed to assistant to push anywhere into the pack. Performer promises the selected card will appear at the very spot where spectator inserts the card.

But things go wrong. In fact the card is not even in the pack. IT IS THE LOCATOR CARD, STILL IN ASSISTANT'S HAND.

Method. This delightful, daring, and surprising effect was typical of Rosini's style.

The chosen card is brought to the top of the pack in the shuffling, and, as the pack is squared, the two top cards are held in readiness for a double-lift (see Note below).

Remarking that it is doubtful whereabouts in the pack the selected card may be, take the two top cards and casually display as one, state that you will have the spectator himself discover the missing card. As you replace the card(s) on top of pack, take your assistant by the arm, as though to command *all* his attention (and this very act provides a natural excuse for having replaced the 'top' card), and tell him **he** can discover the chosen card very simply. Here take the top (selected) card—without disclosing it— and, as you riffle the top right-hand corner of the cards with the left thumb, explain that he is to slice the card anywhere into the riffle. You suit the action to the word as you say 'Like that'.

Leave the card projecting from the corner of the pack for a few seconds, to emphasize the method, but don't show the face of the card. Now, removing the card, but still retaining it for a moment, **slowly** start the riffle, saying: 'Put the card in anywhere you like— you have a free choice.' While saying this, hand the card over. The fact that you have already started the riffle will prevent any pos- sibility of spectator looking at the card. (As you previously showed it to be indifferent (?) he has no reason to look at it, anyway.)

When he has dug the card into the pack, tell him to hold on to the card as you separate the pack. Show the face card above the incision, and ask if that is the selected card. When assistant says 'No', try the top card of lower heap. Wrong again. Take the top heap and fan the cards out, asking if the card is there. 'No.' 'Then, obviously it's here,' you remark, taking up the lower heap. As you fan these out ask the name of the chosen card.

By the time the card is named, you will have gone through these cards, also. As if in despair, ask the name of the card spectator is holding. His surprise is so complete, that it adds a touch of involuntary humour to the effect. You can then tell him you **blame him** for losing the card, so **you'll** take the credit for finding it.

Note. If you are not confident in the use of the Double-Lift, an easy aid is to have the top card of the pack prepared with a crimp at the lower left-hand corner. When the spectator first chooses, he does, of course, have a free choice. As he looks at it, you open the pack for the return of the card, at the same time 'slipping' the top card on to the lower heap. The chosen card is replaced on this and, after a false-shuffle, bringing the crimped and the selected cards to the top, the Double-Lift is very easily handled.

CHAPTER 4

MISCELLANEOUS

♥ ♣ ♦ ♣ ♥ ♣ ♦ ♣ ♥ ♣ ♦ ♣ ♥ ♣ ♦ ♣ ♥ ♣ ♦ ♣

THE SPECTATOR TURNS MAGICIAN. No. 34

Paul Clive

Effect. Performer invites a spectator to become magician. This assistant takes the pack, shuffles it, and fans the cards for a second person to select one card. Card is replaced and the pack shuffled once more.

The temporary magician then spells out the name of the card. The chosen card turns up on the last letter.

Method. You use a one-way pack, duly arranged. Your first assistant, whom we will call A, is given the pack to shuffle and you remark that A will be the performer for this trick: you will merely tell him what to do, to ensure his success as a magician.

With the cards fanned, B makes his selection. 'To make it quite impossible for you to know either this card or where it is placed, will you (A) turn round, and hold the cards behind your back. Now (to B) push the card anywhere you like into the pack. You can shuffle them if you like.'

When A turns round for the card to be returned, the holding of the pack behind him automatically turns the pack. (Fig. 75)

B shuffles, and A faces about. All this while, you stand well away so that you cannot possibly know what card was chosen, or where it may be in the pack. Give the impression that you don't particularly worry, as the success or otherwise of the trick is A's responsibility. (Do not, however, cause A much embarrassment or make him feel ill at ease.)

Proceed: 'Will you (A) take the cards again. Of course you know how to find the card? You don't. I should have told you to slip a rubber-band round it as it was returned to the pack. Now it looks rather complicated. Suppose you spread them out on the table, from left to right, like a long string of cards. Spread them well out—it makes such a nice display, although it doesn't mean a

Fig. 75

thing.' While this spreading has been done you have advanced to the table and, if you don't quickly spot the reversed card, spread them farther out yourself ('it makes such a nice display'). This will give you ample opportunity of noting the position of the card, without making it apparent you are looking for something. (In all reversed-card effects take particular care not to stare, or in any way reveal your interest in the pattern on the backs.)

'Now they're all set out, do you think you could pick out the chosen card? No. Well, there **are** rather a lot to choose from. You could chance it, though. For instance, you could say this is the card.' While pattering, you have counted to the sixteenth card to the right of the reversed card and you now put your finger on the back of the card, and draw it down somewhat—but not clear of the line. 'Again, it could be this,' and you pull down another some way farther along. 'Do you think this is a good idea? No, I can see your point.' Now, to B: 'What was your card?' (Suppose it was the 7 of hearts.) 'The 7 of hearts.' To A: 'Shall we turn them face up? It would be so easy then.' This remark, and the resulting laughter (we hope) will give you ample time to calculate the number of letters in the name of the card—in this case thirteen. Scoop the cards up between the two hands and with the sixteenth card acting as an excellent in-jog, square up the pack, inserting the right thumbtip just over the in-jog. The left little finger squares the near end of pack. Take the pack in right hand, keeping the break at near end, and drop the lower heap on the table, then drop the upper portion at the side. Pick up the lower pile and drop on the second heap, thereby cutting the cards. Do this apparently absent-

mindedly, as you remark: 'I'd like to help you, but, after all, you
are doing the trick.' Then, as though struck by a sudden thought:
'There's always one very simple way out. That is, to spell the card.
Let's see, what was it? The 7 of Hearts you said, didn't you? You
just spell out the name, dropping one card on the table for each
letter, like this, S-E-V-E-N and so on, until you've spelled the whole
name Seven of Hearts.' As you said 'S-E-V-' you put out the top
three cards for these three letters. Drop the pack on to these cards,
then hand the lot to A to spell. The chosen card will be the first
card after the spelling.

Note. If the selected card is near the right-hand end of spread,
proceed as above, counting to the right-hand end of row, then continue the counting from left-hand end. Convert the sixteenth
(drawn) card into a key card (crimp, etc.). Cut several times,
finally cutting at the key card, and bringing it to the top.

THE ELEVEN-CARD SPELLER. No. 35

Buckley

Effect. Any chosen card is returned to the pack, which is shuffled
and cut. The card is named and the performer spells it out, one
card to each letter, and finally produces the card as the last letter
is spelt.

Method. First secretly discard the 3, 7, 8 and Queen of diamonds
and the Joker. In the original working of this method, Buckley
advocated cutting a stack of ten cards from the top of the pack
when having the chosen card returned. To me this seems somewhat pointed and I suggest the following arrangement and routine. Ten cards, somewhere near the centre of the pack, are kept
track of by the ever-useful corner-crimp. The lower left-hand corner is best. Should you not find it expedient to effect this prior to
presentation you can crimp the two top cards at the time you
intend showing the trick, then in overhand style shuffle off the
top card and retain this in the right hand when you lower the pack
to drop the next card(s). (*See* Overhand False-Shuffle)

Then shuffle off nine cards, one at a time: the first, of course, will be the other crimped card—and as you bring the hand down again drop the retained card on top of the nine, at the same time allowing a few to slip off the top of those in your right hand, thereby completely masking the secret operation. Complete the shuffle which will leave the ten cards at the bottom. Have the card selected from anywhere above these ten, and as it is being held up for all to see, under-cut about half the pack; have card returned, and the lower crimped card is thus brought immediately over the noted card. (Fig. 76.) False-shuffle.

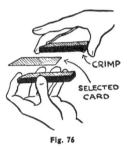

Fig. 76

The audience now cut the pack several times, then finally do so yourself, cutting the upper crimped card to the top of the pack. The chosen card is now the eleventh from the top and may be spelt out as required. You will notice that the spelling is governed by the number of letters in the name of the card. For instance: 2 of clubs would be spelt t-w-o o-f c-l-u-b-s. This totals ten letters so you would turn up the following card. On the other hand, if you had to spell the Jack of diamonds you would have to cut down by omitting the word 'of' and leaving the 's' off 'diamonds'. The best way to work in this case is to say: 'The Jack of diamonds. Suit: D-i-a-m-o-n-d; the value: J-a-c-k' and you would turn up the last or 'k' card. In this way, by adapting your spelling to the needs of the chosen card, you can spell any of the cards which are still in the pack.

THE WRITING ON THE FAN. No. 36

Effect. With a pack of cards fanned in his hand, their **backs** to the audience, the performer marks one card in pencil with an initial, or other requested marking. The fan is closed and the pack shuffled. An assistant from the audience is then asked to think of any card of the fifty-two and to name it.

Going through the pack the magician removes one card, which

he retains, and hands the pack to his helper to search for the marked card. It is not in the pack. The card in the performer's hand is turned over. It is the actual card named and it bears the identification mark.

Method. This most effective trick is performed by the use of a simple piece of apparatus known as the Swami pencil. This is a small piece of pencil lead, fixed in a little crescent-shaped metal, which clips on the thumb nail.

(Throughout this book, endeavour has been made to avoid the use of any conjuring accessory, using only a pack of cards or other item found in any home, but this particular trick is so good that I felt impelled to include it in this collection. The Swami gimmick is obtainable from all good class conjuring dealers.)

When asking in the first case for the mark or initial to be called, you apparently mark one particular card in this way, but in reality only simulate this, leaving the card blank. It is quite a good idea to borrow the pencil, but be sure you do not borrow a copying pencil or your sins will find you out. By borrowing, you create, by inference, the impression that you have no writing tool on you.

Fig. 77

Now, with the pack of cards before you on the table, place your hands in your pockets as you ask for any card to be named. While standing like this, get the Swami pencil on your right thumb nail, and, picking up the pack, you look for the card just named. As you draw this from the pack it is quite easy, as you will find with but little experimenting, to write the initial (or mark) previously called. (Fig. 77.) The pack is passed for examination, while the card you have just marked you place face-down in front of you. Once again your hands go in your pockets. You unload the Swami pencil, and all is set for the grand finale.

ALONE ABOVE REVERSE. No. 37

Effect. While the performer's back is turned the spectator shuffles the pack, then takes any card, turns it face-up, and pushes it anywhere in the pack, again shuffling same. The conjurer returns and, taking the pack, covers it with a handkerchief. Holding the pack through the handkerchief he names the reversed card, and as he does so, all the cards, except one, fall. Remaining is the chosen card.

Method. This is an unusual, and rather fascinating, effect, based on a simple, little-known principle. It is a fact that, with one card reversed, a pack held on its side between the tips of fingers and the thumb, then tilted inwards and allowed to break, while relaxing the thumb pressure, will most readily break at the turned card. Try it and you will find it works every time.

Now if the tilting before breaking is very slight, the reversed card will remain at the bottom of the upper heap, but if well tilted to an angle of about 45 degrees, it will fall with the others into the palm, becoming the top card of this portion.

When performing, everything is quite free from preparation or manœuvre until the moment you pick up the cards to cover with the handkerchief. The pack is held in one hand as just described, and as the other hand draws the handkerchief up and across (so concealing the cards from the spectators), the break is made, with the chosen card at top of the lower heap, which has fallen against the palm of the hand. As the handkerchief is brought into position you have ample time to glimpse the card before you lower the handkerchief over the top of hand. The greater portion of the handkerchief should hang down on the side nearest the audience.

As far as the audience is aware, the complete pack is pushed upwards into the middle of the handkerchief as the latter is brought down over the cards. In effect, you have the pack held flat and facing downwards, covered on all sides by the handkerchief, just like a miniature table spread with a cloth. Now, through the handkerchief, the right hand grasps the 'table-top' well down the sides, thumb at one side, first and second fingers at the other, and

turns them vertical, faces of cards towards the audience. The left
hand at the same time also turns the lower heap in a vertical manner. The top heap is raised just clear, then the lower half pushed
up **behind** for about half their length, the third and fourth fingers
of right hand now pressed against the back of these cards, holding
them in position. The left hand is removed from under the handkerchief and firmly takes the pack from the right hand, holding
the two portions as one (still at the sides). While holding the cards
in this manner, patter to the effect that not only is the reversed
card impossible to know yet or locate, but the fact that the cards
are covered by the handkerchief renders any discovery of the card
by the performer out of the question—or so it would seem. Here
the right hand comes forward, fingers above and thumb below the
cards. The thumb then presses the lower cards up into place behind
the rest of the pack. Do not press the top cards down. To the
audience it will simply seem that you have taken the pack by the
ends. (Figs. 78, 79 and 80 illustrate the initial moves)

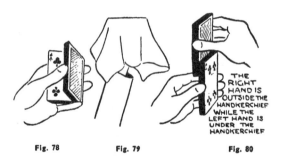

Fig. 78   **Fig. 79**   **Fig. 80**

With left hand, now smooth out the handkerchief and change
the hold of the pack, sides held low over the table, and allow all
the cards except one—the reversed one—to fall away. This is
easily done as a continuous stream.

The above description may seem somewhat complicated but if
you try this out with a pack and a handkerchief in your hands you
will find it quite simple, the different moves blending easily.
Reference to the illustrations will readily disperse any worries.

This is a really worthwhile effect. Some performers prefer to

finish this number with the chosen card rising under the handkerchief from the rest of the pack but this demands that the right hand
be under the handkerchief at the end of the trick. The raising of
the card is effected by pushing it upwards by the first and second
fingers, which move alternately.

PUTTING ON A NEW FACE. No. 38

Effect. The pack is thoroughly shuffled by audience, and the
performer is blindfolded. Holding the pack for all to see, he reads
out the names of a number of cards in quick succession, removing
each card from the face of the pack as it is named.

Method. A number of cards, up to fifteen or twenty, are added
to the top of the shuffled pack, which should at the time of shuffling
consist of about forty cards. It is these added cards that are read
out.

The additional cards are concealed face-down behind the folds
of the blindfold as it rests on the table. As the blindfold is taken
in one hand, the other, holding the pack, drops
it face-down on the cards already there. (Fig. 81)

(Before putting the pack down, shuffle it
yourself and don't show what is finally the face-
card or your audience is likely to remember
later when you pick up the cards that the front
one has changed.) Both hands are used to hold
up the blindfold by its ends, in order to display
it fully. Then, with the cards in one hand and
the blindfold in the other, you walk towards
the spectator, whom you invite to securely
blindfold you.

Fig. 81

The cards should be read off quickly. Hold the pack upright
between the fingers at the top, and thumb at the lower end. This
gives your audience a clear view of the face-card throughout. Keep
this hand well in front of you and draw the face-card off as you
name it, dropping each card on the floor as you stretch out for
the next. (Fig. 82 shown without blindfold)

Many competent performers spoil this type of act by making

Fig. 82

it too slow. Its natural charm and mystery are essentially the product of speedy and, therefore, interesting presentation. Know your sequence of cards thoroughly and you will have no need to hesitate. A slow presentation tends to tedium, and loss of interest on the part of an audience.

SPEECHLESS TELEPATHY. No. 39

Effect. A medium or confederate goes into one room; the conjurer remains with the audience. A shuffled pack is then cut, and several cards dealt out, face-up. Someone names one of these cards and while the magician concentrates on that card a member of the audience goes into the other room. The medium unfailingly names the selected card, even though no word need be spoken by the person who goes to the medium.

Method. Five certain cards are previously agreed upon between the medium and yourself. Let us imagine these cards are the 2 and 9 of clubs, 7 of diamonds, Queen of hearts and the 4 of Spades. Also the names of four of the people present are selected. For example we will take the names of George, Hilda, Mary and Percy. Note that the suits of the cards are arranged alphabetically—that is, clubs, diamonds, hearts, spades. Also the names of the people are thought of alphabetically. The values of the cards rise by five each time, the 9 of clubs being the fifth card. The suits and the names are coupled. The name George conveys the message that the 2 of clubs was selected; the 4 of spades would be indicated by the name Percy, the 9 of clubs is the fifth card, for which no name has been reserved.

Now to present: the pre-selected cards are stacked on top of the pack, which is false-shuffled, then under-cut and the five cards dealt out, face-up. Whatever card is chosen, you ask the corresponding person to go in to see the medium, who will then name the selected card. If the fifth card is called you send anyone, other than the agreed four people.

In the event of your not knowing who will be present you either make your arrangements during your stay there or take the first four people to whom you are introduced, excluding elderly folk or very little children. You cannot reasonably expect an aged person to go and if you did suggest this, somebody more agile might take the journey upon themselves and you would be rather awkwardly placed. If in any doubt and you have no opportunity for private conversation you can seal the arrangement by some agreed remark, even though others are present, such as 'I like Mr. and Mrs. Brown. Mr. Greaves is also rather striking and his daughter Phyllis . . .' (I leave that part to you). If you are faced with the contingency that another person jumps up to go, you suggest that you need that person's presence in the room and ask him or her to hold your hand. (You may get a thrill or a laugh from this!) Again, if the person you wish to go shows some reluctance, insist, on the grounds that he or she is obviously receptive to telepathic influences. This generally satisfies vanity and there is no further demur.

Present this item as genuine telepathy. If pressed for further demonstrations you cay say that you are only beginning your experiments, and that one effort in an evening is all you care to undertake 'just yet'.

THE JESTER REVEALS. No. 40

Glenn Gravatt

Effect. A pack is shuffled, the joker removed, and three cards separately chosen. Each card is placed, **without being looked at,** in the pocket of the person who chose it.

The performer now takes the joker, which he holds to the outside of the pocket in which one of the cards has been placed. Looking intently at the joker, the conjurer then names the particular card in that pocket. This is repeated with the other two chosen cards, and proved correct.

Method. When the joker is being taken from the pack, note the three bottom cards. (Fig. 83.) Have the pack cut into two heaps, the lower section then being counted. This, of course, brings the three cards to the top of that heap. Three people each take one card from the top and you proceed as in the description above. Showmanship will certainly prove an asset in getting the most out of this effect. It is one of a number of versions originally known as 'The Sagacious Joker'.

If you prefer you can, of course, get your three cards to a certain position in the pack, false-shuffle, then cut the pack at this point and offer the lower section for the three people each to select a top card.

POCKET SYMPATHY. No. 41

Effect. The spectator takes one pack, the performer another, and both packs are well shuffled. The conjurer removes one card from his face-down pack and pushes it into his assistant's waistcoat pocket. The spectator then selects a card from his pack and puts it into the magician's waistcoat pocket.

Drawing attention to the obvious freedom of all that has been done, the performer withdraws his card from his pocket and assistant removes his. The two cards are identical. (Fig. 84)

Method. From one pack a known card is removed and placed in your top waistcoat pocket. Its fellow from the other pack is made into a key card. If packs with different coloured backs are

Fig. 83

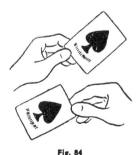

Fig. 84

used in all effects where two packs are necessary, the effect on the audience is greater, and it minimizes any possible thought of tampering with the cards.

You introduce the two packs in their cases and allow the spectator free choice. If he selects the pack with the key card, let him shuffle that while you shuffle the other pack, then exchange. If he takes the pack without the key, shuffle, then proceed without exchanging. The spectator takes any card, which he puts in your pocket without either of you seeing it. This card will naturally go on the inside—that is, nearer the body, leaving the card already hidden there on the outside. If you have any fears, however, that you will get these two cards mixed you can, before secretly placing your card in your pocket, make a little pin-prick at the top. This can easily be felt by thumb or finger and you know immediately which card to draw out. You of course, remove the key card and place in your assistant's pocket. The trick now is done and all that remains is for you to build it up by patter and showmanship into a miracle.

ELBOW GREASE. No. 42

Effect. With the shuffled pack behind the back the spectator counts off a mentally selected number of cards, then looks at the top card of the pack. The counted cards are replaced and the pack shuffled. While this has been in progress the performer has been writing a message on a piece of paper. He folds the paper and hands it to the assistant, with the request that he insert it somewhere in the pack. The chosen card is named; also the position at which it stood in the pack, and, withdrawing the paper from the pile of cards, the message is read. This coincides with the statement just made by the assistant.

Method. When someone removes cards from the top of a pack, or for that matter, from the bottom, with the cards held behind the back, there is bound to be a certain amount of elbow movement, and it is this you watch carefully. (Fig. 85)

The pack is pre-arranged, the top ten to fifteen cards being stacked in, say, numerical order, starting with a 5 on top. Then when you get to the King, which would be the ninth card, you follow on with the Ace. If you count the number of elbow 'jerks', then add four to this number, that will give you the value of the card, and if the first thirteen are all of the one suit, you will have no difficulty in knowing the card. These jerks are often very slight, but are clearly perceptible if you watch closely. In order to do this you have previously written out on the piece of paper you propose using a message somewhat after the following: 'The chosen card will be at the . . . position and will be the . . .' The wording, as you see, is fairly lengthy, thereby giving you good excuse for apparently writing for some seconds.

Don't sit near your assistant, because a reasonable distance permits of better observance than if you are very close.

It is well to ask your helper to first decide on the number of cards to be counted off. State that you are going to predict **while** the counting is done and the card is chosen, but that concentration and silence are necessary. To this end, while you write with the right hand the left hand supports the forehead, and under cover of the left hand you watch the assistant's elbows; at the same time, you simulate the writing on the paper. When he stops, you know the card, and just fill in the two gaps, fold the paper, and the rest is as described under the heading 'Effect'.

A point to bear in mind, if writing in ink, is that when you write out the message beforehand—and it should be done only a few hours before—it should be blotted before it is allowed to dry. Otherwise when you add your two words they may show up in a lighter colour than the rest of the message. Finally, remind your audience that you have not even touched—nor seen—any of the cards, yet you have been able to predict.

ADDING THE PIPS. No. 43

Effect. The pack is shuffled and dropped into the performer's pocket, which was previously shown empty. The spectator then thinks of any card. The name of the suit is given and the performer dives his hand into the pocket containing the pack and draws out one card, which he shows to be of the suit just named. The value of the card is then given and, removing two or three cards, the performer shows that their total value equals that of the thought-of card.

Method. Before presenting the trick you look through the pack, apparently with the intention of removing the Joker, suggesting that that is a card which tends to lead to confusion. In reality you are sorting out four cards to place on the top of the pack. Each of these cards must be of a different suit and one must be an Ace, another a 2, then a 4, and lastly an 8. These go on the top of the pack in a mentally noted order. (You may find it more convenient always to use the same four cards and in a certain order: Ace, 2, 4, 8.)

False-shuffle, then show the pocket empty, and drop the pack inside. As soon as the suit is named you take the corresponding card from your pocket and show it. When the value is named you take the number of cards required to make up that value with or without the addition of the first card. (Fig. 86.) This reads a very

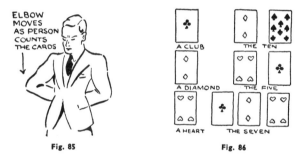

Fig. 85   Fig. 86

simple effect but it has the advantage of being rather different from most tricks and is, from a spectator's point of view, far more puzzling than its real secret would apparently warrant.

Note. It is worth bearing in mind that a great many people think of the 8 of diamonds, or (in lesser degree) the Ace of hearts, or spades.

TEARING A PACK OF CARDS IN HALF. No. 44

Effect. The performer takes any ordinary pack of cards and by merely using the two hands, tears it completely in half.

Method. This is not a trick but it often creates an impression among an audience that colossal strength is necessary, whereas really a reasonably firm grip is all that is required, apart from knowing how to hold the cards. Hold the pack in both hands, each gripping nearly half the pack. The left hand has the first two phalanges of the four fingers on the top, pressing this end of the pack firmly against the lower part of the palm. The right hand grips the other end in a similar manner, but the **fingers** are on the same side as the left-hand **palm**. Holding the cards straight, twist the hands, bringing the elbows down towards each other. (Figs. 87 and 88)

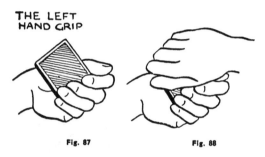

THE LEFT
HAND GRIP

Fig. 87   Fig. 88

A simpler method of tearing the pack is, when using your own, previously to spread the cards out in an oven and leave them there for several hours with a fair amount of heat. This makes them brittle, and tearing is effected very easily.

'UP YOUR SLEEVE, MISTER'. No. 45

Effect. Three cards are separately chosen and put back in the pack by the spectators, who themselves shuffle the pack thoroughly after the return of each card. The performer then holds the pack behind his back and, asking each person to think hard of the card selected, then produces the three cards, each person getting the correct card.

Method. This is simplicity itself and, properly put over, it is extremely baffling to any audience. Before starting, secrete up one sleeve, from another pack, three cards of which you know the order. Three similar cards, also in a known order, are on the top of the pack. These cards you force on various spectators, allowing them to retain their cards. When the three have been chosen, go back to the first person, and hold the pack forward for the return of the card and then, as an apparent afterthought, suggest he takes the pack and puts the card in anywhere he likes, then shuffles the pack thoroughly. Repeat this with the other two selectors; then, taking the pack back, point out the impossibility of your knowing either what the cards are or where they can be in the pack. Then, holding the cards behind your back, ask the first person to concentrate on the card chosen. Whilst

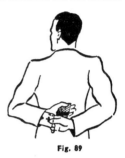

Fig. 89

saying this you draw the three hidden cards from the sleeve and add them to the top of the pack. (Fig. 89.) When you have worked up the concentration business to the extent you consider necessary produce the first card. The second and third cards are treated likewise and the effect concludes to thunderous applause (we hope).

Note. Take care, before putting the cards behind the back, that the bottom card is not one of the selected three.

IT'S IN THE BAG. No. 46

Effect. Three cards are selected, and shuffled back into the pack by the audience. Showing a coloured handkerchief in which the pack is wrapped, the performer dives his hand in among the cards and produces the three previously chosen.

Method. The three cards are forced, and duplicates from another pack are on the table, just behind, or under, the handkerchief. The cards on the table should be in such a position that they are easy to pick up. You can bridge them, or let them rest on a fold or tuck drawn in the cloth on the table.

Should the table be on a level with your audience you can have the cards concealed under a few sheets of paper. The handkerchief which should be of a fairly thick, and preferably patterned, material, is shown clearly on both sides and can be examined if you like.

After displaying the handkerchief, open it out flat on the table with the right-hand corner just covering the three cards completely. (If you have the sheets of paper covering the cards, pick these up as the handkerchief is lowered into place and state that you have only just received the trick and you have forgotten what the instructions were. You pretend to read from the papers and then, satisfied, put them on one side.)

The pack, which till this time has been in full view, you now openly drop on to the middle of the handkerchief. With the right hand take up the corner and the cards with it, and bring the handkerchief over the pack; then fold this corner back, still covering the three cards. As you lower the right hand take the diagonally opposite corner in the left hand and draw that right over. This leaves the handkerchief in appearance like a strip several inches wide, and extending to the other two corners. (Fig. 90.) Lift these

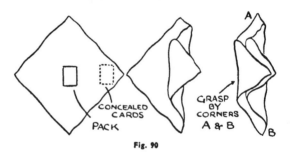

CONCEALED CARDS

PACK

GRASP BY CORNERS A & B

Fig. 90

two corners up and hold in one hand and gently swing the pack for a moment or two while you try to get a 'mental impression' of the chosen cards. Then put your hand apparently into the middle of the handkerchief but really among the three cards and draw them out singly and display.

This effect, although absurdly simple, has a difference in presentation that may appeal, and is another example of 'It's how you do it, that counts'.

FROM PACK TO ENVELOPE. No. 47

Effect. From a shuffled pack a spectator selects a card and, without seeing it, seals it in an envelope.

Calling a number, a second assistant counts down in the pack, notes the card at this position, and writes the name of it on a slip of paper. The pack is assembled, then handed to a third party to shuffle. The first two assistants exchange the envelope for the slip of paper; the name of the card is read out and the pack is examined, but the card just named has vanished. Upon opening the envelope the identical card chosen by the spectator is found inside.

Method. An extra card, from a similar pack, is required. This is placed next to its duplicate. These two cards are at the nineteenth and twentieth positions down in the pack.

After a false-shuffle, one of these duplicates is forced on the first selector. This card is held face-down and slipped into an envelope, which is then sealed and put into the assistant's pocket.

The second helper is then asked to name any number between twelve and twenty. If eighteen or nineteen is called, you hand the pack direct to this person to count down. In the event of eighteen being called, the next card after the count is turned up. When nineteen is the number the last card of the count is indicated. For a number under eighteen, mentally deduct from eighteen, and start to count the cards off. (For instance, suppose fifteen is named—fifteen from eighteen leaves three, which you count off.) When you reach the difference between the actual number and eighteen you suddenly look up and say: 'But perhaps you'd rather count them yourself,' and, dropping the pack on those just counted off, false-shuffle if you think it desirable, and hand to the spectator to count.

In any case, the duplicate of the card in the envelope is 'chosen'.

When the cards are gathered up, see to it that the selected card is on top. An easy method of ensuring this is to let the spectator deal the cards on to your hand when counting. At the finish of the count you take back the rest of the cards and, whichever pile has the chosen card at the top, you place on the other heap, and square up.

You now take a small pad and pencil in one hand and, still with the pack in the other, ask your helper to write down the name of the card just noted, and which no one else has seen. Very naturally, you rest the pad on the pack whilst the spectator writes. Unknown to your audience, however, on the under-side of the pad are two or three dabs of wax. The pressure of the writing causes the top card to adhere firmly to the waxed notepaper. In the event of not being able to use wax to cause the card to adhere, you can manage without it, by the following procedure: As the pad is taken in the right hand and brought up over the cards in the left, the left thumb pushes the top card forward a little and it is held up against the pad by the left fingertips. The spectator now writes the name, as above, on the pad, your left thumb holding the pad from above.

When the name is written, take the pad and the cards away, tear off the top sheet, and hand to the spectator as in the other method; then, with the thumb underneath, fingers on top, the right hand takes the pad **and** the top card, places the pad and card on the table, leaving the remainder of pack in the left hand. (Fig. 91.) Tear off the sheet bearing the name of the card and hand to

Fig. 91

the assistant, requesting him to fold it in four. With pencil and pad in one hand, the side with the **stuck-on** card hidden from your audience, you hand the pack to a third person, with the request: 'Will you look after the cards, please? Shuffle them if you like.' The pad and pencil are dropped on the table or in your pocket.

Briefly state what has been done; then ask the two people holding the envelope and the folded paper to exchange them. The name of the card is now read out and the pack examined. The card has gone. The assistant holding the envelope tears it open and discovers in it the card which only a few moments before he saw in the pack.

Note. The two forced cards can be key cards if desired. You can then keep easy track of them at all times.

THREE FROM SIX. No. 48

Effect. The performer tells the story of having seen a clever conjurer do a wonderful trick with six cards. This conjurer had thrown away three cards and he still had six left. The performer, much impressed, had asked this expert if he could buy the trick.

The story then continues about these six cards which are counted a number of times and three thrown away each time, still leaving six cards. Each step is illustrated by the counting of the cards, then the throwing away of three by the performer as he relates how he sought to acquire this wonderful trick.

Method. Although apparently only six cards are counted each time, a total of eighteen is required for the whole effect.

Preparation. The eighteen cards are in a pocket or other suitable place, in readiness.

Presentation. Take these cards, properly squared up, in the left hand, thumb one side, fingers the other, holding them along their two opposite **longer** sides so that about half their length protrudes above crook of thumb. Hold somewhat to the left, **back** of hand towards audience, cards protruding **directly downwards** (in this position the left elbow will be raised to about shoulder level, or a little higher). Bring right hand to lower edge of cards, fingers at back, thumb in front, the palm being held upwards.

Move 1. During the introduction the back card, i.e. that farthest away from the audience, has been pushed up about a quarter of an inch beyond the rest by the fingers of the right hand, or by means of the 'glide'.

Move 2. Each of the first four cards is drawn singly off the **top** of the stack by pressure from the right thumb, retained in right hand and held against the right fingers (thereby coming **under—**

but **not** added to—those held in left hand each time another card is added). At the count of 'five' **all** of the remaining cards except the one at the back (which has previously been pushed up to facilitate this move) are taken **as one** and added to those in the right hand. The last card is counted 'six' and 'flicked' to show it to be one only. All are now squared up and the last card again pushed up a quarter of an inch.

Move 3. Actually throw away three cards as counted off.

These moves are repeated for the remainder of the trick, and corresponding numbers have been marked in the following patter for guidance.

Patter. 'The other day I saw a good trick. A chap I know took one, two, three, four, five, six cards [**Moves 1 and 2**] and he threw away one, two, three cards [**Move 3**]. Then he found he had one, two, three, four, five, six cards left [**Move 2**].

'I said I liked the trick, so he said: "You can get it at the shop in Town." So I went to the shop, and there in the window was the trick fully described. It said: "Performer takes one, two, three, four, five, six cards [**Move 2**], throws away one, two, three cards [**Move 3**], and still has one, two, three, four, five, six cards left [**Move 2**]."

So I went into the shop and said to the assistant: "I want that trick you've got in the window, where you take one, two, three, four, five, six cards [**Move 2**], throw away one, two, three cards [**Move 3**], and you still have one, two, three, four, five, six cards left [**Move 2**]."

'He said: "Oh, you mean the trick where you take one, two, three, four, five, six cards [**Move 2**], throw away one, two, three cards [**Move 3**], and you still have one, two, three, four, five, six cards left. [*Here throw away each card as counted, leaving the hands empty.*]

' "Would you like to buy it?" Now, I **ask** you?'

Note. The cards should be held so that their **backs** are towards audience throughout.

ACES GET-TOGETHER. No. 49

Jordan

Effect. The Aces are inserted in different parts of the pack yet, on your dealing out the cards, the four Aces are discovered all together.

Method. Place the four Aces on the table and fan the rest of the pack in the left hand, faces towards yourself and the audience. Showing an Ace clearly, push it into the pack, imparting a lengthwise crimp in the act of inserting the card (by holding it from the end, the fingers above, thumb below, and pressing downwards with the fingers at the side of the thumb). At the same time note the value of the card in front of the Ace. Repeat exactly with the other three Aces, putting them in different parts. Then close the fan, and drop the pack face-down on the table, the crimped end away from the audience.

Cut the cards, and take in the left hand, in position for counting and gliding, as described in the last effect (Three from Six). (Fig. 92.) The crimped end of card should be towards the floor. Draw away the bottom face card and lay face-up on the table. Continue this process until you turn up one of the noted cards; then glide back the next card (an Ace) and take the following card, which

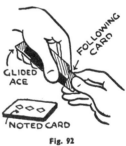

Fig. 92

you place face-up on those already on the table. Continue until you spot another memorized card. The following card (again an Ace) you push up with the right-hand fingers—this is where the crimp will prove of great assistance. The deal goes on in similar fashion with the third Ace and finally you reach the fourth Ace, which you deal; then deal the other three Aces as though they naturally followed on.

A STAB IN THE DARK. No. 50

Effect. The performer is blindfolded yet, after standing for a few moments, holding a dagger poised over a spread-out pack, he stabs one card.

The dagger is thrust right through a previously selected card, although the pack was thoroughly shuffled just before it was spread on the table.

Method. The card is freely selected while the pack is held in your hands. You have a key card somewhere about the middle of the pack, and when the selected card is returned, you note how many cards away from the key it is inserted. False-shuffle; then ribbon-spread the pack on the table. As you do this, spread the cards out fairly well, and see where the chosen card lies.

You now have your eyes covered with a blindfold, taking care that you can still see down the sides of the nose. You will find this a natural and easy procedure with any material that is not of a very fluffy nature. The dagger you already have, either on the table near at hand, or in a pocket. Give every indication that you are absolutely unable to see a thing, and ask a member of the audience to guide your hand along the outside edge of the cards, or at least to put one hand at either end of the cards so that you shall 'know where the cards actually lie' (it's a pity you can't tell them you already know!). If the dagger is on the table, have this put in your hand; then slowly pass this hand along and over the cards. Pass it

Fig. 93

backwards and forwards once or twice; then as it gets near the selected card, cause it to hover; now, putting the other hand to the forehead, as though concentrating, suddenly bring down the dagger and force it through the back of the card. With the card impaled, raise the dagger and point it towards the audience so that all can see you have stabbed the right card. The next moment pull off the blindfold, and the applause is yours. (Fig. 93)

CARD THROUGH HANDKERCHIEF. No. 51

Effect. A pack of cards, complete in its case, is securely wrapped in a handkerchief. At the magician's command a previously selected card falls to the floor, having penetrated the card-case, and the handkerchief.

Method. A chosen card is brought to the top of the pack, which is inserted in the case, backs of cards to the front of the case. The flap is tucked in but goes on the **inside** of the chosen card, thus enclosing all but this card, which, although inside the case, is not secured by the flap.

Hold the pack in the left hand, and, with the handkerchief in right, bring the pack behind the middle of the handkerchief. The fingers of the left hand now ease the selected card a short way out of the case, by means of pressure at the point where the cut-out thumb-grip is. (This thumb-grip is common with nearly all card cases. Should the thumb-grip not be deep enough to permit you to secure a reasonable hold on the end of the card, pare away another quarter of an inch or so by cutting with scissors beforehand.)

The top corner of the handkerchief is now draped over the left hand, which is tilted, raising the pack nearly level, and allowing the handkerchief to hang on all sides. Hold the left hand away from the body somewhat, apparently to see the handkerchief is hanging equally; then, with the thumb, grip the projecting card, and bring the hands together as though to hold the pack through the handkerchief with the right hand. At this moment turn the lower end of the pack downwards, and allow it to fall to the floor, but **retain the selected card** in the crook of the left thumb.

Pick up the pack and, with some such remark as 'Never mind, I'll put the pack on top', drop it on the left hand, which has been all this while extended. The pack is now resting on the handkerchief (with the chosen card directly underneath). Lift up the corner (A) which hangs beyond the left fingertips, and bring it up over the pack, at the same time letting the pack slide down a very short distance on the hand. (This is to make certain the whole of the card underneath the handkerchief is still hidden from view.) (Fig. 94)

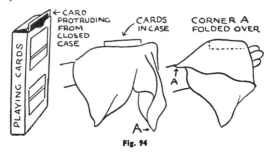

Fig. 94

The right hand takes the lower end of the pack, the fingers below and the thumb above, and raises it clear of the left hand (taking, of course, the concealed card also).

The left hand now grasps the hanging ends of the handkerchief and raises these as the right hand releases its hold.

In effect, the pack is now hanging in a bag formed by the holding of the handkerchief corners.

You ask the name of the selected card and, giving a few gentle shakes with the left hand, the pack facing the audience through the handkerchief, the chosen card gradually comes into view, and flutters to the floor, to all intents and purposes having passed completely through the case and visibly through the handkerchief.

This is a delightful effect, pretty, long remembered, and smacking of real magic.

IN THE ARMY. No. 52

Paul Clive

Effect. Four tumblers are on a table and one of the Kings from a pack is placed in each. One King is shuffled into the pack, then a spectator calls any number under twenty. The performer counts to the number and removes the card at that position, face-down. This card is put into a pocket of some person in the audience.

The three remaining Kings are shuffled into the pack and later discovered face-up. The fourth King is missing and proves to be the very card in the spectator's pocket.

Method. As the story unfolds, the various moves are described in brackets.

[Fanning the four Kings in one hand, you begin] 'This is the Army life story of four good fellows—Bill, the billiards player—he's a lifeclub member [K.C.]; Arty Arthur, more commonly known as "Mate" [K.H.]; Frank, because he always calls a spade a spade [K.S.] and Jim, the Gem man [K.D.].

'These four were close friends and neighbours—well, you can see how much alike they are, because there's practically no difference, apart from their colouring and that was only to suit their purpose, or purse; anyway they were neighbours. These glasses can represent their homes. Of course, they didn't live in glass-houses, although they never threw stones. You don't mind if they turn their backs, do you? [Turn tumblers, so that only the backs of the cards are seen.] Occasionally they would visit each other—just for a game of cards. [Here put all in the nearest tumbler.]

'Then came the shadow of war, and they decided to enlist [return one card to each tumbler, backs still to audience, and leave the K.D. in the glass nearest to you. Pick up the pack in the right hand, take the K.D. in the left, but without showing the face]. This is the Army [show the pack]; not many in it, but there's lots of numbers—and everyone's a number in the Army. So our first applicant trots along [place K.D. on the top] and is soon mixing with the crowd [overhand shuffle while facing the audience, by first dropping nearly half the pack, with the K.D. on top, into the left hand; then in-jog one card and follow by dropping the rest in small packets on top, until the whole pack has been shuffled. Cut at the in-jogged card and drop on top. This brings the K.D. second from top.]

'The medical blokes agreed that some men must be kept at home to do the housework while the wives did the queueing. So they said: "Let's mix this crowd up a bit and then we'll chuck one out." The Authorities—you know, the people who are responsible for the writing on the wall—the Authorities thought the message was "**Mess** this crowd up a bit" instead of "Mix them up", so, delighted with the request, they set to and messed them up [turn to the left and cut the pack, executing a boxed false-riffle-shuffle as described on page 23]. Then someone discovered there had been a mistake, and said: "Well, it doesn't matter; we'll just think of a number." Would you mind giving me a number—anything under twenty. [By now you have turned the pack over, and the K.D. is next to the bottom card in the face-up half. Whatever number is called, you count cards off the top of the pack to within two of that number. If seventeen is called, you count off fifteen; then, holding the fifteenth card face-down in the hand, you lower the left hand to your side and again turn the pack over and say] There we are, sir; the fifteenth card. [This usually causes evident amusement, but whether it does or not, you continue] You did say fifteen, didn't you? I'm so sorry; just like the Authorities, even I can make a mistake. Shall we continue to count from there, or shall we start again? [The usual reply is to complete the existing count but should you be asked to start again, merely gather up the fifteen already counted, put them on top and count down to the required seventeen. In either case your seventeenth card is the K.D.]

'[Leave the pack on the table as you walk over to the spectator and slip this card into his pocket without anyone seeing its value. The leaving of the pack on the table subconsciously creates the impression that you could not have changed the card or "done anything to it". Take the pack and reverse it as you gather up the counted cards, which you place on top. Turn to the three Kings on the table, which is to your left, holding the pack **upright**, and push the Kings—backs towards the audience—separately, at intervals into the **facing** half of the pack; in other words, the Kings are facing the cards among which they were inserted, but only their backs are seen by the audience as they are pushed in among the other cards.] These three have been fretting at home while their companion has been actively engaged, so they go off together, but are separated before they have had time to breathe —and even the Authorities like them to breathe. (Fig. 95)

'Hard times come and they get moved around again. [You are still turned to the left; now raise the knee; separate the two halves

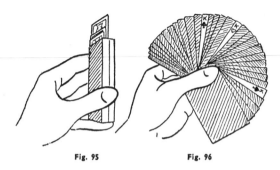

Fig. 95   Fig. 96

of the pack, again reverse the lower portion ready for the riffle-shuffle. Suddenly lower your foot to the ground, as though you had lost your balance; then turn facing the audience, and, if a chair is handy, rest your foot on it. Give a genuine riffle-shuffle for all to see. (The face-up Kings will not be seen, as the backs of the pack run lengthwise towards the audience and the sides are hidden by your hands.)] Greater trials come, and the battle waxes furious . . .

'It's a case of backs to the wall. But what of our heroes? As always in the past, they are triumphant, for they bravely face up to everything. [Saying this you fan the cards, backs towards the audience, and show the Kings face-up. Pull them part-way out of the pack and then look for the K.D. Then turn the pack round and search again through the faces of the other cards.] (Fig. 96)

'Why, there's only three. Where is the other? Could he have been the reject? If so, why? Would you see, sir, what card you have in your pocket? It is! The King of Diamonds! Why didn't they want him? [Look intently, then turn the card face to audience.] I know; he'd only got one eye!'

MENTAL SELECTION. No. 53

Lu Brent

Effect. The spectator thinks of a card as he scans the pack. He is next handed a slip of paper, or card, on which five lines are pencilled, and is asked to write on each line the name of a card—a different card on each line—one being the chosen card. The performer takes the list, then looks intently at the spectator and hands the list back to him, asking him to cross off all except the chosen card. While the assistant does this, the conjurer looks through the pack, removes one card and asks for the name of the chosen card to be read out. Immediately this is done the performer turns over the card he holds, and it is the one just named.

Method. The secret is entirely psychological, and the following points need observing in this order:

1. When drawing the lines on the card (card is preferable to paper, being more rigid in use) make the top, middle and last spaces deeper than the second and fourth. This is one reason for doing the preparation at the moment of presentation. It looks so free from guile.

2. Handing the slip to the assistant, request him to put down the names of any four cards and the name of the chosen card, one card to each space. Now—and this is important—suggest that he may put his mentally selected card 'in the middle space, the last space, or, if you prefer, in the first space. This is, of course, entirely for you to decide, and I want you to feel free of persuasion as to which space your card occupies.'

3. As the five cards are written down, take the pack and begin to look through it slowly, as though seeking one particular card. Whilst apparently thus absorbed, watch carefully how the spectator writes the names. Apart, perhaps, from the first card, and, of course, from the chosen card, he invariably hesitates, sometimes only a fraction of a second, but sometimes painfully long, before writing. (Fig. 97)

WATCH THE WRITER OVER THE FAN

Fig. 97

This done, take the card, note the one you've decided is the chosen card, hand back the list and conclude as already described under the heading 'Effect'.

The reason for drawing the first,

third and fifth spaces wider than the second and fourth is that the spectator shall **not** choose a wide space, that being too obvious. Similarly, by verbal example, you have drawn attention to the first, third and fifth position; so he has a second reason for avoiding them. In writing the five names, the usual choice is second place. The other, but less likely, position is the fourth. The fifth position is the least likely of the lot. If you stand back a little, the slight pause in the writing of the 'wrong' cards, and the no-pause in writing the chosen card, is more easily detected.

Until proficient with this effect, or when faced by an audience of which you feel somewhat uncertain, an additional and almost certain guide to the card is: instead of having the spectator look through the pack to make his selection, let him shuffle the pack, then hand it to you. Sighting the bottom card, hold the pack up, faces of cards to the spectator, and pass the cards in a slow, continuous procession, from one hand to the other, with the request that he think of one. Usually he will tell you when he has done so, but if he does not, just say: 'Have you thought of one yet?' As soon as he intimates he has made his selection, close the pack, and cut at the point just reached. The cards from which the selection has been made are now at the bottom—under the sighted card.

Now, when the list is completed and handed to you, one of the cards near the bottom of the pack, most likely one of the last half-dozen, will be the one chosen.

If, by any chance, two of the cards listed are in the section below the sighted card, you can determine which by 'feeling your way'. (If one is a spade, the other a heart, you ask: 'It was a red card, I believe?' etc.) Generally, it will be the card nearer the bottom. In any event, if you have observed his writing of the list, you can have little doubt when you find the card near the bottom of the pack.

This is a most impressive effect, which should be shown as a mental number, **not** a card trick. Do not hurry the proceedings, but take your time, and see that your helper hears all you have to say about placing the selected card anywhere on the list before you hand him the card and pencil. (Hand him pencil as well as card; this prevents his thinking-up names while searching for his own pencil.)

I ASK NO QUESTIONS. No. 54

Albright

Effect. A mentally chosen card is discovered by the performer, although he 'asks no questions', and does not even see the face of any card, until he picks out the actual card from the pack.

Method. The pack is held, faces of cards towards the audience, and cards passed from the top of the pack, in the left hand, into the right (the order **not** being altered). When the spectator sees the card he thought of, he is, 'in order to save keeping the others in suspense', to call 'Yes, it's there' or just the one word 'stop'.

Then close up the pack, keeping a break with the little finger of the left hand at the spot just reached. Cut at the break and false-shuffle; or cut several times, maintaining position of the bottom part of the pack (i.e. first cut).

Now ask the spectator to remove six cards from the pack, one of them to be the chosen card. Fan the cards slowly, passing them, as before, into the right hand.

Right up to this point you have had no need to look either at your assistant or the cards. Even now you can keep your head turned away until he has chosen five cards. You make sure by your slow, deliberate passing of the cards that he has his first five well before you reach the section in which you know his card to lie.

Then look in his direction and, as you patter, note particularly where he places this last card.

'That is your six?' you ask.

When he confirms this you say, as you take them from him: 'And one of them is your mentally chosen card?' Saying this, you mix the cards up a bit, keeping track of the chosen card, then fan them out, faces towards the assistant, and ask him once again: 'Your card is here? Then will you just concentrate your mind on that particular card. You need **not** look at it, but keep your mind on the card.'

While saying this the cards are held, still fanned, between the two hands. The left thumb presses the lower left-hand corner of the chosen card back against the right thumb and, at a convenient moment, you glimpse the index so exposed.

You now know the position and name of card. Disclose it as you think fit but, as with the previous effect, make it a mental achievement.

CONTROLLED REVERSE. No. 55

Paul Clive

Effect. One spectator chooses a card, which is returned to the pack. A second spectator, holding the pack behind his back, selects a card, reverses it, and pushes it back into the pack. The reversed card proves to be the original, chosen, card!

Method. The pack is 'boxed', with about two-thirds face-down at the top, one-third face-up underneath. (Fig. 98.) Spread the top half of pack for a card to be chosen, taking care the face-up cards are not exposed. As this card is being shown, turn the pack over, then ask your helper to push it back 'somewhere near the centre'. If it is inserted in the top third draw the pack away, leaving the card in the spectator's hand and remarking: 'Not too near the top or bottom, as people think then that I know just how far down it is.' You can, of course, push the card in the pack yourself, but it is better to let your assistant do this. The pack must be held flat, and properly squared; otherwise the faces of the cards will show. Now ask the spectator to hold the pack behind his back. Before

you give the cards, again turn them over and put into the assistant's hands behind his back. A member of the audience now names any number up to ten (or higher if you are sure of the number of face-down cards on top of the pack). Whatever number is called, that number of cards is counted off the pack and the next card turned **face-up** and inserted

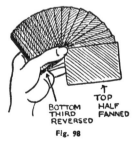

TOP
BOTTOM   HALF
THIRD   FANNED
REVERSED

Fig. 98

'near the middle'. The cards as counted off, were handed to you and, taking back the pack, you now add these cards to the top. Turning to the left you give the pack a boxed-riffle-shuffle (separating the cards where they face and, reversing those in the left hand, riffle-shuffle them into those held in the right hand).

With the exception of the chosen card, the entire pack is now face-down.

Draw attention to what has been done, laying particular emphasis on the freedom of the original choice, also the latitude of the numbers when the card from the pack was counted out.

Holding the pack before you, flat on the hand, address the person who chose the card, like this: 'You are satisfied, sir, that you had complete freedom of choice when you selected your card?' Naturally the reply is in the affirmative. To the person who called the number: 'And I did not influence you in any way in the selection of your number?'

'No.'

'Finally, the number called was counted off by you, sir?'

'It would seem impossible that the card originally chosen was related to the card later reversed. Would you, sir, take the pack and see what card you reversed, then ask the first gentleman what card he chose, and see——' Hand the pack to the spectator and await the applause.

THE FACE IN THE BOX. No. 56

Effect. Any card selected suddenly appears face-up in the pack.

Method. The working of this is almost identical with the last number, Controlled Reverse. It is, however, somewhat simpler.

The pack is 'boxed' at the commencement, and a card selected from the top half, noted, and returned to the lower half of the pack. (Quite a good idea in this direction is to cut the pack **just above** the facing cards and spread those cut-off on the table. Any card is then selected from the spread, looked at and pushed into those still in your hand. The spread is now collected and dropped on those you hold.) (Fig.99)

Now box-riffle-shuffle, which brings all the cards, except the chosen one, face-down again.

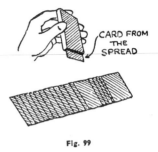

Fig. 99

Conclude as you think fit. Why not hand the pack to the assistant and ask: 'Do you think you'll recognize your card as soon as you see it?' The reply naturally is: 'Of course' or 'Yes', but as the person will certainly look at the faces of the cards, and, on arriving at the selected card, will see only the back of it, recognition is impossible until the card is turned over.

TO GET HIS BACK UP. No. 57

Effect. From a shuffled pack a spectator freely selects a card. The pack is handed to a second spectator. The card is returned and the pack again shuffled.

The performer takes the cards, dropping them into several heaps, then fans each heap, faces of cards towards the audience. The selector is requested to note in which pile the chosen card is situated, but not to give an indication to the performer. The conjurer then correctly names the pile, the number down in the pile, and, eventually, the name of the card.

Method. This is worked with a one-way pack. The cards are all set the one way before commencing. The pack is shuffled, overhand method, and a card selected. The pack is then handed to another person, this automatically turns the pack endwise, so that when the chosen card is pushed back it is the one card reversed in the whole pack.

A further overhand shuffle can be used, then you take the pack and drop the cards into about five heaps. As you fan out each heap, look for the tell-tale reversed card and note its position in the particular pile, and by turning up its lower left-hand corner you expose the index and so you know its name.

Continue with the other heaps as though you really don't know you have passed the chosen card. When you have treated all the piles in this way, pass your hand along the row of heaps, backwards and forwards, once or twice, then hover over the heap containing the chosen card, then bring the hand down on top and say: 'The card is in this heap.' With the hand still on top, appear to concentrate, and slowly state its position down in the heap. Then finally name it.

PASS THIS WAY. No. 58

Effect. The performer cuts a shuffled pack into two heaps and a spectator removes any card from one heap and pushes it into the other. The conjurer then gathers up the pack, which may be shuffled, and yet he discovers the selected card.

Method. Using a one-way pack you cut by holding the cards between the hands, at each end, thumb one side, second finger the other. The right hand draws up the top half and, turning it lengthwise—that is, a narrow end towards you—drops it on the table. The left hand does the same. One heap is now in the opposite direction to the other. Therefore, a card taken from one, and

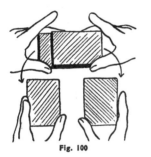

Fig. 100

placed in the other, will automatically become reversed. (Fig. 100)

You can turn your back or go out of the room while the spectator makes the choice. Then when you pick up the cards, take them just as you had put them down and either put one pile on the other or riffle-shuffle them together. This will bring all the cards, except the chosen card, back to the one way.

Quite a good method of discovering the card is to ribbon-spread the pack, and stab the chosen card, first of all pointing out that you cannot know the card, for you have not handled it, nor have you seen its face, nor can you know its position.

CHAPTER 5

TREATED AND PREPARED CARDS

♥ ♣ ♦ ♣ ♥ ♣ ♦ ♣ ♥ ♣ ♦ ♣ ♥ ♣ ♦ ♣ ♥ ♣ ♦ ♣

Some of the most baffling card mysteries are the result of secret preparations—chemical or otherwise. Here is a valuable collection of such subtleties and tricks employing these methods.

PREDICTION BY DEDUCTION. No. 59

Effect. The shuffled pack is placed down and the conjurer writes something on a piece of paper. The cards are cut into two heaps, one of which is chosen by a spectator, who then calls any number between ten and twenty. The slip of paper is next read out—it is the name of a card. Counting down in the chosen pile to the number called, the assistant turns up the card just named.

Method. You use a key card (a short, etc., or, for impromptu use, bridge, crimp, etc.). The key card is at a certain position in the pack. (This trick is ideal to follow any item in which you have counted a portion of the cards, such as 'This is your Card', 'Study in Shade', etc.) With your key at bottom of this pile, drop on remainder of pack and you know how many cards are below it. You also know the bottom card of the pack and it is the name of this you write down.

To present: False-shuffle and cut at the key, which we will presume is the twenty-fourth card from the top. This leaves twenty-eight cards in the pack, with the noted card at the bottom, or face. Now force this twenty-eight-card pile and ask your helper to: 'Give me a number, something between fifteen and twenty-five. I should think there are about thirty-five cards here.' You know there are not, but this makes your suggested range more reasonable. Suppose he says 'Twenty-one'. This is seven short of your noted card. You proceed: 'I want you to count down to the number you have named, like this,' and you count off three cards, singly, saying: 'One, two, three. If, for example, you had chosen seven, you would count down to it—'four, five, six', and the seventh would be the card you look at.' You turn up the seventh card to show the idea, then place it on the other six, and drop the twenty-one you are still holding on top of these.

Continue: 'Let me see, what number did you say? Twenty-one? Right, but before you count, will you read what I wrote on that slip of paper before we began?' He does so, counts down to the twenty-first card and . . . he is so amazed, he doesn't believe it.

However many cards are in the force pile, make your suggested range of numbers fairly near the total so that you will not have many to count off when illustrating this. (For example, if the pile consists of twenty-two cards, suggest a number between ten and twenty, and so on.)

If the number called is rather low, leaving a good number to count off, you get over the difficulty as follows: You start to count

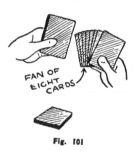

off the cards one by one, then say: 'Don't count them in a bunch,' illustrating this point by sliding off, fan style, about half a dozen or more—taking care to see just how many are in this group. (Fig. 101.) Drop these on the others, then proceed: 'Just one at a time.' As you say this you continue one by one again. 'I want everybody to see the cards are fairly counted, and when you come to the number you named you turn the card up, so.'

FAN OF EIGHT CARDS

Fig. 101

Note. The above is my own routine, but in case you prefer the original, here it is: In this case you work without a key and the whole pack is used, without cutting. You suggest a higher number (between thirty and forty, or thereabouts) and your illustrated count is accordingly more.

THE KEY TO THE DRAW. No. 60

Charles Miller and Jack McMillen

Effect. A card is chosen and shuffled back into the pack, which is now cut into three heaps. Two other spectators each take one heap, shuffle, and select any card, which is then replaced.

The three heaps are gathered up, shuffled again and, with the whole pack spread out on the table, one card is removed. This proves to be the first selected card.

After showing the top and bottom cards to be indifferent, the pack is held in one hand while the other removes two cards at a time, one from the top and one from the bottom until only two remain. These are the other two chosen cards.

Method. The twenty-sixth card down is a key card. Any card is selected and returned to the twenty-sixth position. (If taken from above the key the chosen card is replaced just under it. If selected from below the key it goes back immediately above.) False-shuffle, then hand to spectator to cut into three fairly equal heaps, which we will call one, two and three. The chosen card lies at some point in the middle pile. The two other heaps are now taken by the spectators, shuffled, and any card removed. The holder of heap No. 1 replaces his card at the **bottom** of his pile, the holder of heap No. 3 puts his back **on top** of his cards.

Heap No. 1 is dropped on No. 3 and all on top of No. 2. You can, with advantage, again false-shuffle if you so desire, then ribbon-spread the cards on the table. You can easily find the first-chosen card because of the key card next to it. As you withdraw this, press gently on the next card or two below it, thereby drawing those down a little. Ask the first person the name of his card and turn up the one in your hand. Leave this on the table, then gather up the pack, using one hand at each end. The displaced cards now serve as an 'in-jog'. With the pack roughly squared cut at the in-jog and completely square up.

False-shuffle if you wish.

Hold the pack up, showing the bottom card, and say: 'I don't think that was selected, was it?' Remove the top card, repeat the question and, when you receive a negative reply, **drop the card on the table**. Holding the pack in one hand fairly firmly, fingers over one end, thumb over the other, with the cards facing the palm,

Fig. 102

draw away the top and bottom cards with the other hand by clipping between the thumb above, and the first finger, below, at about the middle of the cards. (As you draw the hand away the two cards come smoothly as one.) Repeat this right through the pack; removing two cards at a time until you have only two remaining. (Fig. 102)

Ask for the names of the other selected cards, turn up the two you hold—and there you are.

This is a most ingenious combination, based on a simple arithmetical formula, although it is so concealed that you will never find anybody realizing how it is done.

STICKING TO CHOICE. No. 61

Orville W. Meyer

Effect. Two packs of cards are introduced, one with blue-backed cards, the other red.

Performer takes a card from the red pack and, without showing its value, has it initialled on the **back** then pushes it in the blue pack, holding the cards behind his back for this purpose.

This pack is then spread out face-up on a table and a spectator invited to put a finger on any card desired, then pull this card clear of the rest.

The pack is gathered up and the **face** of the selected card initialled.

Attention is drawn to spectator's freedom of choice, and the almost impossible odds of his card being the one first selected by the performer. In spite of this, the impossible is achieved. Spectator's card, still bearing the initials, is turned over and it is the red-backed card, originally initialled.

Method. Rough and smooth is the system employed. (Or a dab of conjurer's wax.)

The blue-backed cards are roughed on the backs, and one card from the **red** pack, for instance the 7 of spades, is roughed on its face.

The **blue** 7 of spades is at the bottom of the pack.

Showing the two packs, quite openly, and fanning them, faces towards audience, shuffle the **red** pack then take the 7 of spades and, without revealing its identity, have the back initialled.

Pick up the **blue** pack and, holding it behind your back, declare your intention of inserting the card somewhere in the pack, actually putting it at the bottom. You now have the two 7 of spades at the bottom, the red below the blue.

Turn pack face-up and spread the cards well out on table, keeping the two 7 of spades at the end as one card.

When the spectator is requested to press on one card and pull it clear, if he attempts to touch the 7 of spades, check him by saying: 'Not too far from the middle please.'

The rest will now be evident. Gather the pack, keeping the two bottom cards in position, drop the chosen card on top—all are still face-up—and, after the initialling, take the selected card, with the red 7 of spades adhering, and do your stuff.

THAT'S TORN IT. No. 62

Effect. A card, say the 5 of spades, is selected and shuffled back into the pack. The performer commands this card to leave the pack and travel invisibly to his pocket. He draws the card up from the pocket but it is the 7 of spades. The spectator says this is not the chosen card. The magician inquires: 'Well, what was your card?' The answer, of course, is: 'The 5 of spades.' The conjurer then removes the card from his pocket, saying: 'Well, this has only five pips.' Although the index number is seven, the end of the card has been torn off, and only five pips are on it.

Method. As you will already realize, this is more a joke than a straightforward conjuring effect, but its entertainment value makes it worthy of inclusion in the present selection. You previously secrete in the waistcoat pocket the 7 of spades, from which you have torn off two pips at one end. (The card, of course, faces outwards.) You force the 5 of spades and—the rest is up to you. (Fig. 103)

DOUBLE AND QUIT. No. 63

Paul Clive

Effect. A shuffled pack is cut into two halves, one face-up on the table, the other face-down. The top card of each heap is then taken, and the two held in one hand; thus the one card is seen face-up but only the back of the other is shown. The hand is turned over, showing the face of the other card, and attention drawn to these two particular values. The **face-up** card is then inserted in the **face-down** pile and the **face-down** card pushed into the **face-up heap**.

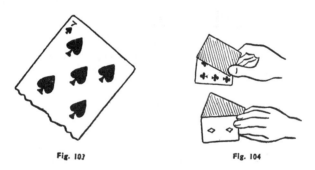

Fig. 103   Fig. 104

The two half-packs are then boxed by dropping the face-down heap on top of the face-up heap. The whole pack is then taken, turned over several times, then cut at the facing cards and, on spreading out the two sections, both the reversed cards are found to have vanished completely. The performer produces these from his pocket.

Method. In addition to the ordinary pack you require a double-face card and a double-back card. The double-face card is at the bottom of the pack; the double back at the top. To present, false-shuffle and cut the pack somewhere about the middle, and reverse the lower half as you place it on the table; the top portion you drop face-down. You now take the top card of each heap (that is, the double cards) and hold in one hand with the double-back card above the double-facer. Draw attention to the value of the card facing upwards, then turn the hand completely over, at the same time gliding the double-backer across the face of the other card, so that when the hand is reversed the back of a card is shown where previously a face had been seen. (Fig. 104)

The best method of holding the cards to facilitate this gliding movement is to grip them at the middle of one end, between the thumb on one side and the second and third fingers on the other. The tip of the little finger is bent down under the lower edges of the cards; the forefinger rests at the lower left-hand corner of the double-backer. In this manner the first and little fingers act as stoppers and prevent the gliding from overreaching itself.

The working will now be apparent. The duplicates of the double-face card are previously removed from the pack and placed in your pocket; the rest is simplicity itself. The double-backer is inserted in the face-up pile; the double-facer goes into the face-down heap; you drop the face-down pile on the face-up cards; take the pack between the hands and turn it over three times, thereby bringing to the top (face-down) the half-pack which was previously face-up. You spread the cards out on the table, separating them at the junction of the boxing and from the face-down cards the face-up one has vanished; likewise from the face-up cards the face-down card has gone.

DOUBLE FORESIGHT. No. 64

Effect. A pack is shuffled and a member of the audience invited to assist the performer. Looking intently at this person the conjurer writes something on a card, which he leaves in full view, the writing side away from the audience. The assistant is now asked to hold the pack behind the back, remove the top card and thrust it face-up in the pack; then to square the pack. The prediction is then read out; it is the name of two cards.

Spreading the pack face-down on the table, the two cards—one above and one below the reversed card—are removed and are found to be the very cards predicted.

Method. Previously reverse a card somewhere about the middle

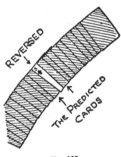

Fig. 105

of the pack and note the card above and the one below it. (Fig. 105.) On the top of the pack have a double-backed card. False-shuffle, then select your assistant and profess to foretell what cards this person will choose. The pack is held behind this person's back and the double-backed card pushed in, somewhere near the middle. You then take the pack, which you spread face-down on the table; thus exposing the reversed card, which is naturally taken to be the one the assistant handled. Remove this and the next card above and the one below, and prove your prediction correct.

ALL OVER THE HOUSE. No. 65

Effect. (For clarity the various effects are numbered.)

1. From a shuffled pack the top card, say the 4 of spades, is turned face-up, then returned face-down. Requesting that all watch closely, the top card is removed and pushed back into the pack, under the next card. The conjurer flicks the back of the top card, turns it up—it is the 4 of spades.

2. Again it is pushed under the next card, another flick and the 4 of spades is back on top.

3. This is repeated a third time.

4. The 4 of spades is now pushed into the middle of the pack, which is riffled and—it's on top again.

5. It is next turned face-up and placed at the bottom of the pack. The ends of the pack are then riffled and—it is reversed in

the middle of the pack. Turning the pack over, the bottom card is still facing the rest.

6. Turning this card over, it proves to be an indifferent card.

7. The obstreperous 4 of spades is put in the performer's pocket.

8. The pack is shuffled and 'just to make sure the 4 of spades hasn't returned, we'll look through the pack'. It's there again! Taking from his pocket the card placed there, this is discovered to be quite a different card.

Method. This is a variation of the 'Ambitious Card', described in *Greater Magic*. In that version sleight-of-hand plays quite an important part. The present method I have devised to obviate this necessity.

In addition to an ordinary pack, a duplicate of one card (in the above instance the 4 of spades) and a double-backer are required. At the bottom of the pack is one 4 of spades, face upwards, with the next card also face upwards. On the top of the pack is the second 4 of spades with the double-backer immediately beneath it. False-shuffle.

1. Take the 4 of spades, turn it face-up and leave it on top of the pack, for all to see; then double-lift, taking the 4 of spades and the double-backer; turn them over and replace on top of the pack. Now slide off the top card (the double-backer) and push it back, just under the 4 of spades. Flick the top card with your fingertips, then turn it face-up, showing the 4 of spades has returned to the top.

2. Repeat the above moves.

3. Again repeat but do not replace the 4 of spades when you show it as having returned to the top. Hold the card up, and lower the left hand, with the pack, to your side, at the same time turning it over.

4. Push the 4 of spades somewhere in the middle of the pack. Again flick the top card (which is the other 4 of spades) and remove it as you turn it face to the audience. Again lower the pack and turn it over.

5. With the double-backer towards the audience, slide the 4 of spades face-up under the bottom of the pack. Riffle the pack by the ends, then fan out, taking care not to expose the two bottom

cards, and disclose the 4 of spades, face-up in the middle of the pack. Remove this card and place face-up on top. Close the fan and turn the pack over, to find 'what card was placed face-up at the bottom'.

6. Double-lift again, exposing the indifferent card, and replace, face **outwards** on the bottom of the pack.

7. Again turn the pack over with the 4 of spades still exposed on top and treble-lift (that is, remove the exposed 4 of spades, the double-backer, and the next—indifferent—card, as one) and, remarking that there is only one sure way of getting rid of the card, that is, to remove it from the pack, you place these three in the pocket, spreading them out slightly as soon as they are out of spectators' sight.

8. Shuffle the pack, separating the two bottom cards and bringing the 4 of spades somewhere near the middle. Or you can, if you prefer, of course, bring it back to the top; then turn the pack face-up to make sure the 4 of spades is out of the way, 'discover' the return of the troublesome card, dive the hand into the pocket and withdraw the indifferent card.

You have in this way unloaded the duplicate card and the double-backer and your pack is now ready for examination, if need be, and a continuation to other effects.

Note. Although it is normally safe to try a double-lift during an effect, and it does not call for much experience on the part of the performer, in this particular effect, where the double-lift is more or less the nucleus of the trick and is so often repeated, it is advisable not to attempt such a trick unless fairly well experienced. In other words, I would suggest, if you are a beginner, that you should not attempt this number until you are more expert in the handling of cards.

SLICK ON THE DRAW. No. 66

Effect. Three freely selected cards are returned to the shuffled pack; after a further shuffle the pack is cut into three heaps; one of these heaps is placed in a pocket of each selector. The three cards are discovered, each in the possession of its respective chooser.

Method. This can be effected in a variety of ways, but perhaps the easiest is by means of a slick card. Three cards are chosen and the pack freely shuffled. With the 'slicker' somewhere near the middle, break the pack at this point and have the **last** of the chosen cards returned under it. Replace the top portion (with the slicker at the bottom); false-shuffle and break again at the same point. Have the second card put back on top of the previous one; repeat for the return of the remaining card. Cut the pack at the slicker and false-riffle-shuffle, keeping the returned cards at the top of the pack.

With the pack lying on its side in the left hand, the top of the pack against the fingers, hold the ends with the right hand as though ready for overhand shuffling. With the left hand, cut about one-third off the bottom of the pack, at the same time slipping the top card on to the top of this cut-off portion, as the right hand lifts the rest of the pack clear. (Fig. 106.) The left hand lays this portion face-down on the table.

TOP CARD
SLIPPED

Fig. 106

A similar move cuts half the remaining cards and slips one card from the top again. These piles held are now placed on the table with both hands, to the right of the first heap. You now have three piles, with a selected card at the top of each. You put the first (left-hand) heap in the first selector's breast-pocket, turning the back or top card upright and laying the rest on their sides; the cards are facing inwards to the body. The second heap you drop in the second selector's pocket in similar manner; the third heap you just drop into the third person's pocket.

Stand beside this third person and appear somewhat concerned; then remove the cards from his pocket, but leave the top card behind; remark to him that you have some doubts about his card —the impression you have gained is not very clear; run through the cards, face-up, and ask all three if they see their cards there. Naturally they reply 'No'. 'Then', you say to the third person, 'that cuts you out. Never mind; we'll just have to pretend with you. When I say "Now" I want you all—and [to third person] you may as well join in, although it will only be a pretence—I want you each to dive your hand into your pocket and take out a card; don't hesitate as there's a prize for the one who does it first. Are you ready? . . . Now.'

Each will remove the actual card he chose and the effect is great if well led up to. The third person usually shows some very real surprise at finding his own card in an empty pocket. If by any chance he does not produce it, just remark 'You're not trying' and, clearly showing your hand quite empty, take his card out. The effect in this case will be all the greater, as your audience will be convinced the pocket was quite empty only a moment earlier—otherwise, the helper must have produced the card.

Have each confirm that he chose that particular card.

ESTEEMED JUDGMENT. No. 67

Effect. The performer cuts a number of cards off the top of the pack and states how many he has cut. Upon counting them this proves correct. He repeats the effect with varying numbers.

Method. A slick card, a short, and a corner crimp is necessary. Before commencing, insert the slicker at, say the seventeenth position, with a short card at the twenty-fourth and a corner crimp at the thirty-eighth position.

To present, false-shuffle, then cut at, and including the slicker. Riffle the end of the cards, cut, and state that you have cut seventeen. Count these cards to corroborate your statement but do not reverse them in the counting; then replace on the top of the pack.

Now cut at the short, leaving the short itself on top of the pack, and, again riffling, claim to have cut twenty-three cards. Hand these to a spectator to count **singly**, thereby reversing their order.

Whilst your assistant is doing this, prepare your next cut at the card above the crimped card (which was the original thirty-eighth card.) To prepare this cut, break the pack by drawing upwards all the cards above the crimped card, with the right thumb tip; then slide this top portion forward about a quarter of an inch and, by thumb pressure against the crimped card, draw it down, or inwards to the body, as you slide the top packet back into place, square with the other cards and close the break. (Fig. 107)

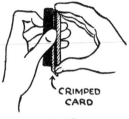

CRIMPED CARD

Fig. 107

You will now have all these cards squared up except the crimped card, which projects on the near side about a quarter of an inch. Square up the counted twenty-three cards and drop the rest of the pack on top, with the left hand. The slicker is now seventeenth from the bottom and the short card is on top.

Lift the whole pack by the sides and square the cards on all sides except the near end.

Again cut with the right hand, pressing the thumb tip firmly down on the in-jogged crimped card and lifting off all those above. This time you have cut fourteen cards, which the spectator counts, again reversing. Replace these on top.

Now false-shuffle, then cut at the slicker. This time you have thirty-six cards; count these without reversing, replace on top, and false-shuffle.

Split the pack at the short, drawing the cards above it inwards about a quarter of an inch. State that you can push some cards out from the centre of the pack in just the same way as you have cut, and still you will know how many have been removed. Hold the pack firmly in the left hand, press the right thumb tip against the near end of the pack, the thumb nail resting immediately under the in-jogged packet. At the same time as you are pressing with the right thumb in this way, swivel the left thumb outwards, still pressing with it firmly on the back of the cards.

The middle packet will break at the slicker and can be easily withdrawn. Immediately hand these cards to a spectator to count, remarking that you have cut twenty-three cards.

In the above routine you cut, in all, five times, and I have suggested this routine simply as a guide. It is up to you whether you enlarge upon it or cut it down, but, however many times you cut, present the whole effect cleanly and crisply; otherwise the counting process will outweigh the entertainment value of the performance.

When cutting at the slick card, have the right hand over the pack and give the impression that you have merely cut the cards with the right hand, thus avoiding any suggestion that the left has pushed these cards into the right hand.

ONE FOR ALL. No. 68

Effect. Several spectators each choose one card, look at it and replace it in the pack, which is shuffled. The performer then takes out a number of cards, which he fans and holds up, faces towards the audience. On being asked if their selected cards are in the fan, all reply 'Yes'. One card is removed and still each person sees the chosen card in the fan. Another card is withdrawn—still the same reply. This goes on until finally only one card remains. All had chosen the same card!

Method. Have about half a dozen cards 'chosen'. These, of course, are forced, the same card each time. Use whatever method you prefer. An extremely simple method of forcing is to use a slick card. This cuts to the bottom of the pile, so hold up the cut pile for the spectator to note the bottom card. Anyone can then shuffle the pack, yet you immediately locate the slicker in the usual way. In order to vary the selection you can force by the knife-blade method, or any of the other forces which appeals to you as applicable.

But let us presume you are working with a forcing pack. You will also need an ordinary pack to match. With the unprepared pack on its side in your pocket, first remove the duplicate of the forced card (say the 7 of spades).

To present, introduce the forcing pack (without showing the faces of the cards) and, suppose you have a fairly large audience, and you decide to force six cards (the number of cards you force will naturally be dependent on the size and distribution of your audience).

Have the first person select, while you pass the cards from the left hand into the right hand, in the usual 'take a card' manner.

For the second person, ribbon-spread the cards on a chair or table.

The third person calls a number and you count down to that

number. (Make sure the counted cards are squared before you hold up the packet for the selector to see; otherwise you may show several identical indexes.)

For the fourth person cut the pack.

The fifth person calls 'stop' at any time while you are dealing the cards, face-down.

The sixth selector takes the top card from any one of four heaps.

The above six methods are merely suggestions, to enable you to vary the selection of the chosen cards.

As each card is chosen, keep the card face-down until it is but a short way from the spectator's face, thereby ensuring that very few people see it, and, by having the six assistants well spaced out, there will be no overlapping.

Request each selector not to divulge the name of the card chosen but to bear it in mind.

False-shuffle. (Overhand style is best; then the faces of the cards are quite concealed.) Drop the pack **upright** in the pocket containing the ordinary pack.

Recapitulate what has been done; six different cards quite freely selected by various members of the audience, and the pack shuffled. Now you propose taking a number of cards from the pack, although you cannot see the face of any. Remove eight cards, in twos and singly, seven of them from the ordinary pack and one from the forcing pack. Crimp or otherwise mark for easy identification the force card, the 7 of spades. Hold these cards face-down as they are taken from the pocket, mix them up, then fan them out, faces towards the audience.

Ask your helpers if they can see their cards. ('Please answer "Yes" or "No".') All state 'Yes' in unison. Lower the fan and run the fingers of the right hand over the ends of the cards and remove one. Raise the fan again, repeat the question; after the 'Ayes', again lower the fan and discard one more card. Continue in this manner until you have only five left. (Fig. 107A)

By now your audience will realize that the chosen cards were not all different. This time discard two of the five; still all say 'Yes'. A further two cards are taken, leaving only the crimped card. 'Whose card is this?' you ask. 'All for one and one for all; yet it is odd.'

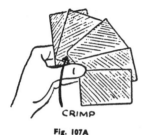

CRIMP

Fig. 107A

Take the rest of the genuine pack from pocket and you are ready to proceed with other effects. You can, if you wish, allow the pack to be examined, but do not allow this to take too long, as the majority of your audience lose interest in such activities beyond certain restricted limits.

THE STAINED-GLASS WINDOW. No. 69

Paul Clive

Effect. Performer shows a fan of five cards, the middle one being the Queen of hearts. This card is removed and put in the pack; the fan is closed. When the fan is opened out again the Queen is back in the middle.

A second time the Queen is removed. There is no doubt it is the Queen, and it is definitely put in the pack. Yet it is back again when the cards are fanned once more.

A third, and last, time the Queen is taken and put in the pack. The fan of cards is even counted and there are only four.

The fan is closed, opened again—and there are five cards with the Queen in the middle, as before.

On the pack being examined not a Queen of hearts can be found—there is only the one in the fan!

Method. Four Queens of hearts are required, all 'roughed' on the faces. Every card in the rest of the pack is roughed on the back.

We will suppose the four indifferent cards in the fan are: 3 clubs, 9 diamonds, 5 diamonds, and 2 spades—this as seen from front of fan, reading left to right with the visible Queen in the middle. There is one Queen hidden behind the 9 diamonds and **two** Queens concealed behind the 5 diamonds.

With the cards in order you can quite easily close the fan, square the cards then, holding the cards faces towards yourself, but with their backs towards the audience (your left thumb is on the face of cards), open the fan out using right hand first and second fingers at back, thumb on face, pushing the top card to the left first, then the next (double) card, then **press** the third card into position (where separating two rough surfaces this pressure will do it without your audience noting anything unusual in the move).

You next push the last—bottom—card to the **right** so that however many cards you have at the fourth position, they are not disturbed. These moves take place each time you fan the five cards, and nothing can slip.

If you wish to present the effect with something of a story, here is an idea:

The performer had a dream, a dream of a wonderful stained-glass window, high up before him. (Fan the five cards, showing the Queen of hearts in the middle.)

As it surpassed in beauty and fascination anything he had ever seen before, he could not take his eyes from it. Suddenly a billowing black cloud arose from below and completely blotted out the window. The smoke, turning a pale grey, dispersed, and the window was gone (remove Queen, close fan and put the Queen on top of pack. Cut off about a third of pack and complete cut.)

Next a pale crimson glow appeared, extending rapidly, then diminishing in intensity. As the glow disappeared, that lovely sight —the window—was visible again, more glorious than ever. (Fan cards, showing the second Queen.)

Once more that strange smoke or cloud rose up and the window was invisible. Once more the air cleared and the stained-glass window had vanished. (Remove Queen and, closing fan, put Queen on top of pack and cut, about a third down, as before.)

Again that mysterious glow, and the eventual restoration of the window. (Fan cards, revealing the third Queen—that is, the last of the Queens behind the 5 diamonds.)

Yet a third time the dark smoke, like a great puff from a witches' cauldron, obliterated the window of splendour, and cleared, leaving nothing but space. (Remove third Queen, drop on pack and cut at the **middle**.) There was no doubt the window **had** gone. (Close fan and count the 'four' cards one at a time, bringing double card into position for the last fanning.)

The crimson glow made its appearance, like a searing, devouring flame, diminished, then disappeared. The stained-glass window was unmistakably there (fan cards showing the Queen returned).

Perhaps it had been there all the time for, if it had gone, there was no sign of it anywhere else (take pack and run through faces of cards towards audience).

If the above is too heavy (dramatic?) for your taste, another notion, in lighter vein, is this:

(Hold up the five cards, fanned.) Introduce as the five senses with vision in the middle. Naturally, anyone would have eyes for a girl with such a heart. She's a good cook, too. Let's watch her go into the bakehouse (put Queen into pack). No, don't hang round the bakehouse door. She knows her onions—oh boy, what a cook— and she's pretty fly, too. In fact, she's flown back indoors. (Fan cards, showing Queen returned.) You weren't watching. I'll show you again. Into the bakehouse. . . . Back into the house. How she gets around.

Try again. You **do** definitely see her go to the cookhouse door. We push her in, and put the lid on. And there are only four senses left.

Yet, she's back again! The bakehouse? No, she's not there. Which just shows what happens when you start seeing things.

Note. Instead of using the pack for vanishing the Queens, you can use the trousers pocket, pushing the cards to the top (but insert hand to bottom of pocket to give the impression each card is placed there).

If preferred, a dab of conjurer's wax on the face of the Queens, can be used, obviating the use of roughing fluid, but the roughing is better in this instance.

REFLECTION ON SELECTION. No. 70

Effect. After choosing a card, which is returned to the pack, a spectator writes its name on a slip of paper. The performer then removes a card from the pack, which spectator agrees is not his card, and this card is placed face towards the audience in a tumbler, then covered with a handkerchief.

Asking a third party to read out the name on the slip, the tumbler is uncovered and there is the very card the spectator chose.

Method. A double-faced card is second from the bottom of the pack. The duplicate of the face-up side is forced and returned to the pack. (The original of the face-down side is previously removed from the pack.)

The assistant writes down the name of the card selected, and hands this slip to someone else.

Cut at the returned card and false-shuffle, but guard against the face of the fake card showing among the backs of the other cards. At the conclusion see to it that you have the double-facer somewhere near the middle of the pack and the selected card on top. Fan the cards, faces to the audience, keeping the chosen card out of sight, and remove the double-facer, stating that 'any card will do'—and asking: 'This is not the card you chose, sir, is it?'

Place this card in a tumbler, which you hold up as you cover with a handkerchief. As soon as the tumbler is covered, give it a half-turn from the wrist, bringing the face of the selected card towards the audience. The rest is straightforward, but you can get a lot of appreciation for this number if you put it over well. (Fig. 108)

Fig. 108

THE CHANGE-OVER. No. 71

U. F. Grant

Effect. The performer takes two cards from the pack and places them in a spectator's pocket. Taking one of these cards, showing it and slipping it in his own pocket, the conjurer now asks his assistant what card was left behind. This is named. With the remark: 'You are right. I wanted to make sure you would remember both the cards,' the magician replaces his card in the assistant's pocket. Again taking one card the performer repeats his inquiry as to which card remains. This time the assistant is wrong, for the very card the conjurer put in his own pocket is discovered in his helper's, whereas the card left behind is produced from the performer's pocket.

Method. A double-faced card accounts for this fine mystery. Let us presume the double-facer is a 5 of hearts on the one side and a Jack of spades on the other. This card is already in your pocket, with the 5 of hearts on the outside. Take the genuine Jack of spades and the 5 of hearts from the pack and slip into the spectator's pocket, the 5 of hearts on the outside, both cards facing **away** from the body.

Stand about twelve inches away from your assistant, both of you facing the audience, and use your adjacent outside coat pockets.

Now take the 5 of Hearts from his pocket and place it in your own. Ask which card remains. Remove the double-facer, the 5 of hearts side showing, and as you place it in his pocket turn it over and take it out again with the Jack of spades showing. Put this in your pocket. Again ask which card is left. Declare that he is mistaken and produce the genuine 5 of hearts and allow the assistant to take the Jack of spades from his pocket. (Fig. 109)

'EXTRA SPECIAL' TORN CARD. No. 72

Effect. Spectator chooses a card and tears off one corner. Assistant's name is written on the face of the larger piece. The torn-off corner is then initialled on both sides.

The conjurer takes the three-quarters piece and tears it into three. Holding all four quarters he puts them in an envelope and burns the lot. Commanding the pieces to return to the pack, assistant finds the three-quarter section restored, but the other corner is missing. This is eventually discovered where it 'must have been dropped'.

Both pieces bear their original signatures.

Method. Prepare for this trick by tearing off the top left-hand corner (as seen from the **face**) from any card. This corner you destroy. The three-quarter piece leave face-down on top of pack, the torn-out piece at the lower (or near) left-hand corner.

Fan the cards and ask a person to take one—the torn-out piece can be concealed quite easily by the hands. If preferred, you can hold the pack up, faces towards audience, for the choice of the card.

As you close the fan, ask your helper to tear off a corner of the card, 'about a quarter of the card, so that everyone can see you're making a real job of it'.

Take the corner from assistant whilst the name is written on the face of the larger piece, then change pieces with spectator, for the corner piece to be initialled. When you take the three-quarter section, place it on top of the pack, **torn corner away from you.**

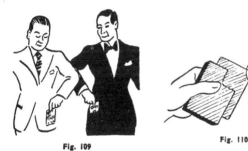

Fig. 109

Fig. 110

The corner initialled, apparently take the torn card off the top of the pack, but actually draw the next card out at the free, top corner, under cover of a turn to the left to put the pack down. Take care not to show the face of the piece you now hold. (Fig. 110)

Place this piece on the table, and cut the pack which you leave in full view, again picking up the three-quarter section. Take back the initialled quarter and, holding it in front of the larger piece— that is, on side nearer audience—tear off projecting end of the three-quarter portion. You now have two quarters and a half-card. Tear the half across the middle, making four quarters in all —keep the initialled corner towards audience throughout, this sub-consciously impresses them that they actually **see** the **original** card mutilated.

Fan the four pieces (count them out if you prefer), backs, of course, still towards audience. Close the fan and, bending the fingers inwards, bring the pieces flat on the palm just below the first and second fingers, thumb now resting on top. Reach over and, with the left hand, pick up an envelope from table, at the same time resting the right hand on the table, a most natural action. While taking the envelope in the left hand, the right thumb pushes the initialled corner off the rest, and it falls on the table. You can either allow this action to be seen, in which case it must be regarded as a 'slip' or 'error' or—preferably—do it secretly.

The envelope is opened out and the pieces obviously dropped inside. Show the right hand empty. Seal down the flap and either burn on a tray or in the fire.

As the burning takes place 'gather' the rising smoke in the hand and 'throw' it towards the pack.

Hand the pack to spectator, and the three-quarter piece is found. Appear disconcerted and look round for the missing quarter. (There is scope for good comedy here.)

Eventually 'find' it—'I must have dropped it; unless it crawled out of the envelope'—and conclude.

A SLICK COUNT. No. 73

Effect. A pack is shuffled after the return of a chosen card. A spectator calls a number (completely free choice up to fifty-two), and counting down, the selected card is turned up at the number named.

Method. The card is forced, 'slicked' on the face and 'roughed' on the back. A very suitable force is the top slip.

When the card is returned, keep a break above it, then separate the pack at this point and riffle-shuffle the two halves together, keeping the forced card on top.

A number is now named, and you openly count down to that number. In counting keep the counted cards in their original order. The force card is then still at the top when the counting is finished. (It is a good plan to count with the cards held up to the left, their **backs**—of course—towards audience.) (Fig. 111)

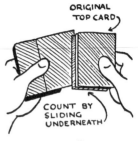

Fig. 111

When you reach the number named, take that card at the bottom of the right-hand heap, but projecting above it, then transfer it to the left hand, where it is gripped between the first and second fingertips. The right-hand cards are now placed on the left-hand pile, and the chosen card is again taken in the right hand. (Backs of all the cards still towards audience.)

Turn towards audience, swinging the cards downwards in front of you, and remark to the second assistant: 'I did not influence your choice of number at all, did I?' Naturally, the reply is 'No'. You continue: 'And this is the card I counted down to?' 'Yes.' Placing the card face-down on top of the pack, that is, on the 'roughed' card, you square all up and, addressing the selector of the card, remark that that choice was also quite free. 'Now wouldn't it be a marvellous thing if the chosen card was at the very spot indicated by the number called?' As you say this, press firmly with the left thumb on the back of the top card and push it out at the side of the pack. The roughed card will cling to it, and the two will move as one. Take this 'card' in the right hand and ask first assistant: 'What **was** your card?'

As soon as it is named, turn your hand over, and show the card!

SIGNED COINCIDENCE. No. 74

Lu Brent

Effect. A spectator cuts a shuffled pack into two fairly equal heaps, retaining one himself. Performer takes the other, and fans his half-pack for assistant to select any card. Performer, in like manner, chooses a card from spectator's half, and each then writes his name across the face of the card he has chosen. Spectator's card is replaced on his own pile, performer doing the same with his card. Each pile is cut several times, then spread face-down (ribbon fashion) on the table. Each participant presses a finger on any card in the opposite spread, pulls it clear, and pushes it into his own. Each pile is then well shuffled, turned face-up and spread on the table.

It is seen that the card bearing the **assistant's** signature is now among the performer's cards, whilst his own signed card is discovered in assistant's spread.

Method. Anything of Lu Brent's is ingenious, and very presentable but I have taken the liberty of introducing one or two twists of my own into the present version.

The fifth card from the bottom of the pack is a locator card. This can be any card with a known and readily ascertainable marking—an age mark, thumbnail edge-marking, or even an added mark in pen or pencil. Two cards below this (third from bottom) is a known card, say the 7 of hearts. Across the face of this 7 of hearts you have previously written your name.

When presenting, give the pack a false-shuffle, and ask spectator to cut it into two nearly equal heaps. Then say: 'Will you indicate one heap?' If he points to what was the lower section, you gather up the other heap, at the same time asking him to fan his cards, face-down, 'like this' and you fan those you are holding.

But should he indicate the upper half, thank him as you pick them up, and ask him to take **his** half and fan them out, face-down.

The effect is, of course, that you have forced the lower section on him. You now take a card from his fan, and he removes one from yours. The fans are closed, and placed, face down, on the table. Next, you each write your name across the face of the card you hold. At least, HE does. You simply simulate this, with pen in hand. Put your card on top of your squared heap, asking him to put **his** card on his heap. You each cut your own heap once, and the other heap twice. With these three cuts the selected cards will be somewhere near the middle of each heap.

Now, ribbon-spread your cards, face-down, and request your helper to do the same. Ask him to place a fingertip on any card in your pile, and to pull it across, and into his pile. You do similarly, except that you take the fifth card below the locator card. This is the card your assistant autographed.

As he already has your signed card in his pile, you have no more work to do, but add showmanship to any already accomplished fact.

Note. If you have the five bottom cards 'left' in the card case, you can make this an effective 'encore'. Apparently having finished your tricks for the occasion, you return the pack to the case, adding the hidden five to the bottom of the pack at the same time. If asked to 'do just one more', here is one that will surely get them guessing.

CHU, CHIN, CHOW. No. 75

Paul Clive

Effect. Four cards are taken from the pack representing four characters—the first Chu, the second Chin, the third Chow, and the last—the wicked man—Hoo Doo.

The rest of the pack is cut into two heaps; and the story unfolds.

It appears that Chu, Chin and Chow are three Chinese who attend an important international conference.

The conference chamber is represented by one of the heaps of cards, and the three 'Chinese' are pushed into this heap.

The villain Hoo Doo shadows them and also gains entry to the conference room—the fourth card goes into the heap.

Chu, Chin and Chow, however, knew of the attempt to steal their Government's secret instructions, so they, also secretly, departed. Hoo Doo, finding his prey had vanished, sought them high and low—but was eventually discovered himself, and was taken away for trespassing.

Upon reaching the point where Chu, Chin and Chow are stated to have 'secretly departed' the pile in which they were placed is taken up and the faces of all the cards shown—and **all four** cards are missing.

Taking the **other** heap, Hoo Doo is found in the middle. Chu, Chin and Chow are produced from the performer's pocket.

Method. Rough and smooth is the principle employed to effect the evanishment of the four cards in the one heap. These four cards are 'roughed' on their faces, and the rest of the pack has 'slicked' faces.

The four cards are: Chu, Ace of diamonds; Chin, 2 of hearts; Chow, 7 of spades; Hoo Doo, Ace of clubs. These are disposed at various points among the top thirty cards in the pack. A duplicate, slick-faced Ace of clubs is placed about ten cards from the bottom, and duplicates of the other three are placed in the top of right trousers pocket.

The working will now be evident. The complete story runs as follows, the various moves being bracketed throughout the patter:

'This is a story of the Far East, but one which can be brought **home** to all, for such things **do** happen [looking through the pack, you remove the four cards].

'We have three well-known characters: Chu, Chin, and Chow [fan these three, faces towards audience]. They are, as you know, Chinese. Take Chu [hold up Ace of diamonds, placing other cards on table]. He's a hungry fellow, with a big mouth and one tooth. He keeps that in the middle so it can cut both ways. Chu works in an American **gum** factory. Well, so much for Chu [if in friendly company, you can glance at a lady and remark] No, madam, not you.

'[Put down the Ace of diamonds and take up the 2 of hearts] Here is Chin. He can take it. A hearty man and hale [here a quantity of rice falls from the card on to the table—*see* Note]. Hmm, that must be the hail [Look closer at it.] No, it's rice: another wedding in Honk-onk [car horn sounds]—that's the honk. Anyway, he's a **hearty** man [hand, just placed in pocket, rustles paper; you stop short, pull paper from pocket, and look at it interestedly, then toss it away]. A bill for liver—**offal** things, these bills. Well, that's Chin, the up-man.

'[Put the 2 of hearts with the Ace of diamonds and take up the 7 of spades.] This is Chow; a doggie little chap, with a black nose, and a dirty tongue. He wanted to dig for gold, but there isn't any in China. So he goes in for Chop Suey, and comes out with chips. He is very fond of drink—you can see he's one under the eight now—and his sense of humour is a **wow**, but as it's Chinese, I can't repeat it. [Put down the 7 of spades and, taking up the Ace of clubs, continue.] Then there's Hoo Doo, son of the Mandarin, Hoo Did. He's the villain of the piece [holding the card up for all to see, peer at it yourself]. Looks like the sign of the three brass balls; and just as close. They're a bit black-looking now, but they're good for a clean-up—anytime. [Place down near other three.]

'Well, those are the characters. [Take up pack.] Now Chu, Chin and Chow are special representatives of their Government at an international conference. You know what an international conference is—a round table in a large room, with lots of men in fancy dress sitting round.

'So our three good men attend the conference carrying secret documents from their Government. Here is the conference room [cut pack into two halves and insert the three cards in top portion in different places to the following patter]:

'First in goes Chu—he got the habit from watching cows when a baby. There he is, complete with his one tooth. He had more when he was a boy; most Chinese children have. Next, Chin goes in, without any rice.

'Now, Chow, with a dark look and a bottle of Scotch. Great Scots, these Chinese.

'The conference is on, and secrets are being compared under the counter. Sorry, I'm talking shop again.

'I forgot to tell you the three Chinese are quite religious. In fact in China they **are** the three Churches (ch—chs)—**Chu, Chin, and Chow.**

'They are, as you must realize, almost inseparable. To such extent that they had a joint banking account. [Pull trouser pocket out and show empty, the duplicate cards remaining at top, out of sight.] Of course, there's nothing in that. I had a joint account with a butcher, but **he** held the joint. [Push pocket back into place.]

'Hullo, here comes Black Maria—er—Hoo Doo. Pity he didn't. He also gets into the conference room; through the roof—he's an eavesdropper. [Place Ace of clubs on top of heap containing the other three cards and cut, bringing it to the middle of this pile.]

'But the three ch—chs knew of this bad man, and when he got there the room was bare. I seem to have heard that expression before somewhere. A statesman's famous utterance, I expect. Hoo

Doo hunted high and low; mainly low, because he was that sort of a man. Besides, he walked with a stoop—saved him looking people in the eye. Yes, he was a really bad man. A bad man, by the way, is the one who **does** get found out.

'Let's see what had happened [take the heap and, showing faces of cards to audience, deliberately go through them all, one at a time, each of the roughed cards clinging to the one in front. Having shown they have gone, take the other half-pack and, going through those in like manner, "discover" Hoo Doo and remove the card.] The last I heard of Hoo Doo was that he was imprisoned for trespass and espionage. For a man of his ambitions it was quite a "cell". The prison governor changed the name from Hoo Doo to Boo Hoo, and wept for joy at the bright idea. Or was it?

'Where were Chu, Chin and Chow?

'They'd gone to the bank to draw lots. [Here withdraw the three cards from pocket.]'

Note. The fall of the rice can be effected by many means. An extremely simple method is as follows: There are a number of cheap 'propelling' pencils on the market in which the lead is **pressed** down and **not** propelled. Most of this type have a fair-sized cavity in the opposite end of the pencil. Prepare by removing the top and filling the cavity with rice. You can replace the cap until ready to perform. The pencil is in the top waistcoat pocket, as usual.

Just before presenting this trick, take cap off pencil, and you're all set.

When you show the Ace of diamonds, indicate it with the point of pencil, keeping top end closed by pressure against the palm of the hand. As you put the card down, lower the pencil and, when you raise it again, hold from the pointed end, keeping the pencil upright. Attention has already been drawn to the 2 of hearts. Point to this card, and at the appropriate moment, lower card and tilt pencil, when the rice will flow out.

CHAPTER 6

PRE-ARRANGEMENT

Involving the use of cards which are in a certain order or
arrangement.

♥ ♣ ♦ ♣ ♥ ♣ ♦ ♣ ♥ ♣ ♦ ♣ ♥ ♣ ♦ ♣ ♥ ♣ ♦ ♦

SUPER THIRTY-CARDS TRICK. No. 76

Zens

Effect. Shuffled pack is handed to spectator, who counts off
fifteen cards. He then selects one of two envelopes and drops his
fifteen cards into it, immediately sealing the envelope and placing
it in his pocket.

Remainder of pack is cut and another fifteen cards counted off.
Shuffling these, assistant goes among the audience, requesting
each of three people to choose any one card. This done, the chosen
cards are replaced and the fifteen again shuffled, then put into the
other envelope, which, after sealing, is dropped in the performer's
pocket.

The assistant is then asked how many cards he put in his own
envelope. Naturally he replies 'Fifteen'. 'And how many in the
other? 'Fifteen.' The conjurer requests him to open his envelope,
where he finds eighteen cards. The performer then opens his and
he has only twelve. The chosen cards are discovered among the
eighteen and are missing from the performer's envelope.

Method. This delightful trick, although sounding so involved,
is really quite easily effected. To commence you need three identical packs, from each of which you take fifteen cards, the same
fifteen from each pack.

First arrange one fifteen in any order you like. Then repeat this

arrangement with the other two sets. Placing these sets together
you have a pack of forty-five cards—top fifteen in one order, this
being repeated twice with the other thirty cards. You also require
three envelopes, in one of which you place any twelve of the
remaining cards from one pack and seal this envelope, placing it
in your inside coat pocket. Another three cards are placed under
the two remaining envelopes on the table. You are now ready to
perform.

False-shuffle the pack, maintaining complete order, then hand
these cards to the spectator, requesting him to cut the pack and
then deal fifteen cards out. These fifteen cards you ask him to
again count to make sure he has got fifteen there. As he counts
these the second time, pick up the two envelopes, also the three
cards secretly underneath, and as he finishes the count toss the
envelopes and the cards on to those he has just counted and say:
'Will you take one of these envelopes—either envelope—and place
the cards you just counted inside, then seal the envelope?' This
done, he places this envelope in his pocket with, of course, the
eighteen cards inside, and you ask him to count out another
fifteen cards from the remainder of the pack. He can, of course,
cut before he does this if he wishes.

These fifteen cards he shuffles, then takes down to the audience
and has three selected by various members. After noting these
cards they are returned to this assistant, shuffled and placed in
the second envelope, which is also sealed. This envelope is then
handed to you and you place it in your inside pocket, where, unknown to the audience, you already have your other envelope
containing twelve cards.

It is a good plan to have the original twelve-card envelope lying
horizontally in pocket, and the second one you should have standing on end. You now remind the audience of what has happened,
stressing the fact that you have not touched the cards and therefore
you cannot have any knowledge of the cards chosen.

Now you ask the assistant how many cards he put in his envelope,
then ask him to check this number again. He tears open the envelope and while he is counting you remove your **original** envelope
from your pocket. He finds eighteen cards, then you check yours
and find twelve. Now you ask for the names of the chosen cards

and show that they have disappeared, and assistant's cards are turned face-up and the three chosen cards discovered there.

Note. You can dispense with the use of the envelopes as follows: Have the three indifferent cards hidden under the rim of a small plate which rests on the edge of the table. When you ask your assistant to recount the fifteen cards 'so that all may see' take up the plate, and with it the three hidden cards, covering their length with the fingers.

When your assistant has finished counting the cards on to the plate, bring the other hand up, fingers underneath, thumb on top, and, tilting the plate, allow the cards on it to fall into the waiting hand, at the same time allowing the three cards at the back to slide down behind the fifteen. The first and little fingers of the hand

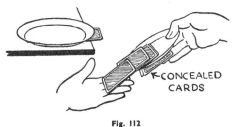

CONCEALED CARDS

Fig. 112

gripping the plate, if held just beyond the sides of the three cards, will guide them into the other hand, preventing their slipping side-ways. The fifteen cards should be dropped from about twelve inches above the plate when counted. They will then spread out and afford ample cover for the three dropped from the back. (Fig. 112)

ODD MAN OUT. No. 77

Effect. The spectator chooses a card, then the pack is spread ribbonwise across the table and spectator pushes his card back, anywhere he likes. The pack is then squared up and cut as required. On running through the cards the performer produces the chosen card without any hesitation.

Method. Have the thirteen cards of one suit together, about the middle of the pack. (Fig. 113.) When the card is chosen see this is taken from the portion above this section. Then, when spreading the cards on the table, see that the centre section is fairly well spread out, and almost inevitably the chosen card will be pushed back in this portion. If by any chance this is not done it is easy to note where it was placed, and in gathering up the cards either crimp this card or one within a specified number above or below— you can easily calculate three, four or five cards to the right or left and that will give you complete track of the selected card. The rest of the working is as in the effect above.

One other contingency may arise; that is, that a card is chosen from among the thirteen. Should this happen, cut the pack while the spectator is noting the card he chose and have this returned in another section. Knowing the suit of the thirteen cards, you can easily find the chosen card when you find one of these out of place.

When discovering the chosen card after the pack has been cut a number of times, run through the pack, faces of cards to yourself; withdraw the card; place it face-down on the table; then as you well shuffle the pack to remove all traces of the preparation you made, name the card, then turn it face-up.

TWO GOOD TURNS. No. 78

Effect. Two packs of cards, still in their sealed wrappers, are introduced and one is selected, the seals broken and the pack cut into two heaps. One of these heaps is counted. The performer then illustrates how he wants the two top cards of this heap turned face-up and placed one on each heap. Then both heaps cut, thus burying the face-up cards.

The cards the magician has just reversed are turned face-down again and pushed into their respective heaps.

The assistant now repeats the reversal process just as shown by the performer. Taking the second pack, still in its sealed case, the performer suggests that all cards possess a certain sympathy, a fact particularly noticeable with new cards for, being untouched by hand, they are as yet not subject to any human influence. As proof of this the assistant is asked to name the reversed cards, then take the second pack, open it and spread it face-down on the table. He does so and the identical cards corresponding to those originally reversed are discovered face-up in the second pack.

Method. Three packs of cards are required, all of similar back design. Before presenting the effect, steam open the seals and in two of the packs place two certain cards at the third and fourth positions from the bottom. (The identical two cards in each pack.) In the third pack **reverse** the same two cards, one about a quarter-way down in the pack, the other a little over half-way down. Re-seal but keep note of the pack with the reversed cards. A small mark (pencil dot, etc.) is an advisable precaution to ensure recognition of this pack.

When presenting, have the reverse-cards pack in lying-down position in right pocket, one of the other packs in an upright position in the same pocket and the remaining pack in the left coat pocket. Leaving the pack with the reversed cards in the pocket, you take out the other two packs, place them on the table and ask

Fig. 113   Fig. 114

your assistant to choose one. When he has done this you place the second pack in your right coat pocket (in an upright position again), then, after he has opened the one pack, and cut it into two heaps, you ask him to count, singly, the portion that was the lower part of the pack (the reason for this is to bring to the top of the heap, the cards you previously placed near the bottom).

Then, taking the top two cards off this heap, and placing one face-up on each of the piles, to show how you want your assistant to put them, cut each pile and state that this is what you want him to do. Now in order to regain the two face-up cards you cut each pile at that point, which of course brings them back to the order they were in before you put these cards on top. (Fig. 114)

These two cards you turn face-down and push into their respective piles. Your assistant now takes the next two cards, which are duplicates of those already reversed (in the other pack), and places these face-up in the two piles.

Place one heap on the other and, taking the pack which is lying down in the pocket—that is the sealed pack with the reversed cards —you hand it to your assistant, reminding him that he previously had a free choice of pack, that you had no control over the cut and therefore you could have had no knowledge of what cards he would ultimately turn face-up.

Here you introduce your story of sympathy among the cards, and ask your assistant to open the pack and see for himself if that sympathy exists in this particular case.

SPELLING BY QUESTION. No. 79

Frank Squires

Effect. A chosen card is spelt, then turned up, although the pack was shuffled after the return of the card.

Method. Fourteen cards, a 3, 4, 9, 10, Jack and King of diamonds, the same six cards of spades and the Queen and 8 of hearts are located from the twenty-third to the thirty-sixth in the pack. It is one of these that is chosen.

The top twenty-two cards are bridged or divided off by a key card. These twenty-two cards are lifted off for the return of the chosen card, replaced and the pack false-shuffled.

To spell it out you ask the following questions in this order:

'Is the card red or black?'

'What is the suit?'

'Is it high or low?' (Seven or over is high.)

'Is it odd or even?' (Jack and King are odd, Queen is even.)

Lastly: 'What is its actual value?'

It will be found that the complete spelling of the answers in every case totals twenty-two letters, including 's' at the end of the suit.

You turn up the next card and that is the card you have spelt.

VICTORY FLUSH. No. 80

Effect. The performer remarks on the frequently uninteresting cards one gets when playing games, particularly if only one part of the pack is used. For instance, take 'Nap'. He thereupon deals from a shuffled pack several hands of nap, then shows them and replaces each on top of the pack. 'Nothing very exciting about those,' he remarks. Shuffling the pack once more, the cards are again dealt for 'Nap' and, once more displaying, the various hands are still without cause for comment . . . until the magician reaches his own hand. This consists of Ace, King, Queen, Jack and 10 of one suit.

Method. The Flush is stacked from the sixth to the tenth positions from the top of the pack, with five indifferent (but preferably low value) cards at the top.

When the five hands are dealt, the Flush will be distributed among the hands, the fourth card down—that is, next to the face-card—in each hand. In holding the hands up for the audience to see, keep the Flush cards hidden as much as possible by the front cards, fanning out the other three and showing rather briefly, but without evident haste. (Fig. 115)

After false-shuffling for the re-deal, deal the hands fairly close to you, then push them out a bit, making sure that you keep the **fourth** hand for yourself. This is easily done without exciting suspicion. (For instance, move the third heap first, then the first, the second, then the fifth, and leave the fourth ready to hand for yourself.) The first hand you pick up to display, is in reality the fifth hand. Then you work round the table through the first, second, third, and finally your own.

Note. When first dealing the cards to illustrate the Nap hand it is a good plan to lay out four cards as though for four people and then remark somewhat along these lines: 'We'd better not make four. Four would play bridge or solo. We'll put in another hand.'

HEAPS OF COINCIDENCE. No. 81

Effect. The assistant chooses one of two packs; the performer takes the other. The helper is then asked to follow the magician's actions.

The packs are cut into two heaps; then into four. The top cards are turned face-up; then, again turning them face-down, pushed into their respective piles.

Now one or more card(s) are moved from one heap to another, this being repeated several times. Finally the top card of every heap is turned face-up and the four displayed. The cards of each heap exactly coincide with those of the other pack, and they are in the same order.

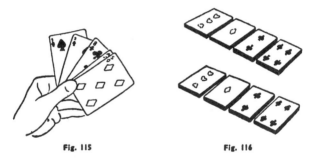

Fig. 115   **Fig. 116**

Method. The working is almost identical with that of the 'Tops' Four Aces'. Briefly, you have four known cards in a pre-arranged order under one indifferent card on the top of each pack. After the cards are cut into the four heaps you have one, two, three or even four moved from one heap on to another, backwards and forwards, keeping mental note of the positions of the four cards, which must ultimately appear at the top of the four piles. (Fig. 116)

MARRIED BLISS AT TWENTY-ONE. No. 82

Frederick Braue

Effect. The conjurer explains that he is about to try an experiment which is well off the beaten track of magic. Many people hold a firm belief in palmistry and phrenology. Others have a leaning towards some other type of pre-determined character—or fortune-telling. Among these, numerology claims many adherents and here is an instance of its application to cards.

A lady and gentleman, courting or married preferred, are selected, and the test is to find whether they are in true harmony, one with the other. A shuffled pack is handed to each, with the request that they follow the performer's instructions in unison.

Each pack is cut about two-thirds down into two piles. A card is then selected from anywhere in the lower portion and turned up. Whatever its value, cards from the top heap are then counted off to make the total up to ten. (For example, if the card turned up was '3', seven cards would be counted on to it. Court cards count as 10.

This is repeated with a second set; then both face-up cards have their values added and whatever the total, that number of cards is counted from the top of the pack. The following card is removed, then turned up at the same time as its partner is revealed. Although the various counts of the man and his spouse (? to be) differ, yet they both turn up the identical card. The performer remarks that the mating is evidently appropriate, for complete sympathy and understanding are indicated. (Fig. 117)

Method. You know the twenty-first card down in one pack, which you have still in its case in your pocket.

When concluding some other trick, such as 'I know that one', 'Study in Shade', etc., you get the duplicate of this card to a similar position in the pack you are using.

False-shuffle while introducing the subject of numerology, then take out second pack and likewise false-shuffle and secure your victims for the experiment, handing one of the packs to each.

When the packs are cut your first twenty-one cards are undisturbed. Should either pack be cut much less than half, replace the cut-off portion on the pack and ask the person to cut again 'well down' as you may need rather a lot of cards in the top heap, 'as you will see presently'.

As you will soon discover by experimenting, the twenty-first card is really forced, but the camouflage is so clever that none will realize this.

If you 'experiment' in this way on a courting couple take care not to suggest that you have given proof that they 'are meant for each other', for some people are most susceptible to any form of fortune-telling and you may easily do more harm than good.

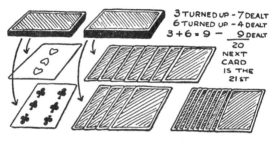

Fig. 117

There is good scope in this item for certain humour, although the effect should primarily be presented as an intelligent effort.

If you wish to try this out twice you can have the two particular cards on top. The first attempt will not come out 'right', in which instance you examine the cards and suggest you see some agreement but not complete unity between the two. Gather up the cards, putting the twenty-first card on the first-dealt pile, then dropping these on the rest of the pack. On top of all, place the remaining cards, but leave the two turned-up cards on the table. 'Having been used once, we'll not use them again,' you remark. You then proceed to repeat the experiment and, of course, turn up the two 'bliss' cards.

THE SEQUEL OF FIFTEEN. No. 83

Elsewhere in this book is a complete chapter on the pre-arranged pack, using my own set-up.

There are, as all experienced conjurers are well aware, quite a number of set-ups, most of which embrace thirteen cards in each complete stacking. This, repeated a further three times, takes in all the fifty-two cards in the pack.

One of the simplest and oldest is that known as 'The Eight Kings'. This runs as follows: 'Eight Kings threatened to save nine fair Queens for one sick Knave.' These words represent the whole thirteen cards in the following order: 8, K, 3, 10, 2, 7, 9, 5, Q, 4, 1, 6, J. The sentence does not make sense but it serves a most useful purpose as a key to this arrangement. Suits usually run 'red, black, red, black' (diamonds, clubs, hearts, spades, for instance) throughout the pack.

A more modern and much more useful version of arrangement is that known as the Si Stebbins 'Three-ahead System'. The cards are arranged: Ace (1), 4, 7, 10, K (13), 3, 6, 9, Q (12), 2, 5, 8, J (11), each succeeding card being three-up on the one before it. (Cards are stacked face-up, Ace first; that is, on the table.) The suit arrangement—red and black alternately throughout the pack— is as in nearly all set-up packs.

Effect. The spectator cuts the pack into two heaps and counts out fifteen cards from the top of one heap (spectator's choice). These fifteen cards are spread ribbonwise on the table and any one card selected. It is then shuffled back amongst the other fourteen cards.

The performer takes this fifteen and, fanning them in his hand, removes one card, which he holds face-down. The assistant names the card he chose. The conjurer turns his up. It is the card just named.

Method. The pack is pre-arranged according to whatever system is preferred.

The cards lie flat on your hand and are cut into two heaps, your

other hand acting as a table for the cut-off portion. The spectator
selects either heap, then counts off his fifteen cards singly. While he
does this you note bottom card of the pile on your hand. The first
card he counts off automatically follows the sighted card. When he
spreads out the pack from left to right the left-hand card is your
follow-on card. As he makes his choice you count from the follow-
on to the space left by the removal of his card and you know in a
moment's calculation just what that card is; so, of course, he can
shuffle the fifteen cards till the pips fall off, but as you already
know the card, he is really only wasting so much effort, though
you'd hate to tell him so. (Fig. 118)

A BEE IN HIS BONNET. No. 84

Tricks of the following type, known as 'The Spelling Bee' have
long been very popular, for not only are they interesting and effective, but they are charmingly simple to perform. This particular
version is rather amusing, in that when your assistant tries, the
effort does not meet with success, whereas your own attempts are
one hundred per cent successful every time.

Effect. Twelve cards are taken from the pack, then the Joker is
added. The performer proceeds to spell out, from this thirteen,
the various cards, commencing with the Ace. As he spells he
removes one card for each letter, from the top, adding it to the
bottom. After spelling several in this way he hands the cards to the
spectator, inviting him to spell out the next number, but when this
is tried the Joker turns up.

The performer then shows how it should be done. The spectator
tries again, and again gets the Joker. Continuing the spelling process, the performer gradually spells through the pack, every so
often permitting the spectator to have another attempt, and every
time the assistant gets the Joker.

Method. Thirteen cards are arranged in among the other cards
of the pack in the following order: 3, 5, Q, Ace, 10, 9, Joker, 2,
8, 7, Jack, 6, 4, the 4 being on top. These cards need not be all
of one suit. (The simplest way to save memorizing is to have these

cards, each with a duplicate of the same colour next to it. For instance, say you are using the 3 of diamonds, the 5 of hearts, and the Queen of spades, you can put next to them respectively 3 of hearts, 5 of diamonds, Queen of clubs, and so on with the others. It is then a very simple matter, as you run through the pack, to remove one of each of these particular cards.) As you place these on the table, **face-down**, this will reverse the order, bringing the 3 to the top of the face-down pile. A King you leave on the top of the remainder of the pack.

With these thirteen cards in your hand, still face-down, you spell out A-C-E for Ace, removing from the top and placing at the bottom of the pile, one card for each letter. At the completion of the word you turn up the next card, which proves to be the one just spelt, and put this face-up **on the table**. (Fig. 119)

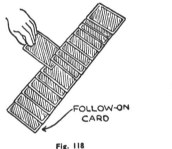

FOLLOW-ON CARD

Fig. 118

Fig. 119

Now here is the full routine:

You spell Ace.
You spell Two.
You spell Three.
Spectator spells Four—and gets the Joker.
You spell Four.
Spectators spells Five—and gets the Joker.
You spell Five.
Spectator spells Six—and gets the Joker.
You spell Six.
You spell Seven.

You spell Eight.
Spectator spells Nine—and gets the Joker.
Other spectators spell Nine—and get the Joker.
You spell Nine.
You spell Ten.
You spell Jack.
Spectator spells Queen—and gets the Joker.

While the spectator is spelling 'Queen' you take the pack in the left hand and slightly push forward the top card (the King). When your assistant turns up the Joker you take the two cards back and, with the Joker on top, you spell Queen and place it face-down on the table without showing. Naturally there is some doubt about this card and your assistant in all probability will wish to pick it up to verify that it is the Queen, but if not, you could smilingly suggest that this be done. While all eyes are on the Queen the two hands are held close together, with the Joker on top of the King. The right hand apparently takes away the Joker, but in reality draws the King from under it, and with the left thumb pulls the Joker back on top of the pack. You hand this card to your assistant and ask him to spell J-O-K-E-R with it. This remark will naturally be greeted with some amusement, as anyone can hardly spell a word with only one card. During this interim, casually shuffle the pack, thereby burying the Joker, and eventually ask the spectator to turn up the card held. This, to the surprise of all (except yourself!) proves to be the King.

In every instance where the spectator turns up the Joker you place this card at the bottom before you proceed to correctly spell the name yourself, except when you spell 9 and Queen. In these two instances only, the Joker is left on top.

A variation of the above, in which the Joker plays further tricks, is effected by the following arrangement: Q, 7, 10, Ace, 5, Joker, Jack, 2, 9, 6, Joker, 4, 8, 3. In this case you spell Ace, Two and Three.

The spectator spells Four—and gets the Joker.
Then you spell Four, Five and Six.
Spectator spells Seven, with a similar result to his previous effort.

You spell Seven, Eight and Nine.
Spectator spells Ten and again turns up the Joker.
You spell Ten.
Spectator spells Jack—same result.
You spell Jack.

You then suggest that, as the Joker has been so much trouble, your assistant should spell Joker and get it out of the way. This is done and the Joker turned up. It is handed to you for safe keeping. The spectator then spells Queen successfully and, turning up the last card, which naturally is expected to be the King, finds it is the Joker again, and the card you are holding is the King. You switch the Joker, handed to you, for a previously hidden King. A simple method of doing this is to slip the Joker up under your waistcoat while you turn sideways during the spelling of Queen, and draw down the King, either from a card-clip pinned just inside coat, or from just inside trousers pocket.

THINK AND SPELL. No. 85

Effect. Spreading a lengthy row of cards face-up on the table, the performer asks the spectator to note and remember any one of them. The cards are gathered and added to the rest of the pack, which is shuffled and cut. The spectator then takes the pack and spells out the card, turning it up on the last letter.

Method. Eighteen cards are pre-arranged on the top of the pack. These are actually three sets of six cards each, the first being an **odd** number, the second **even**, and the third value **10 or higher.**
    The eighteen cards are: A-C, 9-C, 9-H, 7-S, 5-D, 3-D, 2-C, 6-H, 4-S, 2-D, 4-D, 8-D, 10-C, 10-H, Q-C, 10-D, J-D, Q-D.
    Nine cards from the bottom of the pack is a key card.
    False-shuffle, then deal off the top eighteen cards, face-up, each card overlapping its predecessor. When you have dealt the eighteen cards, make as though to continue and then suggest you have already laid enough down. Ask your assistant to think of any one, then you gather up the row without disarranging the order, and replace the cards on top of the pack. Again false-shuffle, then cut once or twice, eventually cutting at the key card, which will leave

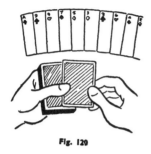

Fig. 120

nine cards on top of the pack, immediately above the eighteen. (Fig. 120)

You now ask the name of the chosen card, which furnishes the key to its position, as to whether it is in the first, second or third group. Should it be in the first group you can give the pack to your assistant to spell off the name of the card, and request that the last card in the spelling be turned up.

If the second group is indicated, remark to your assistant: 'I want you to spell out the name of your card like this: Suppose it was the 9 of Clubs, spell N-i-n-e-o-f . . .' At this point you stop and ask if your instructions are understood. The six cards just counted off are added to the **bottom** of the pack and, as before, the spectator spells out the mentally chosen card.

Once again, if the card is in the last six, proceed in a similar manner, but spell off completely any card of twelve letters, such as 8 of Clubs. These twelve cards then go to the bottom of the pack, the thirteenth (turned-up) card remaining on top.

QUADRANGLE SPELLER. No. 86

Effect. A shuffled pack is cut by the spectator, and the card at the top of the cut is noted. This card the spectator pushes back into the pack, which is again shuffled. Holding the cards, the assistant spells out the name of the selected card, taking one card off the top of the pack for each letter spelt. At the conclusion the last card is turned up and is the very one first selected.

Method. Four packs are required. From each remove the 10-D, Q-H, 3-S, A-D, 8-C, 8-H, 6-D, Q-S, 8-S, 2-D, 3-H, 7-H, 7-S, and place in this order. The four sets of these thirteen cards make up an apparent pack.

It will be seen that, including the word 'of', each of these cards, except the 8 of clubs, spells with thirteen letters. Wherever this 'pack' is cut will not matter, for thirteen cards lower down is a duplicate of the one taken from the top.

You present by false-shuffling, then allowing the spectator to cut and look at the top card. This is pushed into the pack 'well down so that all trace of it is lost', and, gathering the pack, you again false-shuffle. Either you or the assistant can spell, audibly or silently, the name of the card. Provided the bottom card—before the spelling is begun—is not the 8 of hearts, the last card of spelling is the chosen card. If the 8 of hearts is at the bottom, the selected card was the 8 of clubs and the card **after** the spelling is turned up.

A good presentation is, after false-shuffling, subsequent to the return of the card, to put the pack into your pocket and ask the assistant to spell off mentally as you remove one card at a time from your pocket. All you need do is to mentally count till you take the thirteenth card. Then you hold it in the hand, saying: 'You have stopped spelling, haven't you? I can sense it. What was your card? The . . . of . . .' Saying this, you turn up the card you hold. (Fig. 121)

Fig. 121

This is a most effective number, worthy of inclusion in the finest of programmes.

Note. If you adopt the 'Spelling from pocket' method, you can previously place there the balance of one pack (that is, the remaining thirty-nine cards after you have taken the thirteen for stacking). Then at the conclusion of the spelling take out the secreted cards and you have a full pack, ready to continue with further effects. (Place the indifferent cards in a lying-down position, and the stacked cards upright.)

THE SPELLING BEE. No. 87

Effect. This is the straightforward spelling of the cards from Ace to King. In this case as each card is spelt and produced it is placed face-up on the table. The card for each letter in the spelling of the various words is placed at the bottom of the pack.

Method. The pre-arrangement is as follows: 3, 8, 7, Ace, Queen, 6, 4, 2, Jack, King, 10, 9, 5, with the 3 at the top of the face-down pile. It is as well to mix the suits when working this routine.

SIMPLE NAP. No. 88

Effect. A pack is shuffled and cut several times, then four hands of nap are dealt by one of four spectators, who sit at a card table. Standing some distance from the players, the performer asks them to sort their cards. Each player then makes his call, the performer correcting or praising, according to his 'impressions'.

The final call made, the conjurer directs the play, each of the twenty cards being shown as named.

Method. The cards to be dealt, also the next, are stacked on top of the pack. A good selection is as follows (Ace of diamonds on top): A-D, 7-S, J-H, K-H, Q-S, Q-D, A-S, 8-H, 7-D, 7-H, 4-H, K-C, 3-H, 3-S, K-S, Q-H, 10-D, 4-S, 9-H, A-H, 10-S.

The twenty-first card (10-S) is the top card of the pack when the hands have been dealt, and is the optional card for the nap caller.

When dealt, the hands will be as follows:

> First player: Diamonds A, 10, 7; Spades Q; Hearts 3.
> Second player: Diamonds Q; Spades 7, 4, 3; Hearts 7.
> Third player: Hearts J, 9, 4; Spades A, K.
> Fourth player: Hearts A, K, Q, 8; Clubs K.

The whole twenty-one cards, of course, have to be memorized as has the order in which they are to be played. The easiest method of doing this is to visualize a table with the four sets of cards placed face-up. If you are a card-player you will not have much difficulty in the playing of the hands. (Fig. 122)

You could suggest to the first caller: 'What do you think you can call?' Whatever the reply may be, suggest three. To the second player again ask, but advise passing. With the third player propose a call of four. To the fourth player enthusiastically suggest trying nap.

Fig. 122

Have the top card of the pack looked at by the 'nap' caller and remark that it isn't worth using. Should you find one of the players wishing to make a call different from what you suggest, appear to concentrate and then rule out the player's desired call, on the grounds that the opposition is too strong. This will get a laugh, and in no way detract from the effect.

When the play begins, direct the caller to lead the Ace of hearts, the next player the 3 of hearts, the next the 7 of hearts and the last the 4 of hearts.

Don't hurry the effect, but under no circumstances pause too long or your audience will tire. The playing of a hand of nap or poker, under conditions which make it 'impossible' for the performer to control or know the cards, is an everlasting source of entertainment and real magic to any audience.

The method suggested above is of the simplest character, but provided your audience is convinced the cards have been thoroughly shuffled—and this is a first essential—you will have no difficulty in creating a great effect. This type of trick should be treated seriously. Give the idea that you are doing something that calls for concentration, without directly claiming to be a mind-reader.

Make the top and bottom cards key cards—for instance, the top a 'short', the bottom 'crimped'. False-shuffle, and allow each of the players to cut as they come to the table. Then you cut and place the pack down ready for dealing. Your cut, of course, is at the short card.

If you wish to have the pack shuffled and cut by the spectators, your procedure is somewhat different. You have a pack of about forty cards handed out, including nine (not of the stacked denominations) from another pack. The twenty-one stacked cards are on the table face-up, and can be concealed behind a packet of cigarettes.

The pack of forty cards can be thoroughly shuffled and cut if desired; then you place them on the table, face-up on top of the stacked cards, and invite four nap players to come and try a hand. As they come up, offer each a cigarette. Hand the cards for dealing. It is as well in this case to have the top card crimped, just as a precaution against possible cutting, when you must again take the pack and cut at the crimped card. For dealer, you can ask the first person who came up to officiate.

THE PIPS IN THE NEWS. No. 89

Effect. From a shuffled pack, a card is selected and replaced. The conjurer takes a sheet of newspaper, folds it and while he patters, tears pieces out of it. The assistant is asked to find the chosen card in the pack. This is done, and as he displays it to the audience, the conjurer opens out the sheet of newspaper, which is now a giant replica of the selected card.

Method. Have the 2, 4 and 6 of the **three** suits—diamonds, spades and hearts—in the middle of the pack, in a known rotation. False-shuffle, and spread the pack on the table, allowing a member of the audience to take any card. This will be taken from somewhere near the centre (if you have any fear in this direction, force one of the diamond suits).

You gather up the cards while the person is holding the one chosen, noting as you do so the next card in the spread. You know immediately just which card is held; now hand the pack to the person with a request that the chosen card be put back and the pack shuffled. While this is done, you fold the newspaper and tear out the pips to represent the value of the chosen card.

The actual folds of the paper will vary according to the number of pips to be torn out. Let us suppose the 6 of diamonds has been chosen. Fold the paper lengthwise in half, then lengthwise in half again, then double it along its length—making eight thicknesses of paper. You then tear a small triangle from the last fold. This will give the two centre diamonds; then you tear out another triangle which bites into the paper on the sides of the previous fold, rather near to the end. When opened out this will give you the 6 of

diamonds. A little experimenting will soon show you how to produce the hearts and spades. (Fig. 123)

Mould your patter along whatever lines you like, but try to
give some reason for tearing the paper. You can, for example,
suggest it's a matter of temperament and temper, so you want to
tear 'em up. Again, you can offer your assistant a chair while

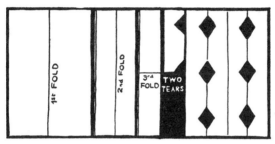

Fig. 123

shuffling the pips off the cards; then rock the chair as though it
had one leg shorter than the rest, and tear the bits out of the paper,
putting them under the short leg to give the chair balance.

Finally, ask the assistant to find the card, if it is still in the pack,
and hold it up for everyone to see. As this is done, open out your
paper and remark: 'It must be right; it's in the news!'

STUDY IN SHADE. No. 90

Paul Clive

Effect. The pack is cut into two heaps by a spectator, and one
section taken and cut again. The performer now states he can
determine by feel, the colour of almost any card without looking
at its face. He thereupon names the colour of half a dozen to a
dozen cards, turning them up in quick succession. The two halves
of the pack are now passed for shuffling and, as further proof that
vision is not necessary, he places the pack in his pocket and names

Fig. 124

the colour of half a dozen cards, taking each from his pocket as named. (Fig. 124)

The pack is next cut into two heaps and the spectator deals one pile into four heaps. The conjurer says he will try to go even further: he will try to name the exact value of each of the top cards. He does so.

One step further still. He will name how many more **red** cards are in the four smaller heaps than there are **black** cards in the large pile of cut.

He names a number and, checking up, his forecast is found exact.

Method. Although the routine and presentation are entirely original, I must admit the finale comes from an unknown source. The ingenious wording of the 'so many more red cards here, than there are black cards there' hides a fine, and very little-known, mathematical equation.

Before you begin, stack a dozen or so cards in some particular order, so you can readily read them off, and crimp, bridge, or otherwise keep location of, top card of the stack. Place these cards near the bottom of the pack.

In your pocket are ten cards from the pack, faces towards your body. The first six you know by colour, the last four by name—reckoning all from the faces.

To present, false-shuffle, and have the pack cut in two 'somewhere about the middle'. Take the lower half and have this cut again, completing cut. Lastly, cut at the crimp and read off the colours of the known cards, feeling the face of each card briefly before naming, then turn it over to confirm.

Gather up all the cards and hand for shuffling. Then place them in the pocket containing the ten cards, keeping these at the bottom (face) of the pack.

Proceed to name the colour of the bottom half-dozen cards, producing each as named. Then suggest an improvement which you 'have been trying lately', and, squaring all the cards from the pocket, have the pack cut into two heaps, as before, and hand the lower half to the assistant to deal into four heaps, a card to each at a time.

When the cards are dealt out, count the number as the cards fall. The last four cards are the ones you previously memorized. These you now name, first placing each card on the palm, then, as naming it, turn the hand over and slap the card down on the heap from which you took it. After naming all four, turn them face-down, and gather the four heaps into one pile, pass it to the person who dealt them out and state your final effort in colour-display. Pick up the remaining pile and, riffling once or twice, state the relative strengths in the two sections. To arrive at these you have recourse to the number of cards in the four-pile heap.

Whatever quantity above or below the half-pack (twenty-six) is your key.

For instance, if **you** hold thirty cards you proceed as follows: 'If you will look through the cards you hold you will find you hold four less black cards than I have red cards.' Your assistant goes through his cards, counting the black cards, and your cards, handed to a second person, are examined for the red cards. You are right. Indeed you must be.

(As further examples, if the cards dealt out total twenty-four, you must hold twenty-eight; therefore you have two more (twenty-eight minus twenty-six) red cards than the spectator has black. Similarly, if assistant holds thirty-one cards, he has five more black than you have red.)

It doesn't matter whether you name the spectator as holding so many more—or less, as the case may be—**red** or **black** cards, but whichever colour you mention in his hand, you must name the **opposite** colour in yours.

The reason behind this, although obscure, is that each colour accounts for exactly half the pack. So, however many cards of one colour the spectator holds, **the balance of that colour** in your hand completes half a pack. Also, the remaining cards in your hand, coupled with those of the same colour in the spectator's hand, make up the other half-pack.

Therefore, supposing you each hold just twenty-six cards and that your assistant has fourteen red cards: you hold the other twelve red; your balance, fourteen, are black. If you hold a total of twenty-seven cards, then, with the reds divided as above, you would have fifteen blacks. And so it goes on, whichever way the excess lies, and the difference is always in precise relationship to the half-pack (twenty-six).

This effect should be presented crisply, NOT slowly.

Note. If the suggested routine above, is too much 'pre-arranged' for your taste, a simpler, shorter routine is easily effected by noting the two bottom cards while gathering up after a previous trick.

Square the pack, false-shuffle, and hand the pack to be cut into two heaps. Hand the lower pile to the assistant to deal into two heaps, noting how many cards are dealt. Now 'read' the top card of each heap, and follow on with the 'You have so many more reds than I have black'.

SUPER-THOUGHT CARD. No. 91

Dai Vernon

Effect. Five cards are placed face-up on the table and a member of the audience invited to think of one. This done, the magician takes the cards, mixes them up, then places one face-down. The assistant is asked to name the selected card. Turning up the one on the table, it is found to be the very card thought of.

Method. In a row, put down the following five cards: Q-H, 5-S, A-D, 2-H, 10-D. Note that the Queen of hearts is the first, or left-hand card, and the 10 of diamonds the last, or right-hand; this as viewed by the spectators. (Fig. 125)

The whole routine is essentially psychological, and careful presentation is accordingly necessary throughout. But do not on this account avoid it. The effect on an audience is really great, and your prestige will stand at its peak.

Observe carefully the trend of the following patter, and mould your own on these lines.

'I want you to take note carefully of each of these five cards. I

am going to ask you to mentally
choose one, and that one I shall
later remove from the five and
place on your hand.

'Your choice is quite free, of
course. For instance, you may
fancy the Ace of diamonds. [Here
you lightly touch the card]; you
may prefer the 5 of spades [Indi-
cate by touching again]; the
choice is entirely as you fancy.
You may even wish to change your
choice. This again rests with you.

Fig. 125

'Will you look at them and consider, then tell me when you have
selected one.'

The choice made, gather the cards, mix them up, and remove
the 2 of hearts, which you place, face-down, on your assistant's
hand.

Ask him to name his thought-of card, then to turn up the one
on his hand; they are identical.

The selection hinges on a process of abstract deletion, or rejec-
tion.

In your patter you draw attention to the Ace of diamonds and
the 5 of spades, so these two are subconsciously ruled out. The
Queen of hearts is far too conspicuous, for not only is this the only
picture card, but it is also prominent in legend. The Ace of diamonds and 5 of spades are also rather prominent, the Ace because
of its position, also its frequent reference in everyday language;
and it is much favoured in conjuring tricks. The 5 of spades stands
out as the only black card. Therefore, this is mentally rejected.
The 10 of diamonds is another card of some prominence. Not so
prominent as the others, but still much in evidence; look at all
those pips on it!

Conveniently close to the 10 of diamonds is the 2 of hearts; a
simple unpretentious card. This, then is the choice. And it is so,
unfailingly. Well, I say 'unfailingly', but you **can** fail if you don't
observe the necessary points.

In the first case, don't hurry the effect; take time to drive your remarks home, and allow your subject to consider each card on its individual merits.

Secondly, let him know **before** he chooses a card, that you intend discovering that card and that he cannot frustrate you. (Note the element of challenge here—one of the strongest points of the trick. The spectator instinctively counters the challenge by rejecting any card which he feels is a force-card.)

Speak with conviction, certain in the knowledge of success. But avoid any tendency towards aggression. You can imply a challenge without being aggressive.

Finally, do try this effect. I speak here to conjurers of some experience rather than to beginners, for this is not an effect to be tried out before you have gained some experience in presentation.

The secret of this grand number is attributed to Dai Vernon, I believe.

If you prefer to think out your own five cards, be careful what you choose.

I have the five cards on top of the pack before commencing, and just count them off.

You will sometimes come up against the person who will not be guided. If you sense that you are dealing with such an individual, or that the card has been selected before you have told your story, you will invariably find the choice to be the Ace of diamonds.

THE ONE I LEFT BEHIND. No. 92

Effect. Seven cards are dealt out, face-down, from the shuffled pack. While the performer's back is turned, one card is looked at. They are then collected with the others and put into the performer's pocket. One by one six are removed, then, on the chosen card being named the magician produces the last card from his pocket. Right again!

Method. Stack the top seven cards in any desired order. There is no need to memorize suits, just carry the denominations in mind, as a 'phone number. False-shuffle, retaining these seven cards in the same order on top of the pack, and deal out—or invite an assistant from the audience to deal—the top seven cards in a row, face-down. (If preferred, of course, the spectator can shuffle in the first instance.) You then shuffle, noting the top seven cards; if you cannot do this satisfactorily, openly look through the pack 'to locate and remove that awkward card, the Joker', at the same time memorizing the seven cards: for instance, if the cards were the 7-D, 9-C, 3-S, 2-H, 10-H, 5-D, 6-S, you would memorize them as 7932056, tens and court cards being represented by 'O'. If there is a court card and a ten, put the initial of the court card in instead of 'O'.

While you retire, or turn your back, a spectator looks at one of the cards, and replaces it. You return and collect the seven into a heap, apparently casually as you patter, but carefully keeping the memorized order.

Unknown to your audience you already have six other cards from the pack in your trousers pocket. If these are secreted right at the top, the pocket can be pulled out and 'shown' empty! It is as well to have some coins and perhaps a handkerchief, in this pocket. Remove the coins, etc., show the pocket 'empty', then place the seven cards **upright** at the bottom. The middle (fourth) card can, with advantage, be turned sideways, thus making a 'break' in the cards. (Locate this fourth card when the seven are handed to you, and keep track of it by inserting the little fingertip. Once the cards are out of sight, it is a simple matter to turn the fourth card.) As you ask the spectator to concentrate on his card, you draw down the other six—all the cards are backs outwards— and as though contemplating which cards to remove, take out the six, one by one, but do not show them at this stage; merely say: 'One'—'Two'—'Three', and so on. Hold these cards fanwise in the left hand.

When the six are in your hand, ask your helper to name the selected card. Stand with your right side towards the audience, the right hand in trousers pocket, the left hand holding the fan of six cards downwards. As the card is named, the left hand turns the fan, faces towards the audience whilst the right hand seeks the appropriate card from among the seven in the pocket. You will find that, in the majority of cases (by no means always, but still in most cases), the fourth card is the one selected. As soon as the audience have had time to see the card named is not among the six, you withdraw that one from the pocket, remarking: 'No, it's not there; it's here—the one I left behind.' (Fig. 126)

Note. It is perhaps needless to point out that the faces of the seven cards must not be seen by the audience, until the final stage.

The above effect is, as you will readily note, a variation of No. 6, on page 66. While, however, 'Five in harmony' is to be preferred for its subtlety and perfect misdirection, 'The One I Left Behind' will often be found more suitable as it can be performed with any ordinary pack of cards.

FOUR IN LINE. No. 93

Paul Clive

Effect. Four cards are dealt off from a shuffled pack. While the magician turns his back, or goes from the room, a spectator looks at one card—they were dealt face-down, as usual—then drops it on top of the next card, finally putting the other two cards on the top of the chosen card. Without even touching the cards, and while the assistant is shuffling them back into the pack, the conjurer names the card chosen.

Method. Five cards are already on top, in a pre-arranged order. The first (top) card and the fourth are red; the second and fifth are black. The third is an indifferent card.

False-shuffle, keeping the top five cards in position; then either hand to the assistant to deal, or do so yourself. If the assistant deals, take back the pack while pattering. Place the pack on the table with the top left-hand corner directly in line underneath the space between the first and second cards, judging the space from the pack to the nearest corners of these two cards, to equal the distance from the far corner of the last card to the space between the first and second cards, as shown in the illustration (Fig. 127).

This must, of course, be done without any evidence of care or precision, and, indeed, only needs to be reasonably approximate. But you will find it extremely simple to do this, as you say to your helper: 'I shall turn my back so that I can have no knowledge of your choice.'

Now patter along these lines: 'I want you to take any one of the four cards. Look at it. Drop it on the next card, like this . . .' Turn up the third card, then place it face-down on the next, by way of illustration. Again take this card and return it to its original (third) position; then, apparently as an afterthought, pick it up, show it again and push it into the pack. Deal the next card into the third space.

Do not move the pack from its position in doing all this. You can, of course, give this illustration **before** putting the pack in place, if you desire. Now walk away a few paces, turn your back,

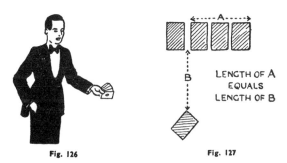

Fig. 126   Fig. 127

and instruct: 'Will you take any one of the four and look at it. Show it to others, if you wish. Now drop it on to the next card. Have you done that? Now, pick up the other two cards and just drop on top.' Don't stress the word 'other' too heavily, yet make it evident. Don't forget to say '**Just** drop on top'. This implies, without stating, that the cards are not to be touched any further. Now face the table and glance at the heap of four and note its relative position to the pack. If you have any doubt as to whether the small heap is on the first, second, third or fourth position originally occupied, walk up to the table (when you will see without doubt).

If you have returned to the table, pick up the pack and hand it to the assistant. If not, ask him to take it. Have the heap of four shuffled into the pack.

To determine which card was chosen: should the pile of four lie where the first card was originally placed, the chosen card was the second one dealt. With the pile in the fourth position, it was the third card. If the second position, the card was the first, or third; more probably the third. Finally, if the heap lies at the third position, the card was the second or fourth; more likely the second. (The normal choice is the second or third card.)

When the heap lies at the second or third position you determine which card was chosen by throwing out a feeler. For instance, if you see the small pile at the second position, you suggest: 'You chose a black card?' According to usual choice the card would be the third, so you suggest black as the colour. If the answer is negative, then you know the first was the chosen card—red.

IT'S A RESERVATION. No. 94

Effect. The performer writes something, leaving the message, face-down, on the table.

A shuffled pack is cut into two fairly equal heaps. One heap is fanned, faces of cards to the audience, showing the cards well mixed. The other heap is then spread out and the assistant draws out four cards, without seeing their faces.

The performer now names these four cards and the spectator chooses one. This one is inserted in the spread-out pile and the other three turned face-up.

The spectator now reads the message. This is a prediction that the selected card now lies at a certain position in the heap which was originally fanned-out.

Such proves to be the case, the card having vanished from the heap in which it was placed.

Method. First write your prediction. You know the top (or bottom) card of the pack, and you decide on a number, say nine. So your prediction runs something like this 'The . . . of . . . will be the ninth card down in the other heap'. Then leave the message, face-down, on the table. False-shuffle, leaving the card you intend to force ninth from the top. Cut the pack and fan, briefly, the top half, afterwards squaring and leaving these cards near the prediction.

An assistant from the audience now places a finger on the back of any card from the lower part of the pack—which is spread out on the table—and draws this card clear. (Fig. 128.) He repeats this with three other cards. You take up these cards and look at them yourself, but do not expose the faces to the audience. Smiling with evident satisfaction, exclaim: 'I knew you would.' Name the first card and show it with some flourishing, placing it face-down. Name the second, quickly show, and drop alongside the first. For the third, name the card mentioned in your prediction, flourish, **but don't show**, and drop beside the second card. Name the fourth, correctly, and drop, **face-up**. Apologizing, turn the card face-down.

Force the third card, turn the other three face-up and leave on the table, then insert the chosen card among the spread-out heap. Square up this pile and hand to the spectator, asking him to read the prediction aloud. He does so, and 'the miracle is done'.

The fourth card is dropped face-up accidentally (?) so that, even if the first two cards were not very clearly seen in the flourishing process, this last one is, and a definite impression is left on the minds of the audience that all four cards were shown, as named.

'DRAWN' FROM THE SPREAD. No. 95

Annemann

Effect. The pack is spread out, face-down, on the table. The spectator removes any card, which he proceeds to draw on a slate.

The performer also writes something on a slate. Both slates are shown, and the two illustrations are identical.

Method. Using a pre-arranged pack, false-shuffle, if desired, then spread the cards along the table. Do not extend the spread, but leave them somewhat compact, with only a small space between the edges of the cards. When the spectator draws a card he inevitably disturbs the card above it. (Fig. 129.) If, as is usual, he draws his card downwards, the card over it is also drawn down somewhat, thereby making an excellent locator card. Scoop the pack up, then, holding firmly to prevent locator slipping back, cut

at this card, casually note it, then proceed to cut several times again
as you patter.

Have the spectator stand well away from you while he draws his
picture of the card, and allow him to start his drawing just before
you commence yours. The audience will thus have the impression
that you are **following** him. (Complete your own picture quickly,
but do not show until after the assistant has finished his.)

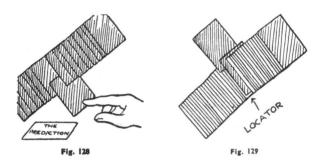

Fig. 128   **Fig. 129**

Note. In the original version, Annemann had the cards strung
out loosely. In this instance the performer noted the break and
collected the cards **below** this point first, then gathered up the rest,
noting the card previous in sequence to the chosen one—i.e. the
card above the break—in the process.

CUT AND CHOOSE. No. 96

Effect. The spectator cuts the pack, looks at a card, then shuffles,
finally cutting the pack again. The performer locates the card.

Method. With the bottom card of the pack noted, assemble all
the picture cards together, from the twentieth to the thirty-first
positions in the pack. Request your helper to cut the pack 'near
the middle', look at the bottom card of the cut, then to **riffle-
shuffle** the two heaps together.

You now look for the original bottom card and the first picture
card above, or just below, is the noted card. (Fig. 130)

If you prefer to increase the number of known cards near the centre of the pack, include the four Aces. Your assistant can hardly fail then to cut within this section.

A riffle-shuffle is, of course, essential. Should you not know whether your helper will, or can, use this shuffle, do this yourself and then have the assistant cut two or three times.

Note. When locating the chosen card, if you find several Court cards just below the key card, the one you seek will, naturally, be the lowest of these.

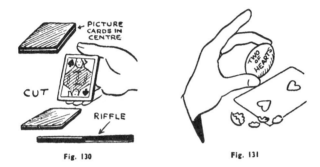

Fig. 130   Fig. 131

HARD-BOILED MYSTERY. No. 97

Effect. A card is chosen and shuffled back into the pack. A hard-boiled egg, previously inspected, is shelled by the spectator, and the name of the chosen card is discovered WRITTEN ON THE EGG. (Fig. 131)

Method. Prepare by dissolving a little alum in vinegar (proportion one ounce of alum to one pint of vinegar). Apply this solution to the egg-shell by printing the name of the force-card. When **quite** dry, with no sign of writing remaining, boil the egg for about twelve or fifteen minutes and it is 'ready to serve'. The writing will have penetrated the shell to the inner surface.

The forcing of the card is left to you, to use your own pet method.

THIRTEEN'S A SUIT. No. 98

Effect. About a third of the pack is cut off and the spectator is invited to cut this again. The card at which he cuts is intended, as far as suit is concerned, to guide him in selecting a card from the other, larger heap. So, if he cut at a spade, he takes any spade from the other heap. The performer now names the suit and value of the chosen card.

Method. Using some easily get-at-able key card in the sixteenth position, you have previously arranged seven—any seven—cards of one suit together in the sixteen, with five cards of other suits above, and four below. (Fig. 132.) Further, you know the **total** value of the pips on these seven cards. (Reckon Jack and Queen as 11 and 12 respectively. Ignore King.) Divide the total by 13, remembering only the remainder. (Thus the 8, 5, 9, K, 10, 2 and 7 would total 41, divided by 13 equals 3 plus 2. You just remember 2.)

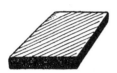

FIVE INDIFFERENT CARDS
SEVEN OF ONE SUIT
FOUR INDIFFERENT CARDS
KEY CARD
THE REST OF THE PACK

Fig. 132

Commence by false-shuffling, keeping the sixteen cards in position. Put back on the table and cut at the key card. Ask the spectator to cut again. He is almost **certain** to cut within the seven-card radius, but if not, or you have any doubts, replace his cut with a correcting remark such as 'Yes, but cut them—don't skin 'em' or (if this drastic humour is not in keeping with the moment) 'Not too near the top or bottom in case others think I can later locate the card'. When the card from the main heap has been chosen, scan through this pile, mentally adding the values of the particular suit, adding also the remainder left over from the seven-card sequence. Divide this total by thirteen and deduct the remainder from thirteen. This gives the value of the chosen card. As you know the suit, you can name the exact card. (For instance, if the remainder you are carrying in mind from the first heap is three, and the total in the second heap is forty-two, this gives a combined total of forty-five. Divide by thirteen, equals three, with remainder of six, thirteen minus six equals seven. The chosen card is the 7 of the suit.)

If there is no remainder, the card is the King.

Alternatively, you need not total the seven cards; after the choice is made have both heaps shuffled together (the chosen card being, as before, retained), then run through the pack, totalling the values, and deduct the final figure from seventy-eight.

THE SANDWICH. No. 99

Effect. Deliberately, and rapidly, running through a pack of cards, a few at a time, and repeatedly 'boxing' them in little packets as he goes along, the performer finally spreads the cards out, showing that half of the pack is face-up, and the other half face-down.

Method. As a piece of magic, this is of but casual interest, although it is puzzling. But this effect has been put here specifically to enable the performer openly to stack the cards before the eyes of the spectators. (*See also next effect*, 'The Parting of the Ways'.)

Hold the pack well up in front of you, and facing you. Run three or four cards into the right hand. Then turn the back of **right** hand to you, so that the cards are facing audience. (The right hand moves throughout **from the wrist**.) Run a few more cards on to the **face** of those held in the right hand, thereby boxing them. Now turn right hand back to original position, and pass a few more cards into the right hand. Note that **all** additions are made to the side nearer audience. Spectators will have the impression that you are making a chain of little boxed packets in the right hand (as **would** be the case if the additions were made to the **thumb** side). When all the cards have been transferred to the right hand, you show one half all facing one way, the other half facing the other (or, in other words, the two halves are 'boxed').

Note. When the little packets are being dealt into the right hand, speed is essential. Patter also helps.

THE PARTING OF THE WAYS. No. 100

Paul Curry

Effect. Performer begins dealing the pack face-down, in two columns. One column is headed by a face-up red card (RC), and the other by a face-up black card (BC). The magician declares he will deal all the red cards on to the one column, and all the blacks on to the other, **without once looking at the faces of the cards.**

But, changing his mind, he returns all but the original two cards to the pack, and secures the services of an assistant, who is requested to deal the cards one by one, putting what he feels 'instinctively' is a red card, on to the red column. If he 'feels' it is a black, then it goes on the black column. He may put several in succession on to one heap, as the urge takes him. If he feels the performer is in any way influencing him, he may follow, or go counter to, that influence.

After a while the performer calls a halt, and takes another red, and a black, card from those held by spectator, and places these two, face-up, on the columns, **but the RC goes on the BC column; the BC is added to the RC column.** Assistant is asked to follow **these** colours in the placing of the remaining cards. (In effect, the colours will now be transposed.)

When all the cards have been placed out, the assistant takes one column, turns up the cards under the lower indicator (face-up) card and, sure enough, **every card is of the same colour,** as indicated. The upper section is, likewise, all of the one colour, thereby matching the original indicator. Performer spreads the other column, with equally astounding results.

Method. This was put out by Paul Curry under the title of 'Out of this World' and has ranked as one of the greatest sensations in easy, intimate card magic ever to confound the public. I urge you to try this. It is far too good to be missed. It is entirely without lengthy preparation, and you can use a borrowed pack, if you like.

At the top of the pack are five assorted cards (say three red, two black. Then follow all the remaining reds and, lastly, all the other twenty-four blacks. (*See* Note.)

False-shuffle, keeping the pack in its entire order. Explain to the audience that it is possible to **sense** the colour of cards, without ever needing to look at them. Take the first red, and the first available black card, and leave them face-up, side by side, but about six to eight inches apart. Knowing the rotation of the first three cards, you take the next card and say 'That's black' (or whatever it is), turn it up to show, then place face-down on the black card, but overlapping, so that nearly an inch of the face-up card is visible at the top. Repeat this manœuvre with the next two cards, then suggest: 'I have a better idea.' Collect up the last three cards, and push, face down, the two RC separately into the top half of pack, and the BC into the lower half.

Ask for the assistance of a member of the audience. Tell him you would like his help, but that, even with his best co-operation, this is not an easy experiment to ensure a hundred per cent success.

Standing together, facing audience, point to the face-up cards, hand the pack (after another false-shuffle, if you wish) to the assistant, and tell him, as indicated above in 'Effect' that you want him to place the cards out on the table, **one at a time**, into two vertical columns. (It should be noted here that you stand beside your assistant on the side nearer the **wrongly placed** cards: i.e. if the top half of pack is of RC, you stand by the column headed by the black card.) Stress that, without looking at any of the cards, what he **thinks**, **feels**, or **hopes**, is a red card, he is to put on the red side, the first card overlapping the face-up red (and leaving about three-quarters of an inch exposed). Every following red card is similarly to overlap its predecessor. If he 'thinks' it is a BC, it is to be placed in similar manner on the black side, building an overlapping column as he goes.

Without revealing the fact, you count the cards as they are placed out. When twenty-four cards have been added to the two indicator cards (making a total of twenty-five RC), stop your assistant, saying: 'I think you are getting a little tired,' and pick up the last card from the BC column, and show it to be red. Replace it, face-down on the red column, remarking: 'Perhaps a switch will help you.' (*See* **Note** *f.*) At this point you look, without others observing the value, at the top card of those held by spectator. It is, of course, the last RC in the pack. You put this, **face-up**, at the base of the **black** column. Look at the next card, but return it (as apparently the wrong colour). Take the next card, look at it, and place it at the foot of the red row.

Spectator deals as before, except that the black cards are now under the previous red, and vice versa. All cards apart from the indicator cards, are face-down throughout the dealing process.

When all the cards have been distributed, ask your assistant if he felt any influence from you at any time. Whatever the reply, point to the column on his side and ask him to look, and 'see how you made out'. After he has turned over a half-dozen cards or so, you scoop up the other column and, after squaring them, wait until he has practically finished going through his cards, then ribbon-spread yours, **face-up**, from left to right, until you come to the first indicator card. Leave that at the end of the spread, then ribbon-spread the remaining cards parallel to, but **above** your first spread. (That is, nearer audience.)

There is now no likelihood whatever that the reversal of the colour-sequence of your cards will be observed. Pick up the two face-down indicators from your spreads, as you turn to the assistant, and remark: 'You see, you did a pretty wonderful job all around. Not a single mistake.' Saying this, you carelessly toss the indicator cards on the table, still face-down, flicking them apart so that all tell-tale evidence is lost.

Note. The above instructions are for close-up, intimate, work. If your audience is seated, and at a distance, or if you're working on a stage, proceed as above, until assistant starts checking to see if the colours have been successfully segregated. At this point ask him to take the section that should be BC, and fan them out for the audience to see. He does similarly with the RC. You have, in the meantime, scooped up your column, first taking the cards from, **and including**, the lower (or second) indicator card. With these squared in the left hand, you gather the remainder and add on top of the first pick-up. This effectively reverses the two colours in your heap. When spectator has displayed his card, hold yours, facing audience (the cards being held well up). It is most effective if you hold the cards, squared, with the thumb across the middle of one longer side, the second, third and little fingers spaced out along the other longer side—the little finger by the right-hand corner. The first finger rests across the narrow end. In this way the cards are easily held compactly, with the bottom card always in full view of the audience. The thumb is at the **upper** long side. The card nearest audience is, of course, the first indicator card, and is back outwards. Simply slide this card off and place it, without showing the face, behind the others.

Now slide each card off the face of the pile, allowing it to fall to the floor, as you clearly call 'Black'. You start without haste, but increase the tempo as you continue, pausing only at the second reversed card, which is added to the first, inside the pile. From here on you call 'Red', of course. When only three or four cards remain, fan them out, drop them on the floor—and with them the two indicator cards—then turn to the assistant, and gesture in his direction, as though to suggest he deserves some applause. (He may get it, but you will have the credit.)

Various additions and alleged improvements have inevitably cropped up, among which one or more of the following may appeal to you:

(*a*) Suggest to assistant, as he places the cards out, that if he at any time feels a definite uncertainty as to the colour of any one particular card, he may hand it to you. This may only apply to one card. If he does hand you a card, put it in your outside breast pocket, back to audience, and leave an inch or so showing. Near the end of the trick, just before you show your column of cards, remind assistant of the card he handed to you. 'Remember how uncertain you were of the card you gave me?' you say. Then remove it and, as you turn it over, add: 'This is why . . .' and you reveal the Joker. This is only possible where you are able secretly to remove the Joker beforehand. It is pushed, back outward, down below the top of pocket. When spectator hands you his card, you push it down into the same pocket—on the near, or body, side— holding it between the thumb and first finger. As soon as the finger-tip touches the hidden Joker, it slides that card up, the unknown card remaining out of sight, at the bottom of the pocket. The thumb aids in raising the Joker into sight, and the whole move is done without comment or ostentation, while you appear to concentrate on assistant's dealing.

Where you are using your own pack, there is considerable latitude for making things even easier. For instance:

(b) You can have the twenty-second card marked, and so save yourself the trouble of counting while the cards are dealt. This has the added advantage that you can patter a little, while the cards are being placed out. But if the effect is being presented as a serious effort in mind-control, or any other serious manner, patter should be kept to a minimum.

(c) Using your own cards you can, of course, work with two packs, substituting the stacked pack for the genuine pack used hitherto.

(d) To arrange a pack right before spectators' eyes, you use the last effect see p. 206, but, as you run off the cards into the right hand, you transfer only one colour at a time. When you've finished you'll have all reds in one half (except for the few top intermingled cards), and all blacks in the other, facing, half. The mixed cards can be either 'set' at the **top** of the pack before the 'facing' is started (they will then be the last to be disposed of), or you can take them as they come in the **first** few cards dealt into the right hand. In any event you need to remember their order. If they are the **first** cards 'faced', wait until you are ready to show the cards in two half-packs, then separate them at their juncture, put down the half facing audience, and ribbon-spread the others, face-down, making a long spread so that, as you gather them up, you can detach the assorted cards, and add them to the **top**. You then spread the other half-pack, gather it up, and add to the **bottom** of the first half.

(e) Using a Wizard, or Stripper, Pack, spectators can shuffle the pack, provided they do not use the riffle-shuffle. And, the pack can be used for other effects beforehand. A couple of cuts, and you have your stacked pack—but you will not be able to pre-arrange the top few cards for mixing the colours. (Unless you precede this 'facing' trick with one in which you place the pack in the pocket—where you have already secreted the few assorted cards.)

(f) When you reach the point (at the dealing of the twenty-fourth card) where you show your assistant has made a 'mistake', you may prefer to suggest your powers are wearing thin with this assistant, and take a second helper in place of the first. I do not, personally care for this changing of an assistant, for various reasons, but there are some to whom it appeals.

(g) By having the **final** six or eight cards in mixed colours, you can take over at that point, and say how very simple it would have been to place the cards out **face-up**. This you do, clearly showing, without words, that they are mixed. Again, this doesn't appeal to me. It's an attempt to add finesse, where none is necessary: this effect is loaded with impact. Nothing **needs** to be added.

ONE LITTLE BIRD STAYED AT HOME. No. 101

Paul Rosini

Effect. Two packs, a red-backed and a blue-backed, are introduced. One spectator freely selects any card from the red-backed pack. A second person freely selects a card from the blue-backed pack. Performer takes about a dozen cards from the red-backed pack, and first assistant pushes his card among them. These cards are then dropped into his inside breast pocket.

Second spectator is dealt with similarly with the blue-backed pack.

Each assistant holds a card of identifying colour in front of himself.

Performer now asks both spectators to concentrate on the selected cards, and declares he will cause all the cards in each assistant's pocket to be transferred to the other spectator's pocket, WITH THE EXCEPTION OF THE CARDS CHOSEN.

This, in fact, proves to be the case. The assistant who chose a blue-backed card finds it is the only one that has not changed colour, all the others in his pocket now having red backs. In similar fashion, the other assistant finds his cards transposed.

Method. Prior to performance, remove a dozen cards from each pack. Add the red-backed cards to the bottom of the blue-backed pack (all cards face-down), and return to the blue-backed card case. The loose blue-backed cards are, of course, added to the bottom of the red-backed pack, and returned to that case.

When card is selected, a perfectly free choice is allowed, but do not fan more than about two-thirds of the pack, for fear of exposing the bottom cards, with their contrasting backs.

Ask spectator to note his card and, as he does so, you turn towards audience and hold the pack well up in front of you, faces to audience. Let us suppose you are using the blue-backed pack first. Spread the pack, fanwise, **from the bottom** of the pack. Remove all the red-backed cards **and the first blue-backed card,** remarking that you no longer need the whole pack. Drop the bulk on the table and, with the thirteen fanned cards facing your assistant, and the audience behind him, ask him to push his (blue-backed) card into the fan, anywhere he wishes, without letting you see the face. The moment he does so, close the fan, which is still held up facing audience and, with the cards squared, ask him to empty his inside coat pocket, into which you then drop the cards.

The rest of the blue-backed cards are returned to their case as you patter.

Repeat the procedure with the second assistant.

Now suggest that, if each assistant will concentrate on the card he chose, you will try to transfer all the cards, **except the ones chosen,** from each man's pocket to the other. As an apparent afterthought, go to the first assistant and, dipping your hand into his pocket, take out the only red-backed card, and hand it to him with the request that he will hold it up, colour towards audience, so that no one may later confuse the situation. From the second spectator's pocket you produce the (only) blue-backed card, which he holds in full view.

With a little showmanship this can register as a particularly clever piece of magic. The late Rosini regarded it as one of his best.

Note. When the twelve cards are fanned for the insertion of the chosen card, do not have this fan too widespread, or open. The individual values of these cards will not then impress themselves on the audience. Also, on removing the cards from the pockets, show the backs first, and either cut at the selected card, or reverse their order by passing from hand to hand. This will effectively change the face card.

CHAPTER 7

THE IDENTITY PACK

♥ ♣ ♦ ♠ ♥ ♣ ♦ ♠ ♥ ♣ ♦ ♠ ♥ ♣ ♦ ♠ ♥ ♣ ♦ ♠

It was during the final years of the last war that I first published, under the above title, my 'set-up' system, together with some effects incorporating that system.

The whole method, from first to last, is original. I have since received some very gratifying testimonials regarding its practical utility and quality, and ease of accomplishment.

But I cannot claim it to be of the very high standard of 'Nikola's Card System', which I consider the finest system yet devised of the stacked pack. It does, however, entail far less memorizing than Nikola's method, and for this reason I feel justified in including it in the present volume.

Whatever method you care to use, there is no doubt that the marvellous results very well repay the time spent in becoming master of this branch of card magic.

THE IDENTITY PACK

Paul Clive

Preliminary Observations

First, an explanation of the term 'Identity Pack'. This has been so named because as the whole pack is in a pre-arranged order, the name, or identity, of every card, at whatever position in the pack, is known to the performer.

The pre-arrangement and the presentation of the effects are, of course, readily done with any ordinary pack of cards, but there is an undoubted advantage to using a Conjurer's Marked Pack (in which all the cards have their values secretly marked on the backs —markings immediately distinguishable to the performer's eye, yet totally invisible to the untrained eye); this advantage is so considerable that if you do not already possess a marked pack, you are strongly advised to obtain one—or even more. As you will read, farther on, two packs, of similar back-design are desirable, though not essential, when performing with an Identity Pack. The price of marked cards varies, but it is generally about twice the price of an ordinary pack, or it may be a little more. This is due to the special printing of the backs, each back necessarily being coupled with its own particular face-value. Also, there is not the mass-production of marked cards that there is of ordinary cards. All marked packs include full instructions for many fine tricks, quite different in character from those described in this work. Marked packs can be obtained from any reputable magical dealers.

Without any previous knowledge of conjuring you can read through this chapter and, applying the ideas set out, give a good convincing performance of card conjuring in far less time than by most other means. The actual time required to learn the card sequence need not exceed five minutes! Naturally, you would not be equipped to go and give a performance in so short a time, but a thoughtful evening spent on this section should leave you fully prepared to give a creditable performance.

THE IDENTITY PACK

Now as to the arrangement of the Identity Pack:

The suits run in the same sequence as the marked cards, so that, if you are using a marked pack, you will find nothing confusing in the rotation of the suits.

The sequence is diamonds, clubs, hearts, spades. A good expression to facilitate memorizing the sequence of the suits is 'DarK HorSe', the large letters being the initials of the suits— Diamonds, Klubs, Hearts, Spades.

It will be observed that, owing to the nature of the arrangement, the pack does not bear close examination by an audience. With the cards in your own hands you have nothing to fear, but if the pack were examined by an audience, you might be in trouble. There is, however, no reason for anyone to wish to examine them, for, to your audience, it is 'just a pack of cards'. But here is a very evident reason why you should have two packs in use. The first is unprepared and you do various tricks with that pack, **allowing your audience to handle and shuffle the cards** with reasonable freedom.

Then you 'switch' for the Identity Pack, and proceed with your further tricks, **giving the pack a (false) shuffle** as often as one could normally expect. In this way, an audience has no good reason to even suspect the use of more than one pack, for they are witnessing one continuous performance with a pack of cards and they've handled the pack themselves!

Here is the actual arrangement of the pack:

1	2	3	4	5	6	7	8	9	10
6 D	11 C	1 H	6 S	11 D	4 C	7 H	10 S	13 D	3 C

11	12	13	14	15	16	17	18	19	20
4 H	7 S	10 D	13 C	3 H	4 S	7 D	10 C	13 H	3 S

21	22	23	24	25	26	27	28	29	30
4 D	7 C	10 H	13 S	3 D	9 C	12 H	2 S	5 D	8 C

31	32	33	34	35	36	37	38	39	40
9 H	12 S	2 D	5 C	8 H	9 S	12 D	2 C	5 H	8 S

41	42	43	44	45	46	47	48	49	50
9 D	12 C	2 H	5 S	8 D	1 C	6 H	11 S	1 D	6 C

51	52
11 H	1 S

Note that the suits are shown above by the initial letter. Over each card is the number of its position in the pack. Thus, the first three cards are: 1st card, 6 of diamonds; 2nd card, Jack of clubs; 3rd card, Ace of hearts.

Note also, that Ace is referred to as 1; Jack as 11; Queen, 12; and King, 13.

The first card is the top card of pack, when pack is held face-down.

When putting the cards in above order lay the 6 of diamonds on the table, **face-up**. Place the Jack of clubs on this, and so on.

The first five cards, and the last seven, run in groups of three, really Ace, 6, Jack, repeated, but the first card is a 6, as it is less likely to stick in the mind of an audience than an Ace; also it facilitates the easy placing of the other cards. These groupings of three cards, you will notice, are stepped up in fives [i.e. 1 (Ace) plus 5 = 6; 6 plus 5 = 11 (Jack)].

All the other cards in the pack are grouped in fives, the value of each succeeding card being three more than the last.

Each set of five cards is referred to as a 'Group' and the **rotation** in the Groups as a 'Sequence'.

Thus the five cards, the sixth to the tenth, are 4, 7, 10, 13 (King), 3 respectively. This sequence is repeated up to the twenty-fifth card, after which the second five-card sequence commences, and continues until the forty-fifth card. This second five-card sequence, or series, runs: 9, 12 (Queen), 2, 5, 8.

So, the only memorizing you have to do to determine the **value** of any card in the pack, is:

> Cards 1 to 5: 6, 11, 1, 6, 11.
> Cards 6 to 25: 4, 7, 10, 13, 3.   Repeated.
> Cards 26 to 45: 9, 12, 2, 5, 8.   Repeated.
> Cards 46 to 52: 1, 6, 11.   Repeated.
> The three-card group is stepped up in fives.
> The five-card group is stepped up in threes.

However, you must know both the value **and the suit** of every card.

So, the suits: These run, as already stated, in the order of diamonds, clubs, hearts and spades, which you also think of as suits 1, 2, 3, and 4 respectively.

To quickly memorize the three-card group you make use of mental pictures. This may sound formidable, but read on and you'll find you can memorize them as you go (there are only twelve in all).

Take them in order, and this is the procedure:

1st card, the 6 D.	One sick diamond (*see below*).
2nd card, the 11 C.	Two-eleven club.
3rd card, the 1 H.	Three. One heart.
4th card, the 6 S.	Four sick spades.
5th card, the 11 D.	5/11 diamonds!
46th card, the 1 C.	For to seek one club.
47th card, the 6 H.	For seven sick hearts.
48th card, the 11 S.	Forty ate eleven spades.
49th card, the 1 D.	Forty mine one diamond.
50th card, the 6 C.	Five o'Six club.
51st card, the 11 H.	Five won eleven hearts.
52nd card, the 1 S.	Five to one spade.

Your mental picture takes the form of the easiest association you can picture.

Take No. 1 for example. You think of a diamond or diamond ring of exceptional size lying in a gutter, with the diamond badly crushed. A valuable diamond in that condition would certainly look 'a bit sick'.

No. 2. Think of two football teams. Two clubs, each with eleven players.

No. 3. Three men in love with the same girl (she's 'tops', so must be an Ace).

No. 4. Picture four battered spades discussing how badly they'd been used, and how ill they feel.

No. 5. Diamonds, 5/11 each!

No. 46. Think of yourself in a strange town seeking one particular night-club (there's a guy running the place who owes you £200). So you go 'For to seek one club'.

No. 47. You have seven girl-friends, one for each day of the week, but they all pine for you on the other days (?). What would you give 'for seven sick hearts'?

No. 48. Forty ravenously hungry wolves come across what had been a camp site. All they could find was eleven spades, which they ate!

No. 49. Forty men share a mine and discover only one diamond.

No. 50. A club for the sale of intoxicants opens at 5.0 p.m. or 6.0 p.m., but you're not sure. Is it 5 o' 6?

No. 51. Five handsome folk had eleven ardent admirers.

No. 52. Five to one spade. Five energetic workmen sharing a spade.

The sillier the association of the various ideas the more easily and definitely they will stick in the mind. If the three sentimental heart pictures are too much for you, you can doubtless make your own, more acceptable, pictures. The above are only suggestions. Whether or not you accept them is entirely a matter for you to decide.

For the other cards (Nos. 6 to 45 inclusive), two very simple mental calculations give you the identity of the card at any named position.

1. Divide the number called, by five, and the **remaining number**, if any, gives its position in the 'five' group. Thus, if three remains, it is the third card. For a number **under twenty-five** this would be a ten. For a number **over 25** it would be a two. If there is nothing over (that is, if it's a multiple of five) it is, of course, the last card in the sequence.

2. Divide the number called by four, and the **remaining number** (again, if any) gives the **suit**.

For example, say 'twenty-two' is called, twenty-two divided by five leaves two. The second card (first sequence) is seven. Twenty-two divided by four also leaves a two—a club. Therefore, the twenty-second card down in the pack is the 7 of clubs.

Again. Thirty-eight is called. Divide by five leaves three. This is a two. Thirty-eight divided by four leaves two. The second suit is clubs. So the thirty-eighth card is the 2 of clubs. Similarly, the twentieth card is fifth sequence (3), fourth suit (spade), the 3 of spades.

All this takes a long time to write out, but in actual practice it takes very few seconds.

Even to begin with (once the sequence has been properly committed to memory), any card should be easily named within ten seconds. With a little use this can be brought down to three or four seconds, and that without mental exertion. Quite a good subterfuge in the earlier stages is to ask for any number 'up to twenty or twenty-five. If a higher number is given it rather wastes time while the cards are being counted.'

Naturally, after you have named the card, you count down to that number and exhibit the card, for all to see you have correctly named it.

The cards are counted off quickly from the left hand, and are gathered into the right hand, the fingers drawing each succeeding card in front of the last, thereby preserving the order. Afterwards, the counted cards are placed back on top of pack, and you are ready to proceed.

Where you know the name of a card, or where your audience is giving you the names for you to state the positions, two processes will give you this, as follows:

1. You take the **sequence** number, deduct it from the **suit** number, and that gives the **group** number (i.e. the number of groups preceding this card).

For instance, take the 7 of spades: 7 is second sequence; spades is fourth suit. Thus 2 from 4 = 2. 2, then, is your group number.

2. Multiply the group number by five (the number of cards in each group), and **add** the sequence number. This gives you the position of the card. In the above instance your 7 of spades is second group, second sequence: therefore $2 \times 5 = 10 + 2 = 12$. The seven of spades then, is the twelfth card.

Two more examples:

4 of spades is called.

4 is first sequence; spades fourth suit. 1 from 4 = 3. $3 \times 5 = 15 + 1$ (sequence) = 16. The 4 of spades is the sixteenth card down in the pack.

10 of spades—10 is third sequence: spades, fourth suit. 3 from 4 = 1. $5 \times 1 = 5$; + 3 = 8. Eighth card.

Where the sequence number is **less** than (or the same as) the suit number, add four in order to subtract.

Examples: 10 of clubs; third sequence, second suit. Therefore deduct as follows: 3 from (2 + 4 =) 6 = 3. Third group. The position of the card then is: $3 \times 5 + 3 = 18$.

King of hearts: fourth sequence, third suit. 4 from 7 (3 + 4) = 3. $3 \times 5 + 4 = 19$.

In all fourth-card sequences, the group number and the suit num-

ber are identical. In the example just quoted you will see the card was fourth sequence. It was **third** suit and **third** group. Take the King of clubs: fourth sequence; second suit. Therefore second group. Its position, then, should be $2 \times 5 + 4 = 14$. This is correct.

For the second sequence series (that is, the twenty-sixth to the forty-fifth cards; the 9's, 12's [Queens], 2's, 5's, and 8's) you add 20—NOT 25—to the final figure. If the Queen of hearts is called, your calculation runs thus:

Sequence 2. Suit 3. Deduct 2 from $3 = 1$. $5 \times 1 + 2 = 7 + 20 = 27$.

The last, or fifth, card in each sequence is the easiest of all. With two exceptions, **you only have to multiply the 5** (that is, the sequence number) **by the suit number, and you have the position of the card!**

The 3 of hearts is fifth sequence, third suit. $5 \times 3 = 15$. The 3 of hearts is the fifteenth card. Similarly 8 of clubs is fifth sequence, second suit. So $5 \times 2 + 20 = 30$.

The two exceptions are the twenty-fifth card, the 3 of diamonds, and the forty-fifth, the 8 of diamonds. These two you can easily remember specifically. Alternatively, just remember that the fifth sequence cannot be multiplied by one (first suit). You must add 4 to the suit number, making it 5.

The following table sets out the position of every card from the sixth to the forty-fifth, and a little attention given to it will settle any queries you may have on the foregoing description of 'Find the Number'.

First Series

Card *Name of Sequence*

No.	Card	No.	Suit No.	Group
6	4 C	1	From 2	$= 1 \times 5 + 1$
7	7 H	2	From 3	$= 1 \times 5 + 2$
8	10 S	3	From 4	$= 1 \times 5 + 3$
9	13 D	4	From $(1 + 4 =)$ 5	$= 1 \times 5 + 4$
10	3 C	5	$\times$ 2	$= $ 10th card
11	4 H	1	From 3	$= 2 \times 5 + 1$
12	7 S	2	From 4	$= 2 \times 5 + 2$

13	10 D	3	From $(1 + 4 =) 5$	$= 2 \times 5 + 3$
14	13 C	4	From $(2 + 4 =) 6$	$= 2 \times 5 + 4$
15	3 H	5	$\times$ 3	$= $ 15th card
16	4 S	1	From 4	$= 3 \times 5 + 1$
17	7 D	2	From $(1 + 4 =) 5$	$= 3 \times 5 + 2$
18	10 C	3	From $(2 + 4 =) 6$	$= 3 \times 5 + 3$
19	13 H	4	From $(3 + 4 =) 7$	$= 3 \times 5 + 4$
20	3 S	5	$\times$ 4	$= $ 20th card
21	4 D	1	From $(1 + 4 =) 5$	$= 4 \times 5 + 1$
22	7 C	2	From $(2 + 4 =) 6$	$= 4 \times 5 + 2$
23	10 H	3	From $(3 + 4 =) 7$	$= 4 \times 5 + 3$
24	13 S	4	From $(4 + 4 =) 8$	$= 4 \times 5 + 4$
25	3 D	5	$\times$ $(1 + 4 =) 5$	$= $ 25th card

Second Series

Card	Name of Sequence			
No.	Card	No.	Suit No.	Group
26	9 C	1	From 2	$= 1 \times 5 + 1 + 20$
27	12 H	2	From 3	$= 1 \times 5 + 2 + 20$
28	2 S	3	From 4	$= 1 \times 5 + 3 + 20$
29	5 D	4	From $(1 + 4 =) 5$	$= 1 \times 5 + 4 + 20$
30	8 C	5	$\times$ $2 = 10, + 20$	$= $ 30th card
31	9 H	1	From 3	$= 2 \times 5 + 1 + 20$
32	12 S	2	From 4	$= 2 \times 5 + 2 + 20$
33	2 D	3	From $(1 + 4 =) 5$	$= 2 \times 5 + 3 + 20$
34	5 C	4	From $(2 + 4 =) 6$	$= 2 \times 5 + 4 + 20$
35	8 H	5	$\times$ $3 = 15, + 20$	$= $ 35th card
36	9 S	1	From 4	$= 3 \times 5 + 1 + 20$
37	12 D	2	From $(1 + 4 =) 5$	$= 3 \times 5 + 2 + 20$
38	2 C	3	From $(2 + 4 =) 6$	$= 3 \times 5 + 3 + 20$
39	5 H	4	From $(3 + 4 =) 7$	$= 3 \times 5 + 4 + 20$
40	8 S	5	$\times$ $4 = 20, + 20$	$= $ 40th card
41	9 D	1	From $(1 + 4 =) 5$	$= 4 \times 5 + 1 + 20$
42	12 C	2	From $(2 + 4 =) 6$	$= 4 \times 5 + 2 + 20$
43	2 H	3	From $(3 + 4 =) 7$	$= 4 \times 5 + 3 + 20$
44	5 S	4	From $(4 + 4 =) 8$	$= 4 \times 5 + 4 + 20$
45	8 D	5	$\times$ $(1 + 4 =) 5$	

$$= 25 + 20 = \text{45th card}$$

The pack contains two locator cards, or, at least, it will be found a great advantage if they are included. These locators are the top card, the 6 of diamonds, which is made into a 'short', and the twenty-first card, the 4 of diamonds, which is 'short-cornered'— this is done by removing from each corner of the card a thin slice (in width equal to about the thickness of a 6d. piece). This must be done neatly, and care taken to leave the corners nicely rounded. Experiment first, if you can, on an old, disused pack. Well done, there is nothing perceptibly wrong with the card. But riffle the pack at a corner, and you can detect it at once.

TRICKS WITH THE IDENTITY PACK

102. How many cards cut? Request spectator to cut the pack and place the top (cut) portion on your outstretched hand. Professing to calculate the number of cards by weight, the hand is gently moved up and down, then the number stated. Counting the cards, the forecast is proved to be correct.

All you need to know, of course, is the value of the bottom card of the top heap, which you glimpse, or, if using a marked pack, you know the value of the top card of the lower heap, and, by easy calculation, you know how many were cut.

103. Choice and Position. Have a chosen card replaced in the pack in its original position (apparently close the pack after the choice is made, but keep a 'break' at the spot, then cut the cards at this point for the return of the card). Name the card, state its position, then count down to it. (Fig. 133)

HOLDING
BREAK

Fig. 133

104. Naming Bottom Cards. Have the pack cut into about five heaps, name the bottom card of each heap, then turn the heaps face-up, and show.

Be sure to replace heaps in correct order.

This effect is miraculous if done with marked cards, for you don't even need to touch the cards at all. If done with an ordinary pack you must 'sight' the top cards. A good way of doing this is to take each top card and insert it face-up at the bottom of its own heap, saying: 'When they come face to face these cards talk, and I want to hear them talk.'

105. Request an assistant from the audience to count off, face-down, any number of cards desired—any number under twenty is preferable—and then to replace them on the pack. The cards are to be counted out (silently) singly and deliberately so that everyone can see clearly how many cards are counted. Particularly mention that no one must count aloud. Stand some distance away and turn your back while the counting is in progress.

This done, go over to the table and state your intention of re-peating what has already been done. Pick up the pack, cut at, and include, the 'short', then count out the cards singly. (If using marked cards, just count till you see the coding of the 6 of diamonds, and that is the last card you count off.) Alternatively (when **not** using marked cards), riffle the pack to locate your short, and draw the cards **above** it over the near end of pack, making a slight 'step'. Then count these off, also the short.

Do your counting silently, and hesitate once or twice. You will find that, simple though the trick is to perform, it can be most impressive. To sight the top card a simple ruse is to place it down face-up when you start counting. Then, apparently recollecting, turn it face-down, and proceed.

Your pack is once again in order.

106. Cut at the Cut. A member of the audience cuts the pack, looks at the top card at cut, **replaces this card on top of the other heap,** then completes the cut.

This is done while your back is turned. You now step forward, take the pack, look at your assistant as though trying to read his thoughts (this gives you convenient and ample time to calculate the number of cards cut), and you next state the name of the chosen card, also its present position in the pack.

Note. If the card's original position in the pack was twenty-two, it will now be the thirty-first card: 52, less 21—the cards actually removed in cutting are one less than the position of the chosen card.

Now, cut at the short card, put down all the cards below the cut, and count those still in your hand. You have named the chosen card, foretold its position in the pack and then cut the pack at that very card! ! ! Most impressive, but so simple when you only know how to do it.

Of course, you replace the chosen card (when you have counted down to it and held it up for all to see) on top of those in your hand. The cards on the table now go on top of those in your hand, and you're ready for more miracles.

107. Spelling Cards Named. Certain cards can be spelt out. These are listed below. Note that the 'spelling' method varies according to the particular card and its position. These spelling effects should not be attempted until you have thoroughly familiarized yourself with the cards to be spelt, so that, as soon as one of these cards is named (as in the case of the following effect, 'Call a Card'), you can say, 'by way of variation, let us spell it out'.

Here are the cards, and how spelt:

Tenth card: 3 of clubs. A person calls 'Three of clubs'. You spell T-H-R-E-E C-L-U-B (Remark: 'You want the three—T-H-R-E-E. And it's to be a club—C-L-U-B.') It will then be the first card following the spelling.

Eleventh card: 4 of hearts. Spell F-O-U-R H-E-A-R-T-S. It is the **next** card.

Twelfth card: 7 of spades. Spell S-E-V-E-N S-P-A-D-E-S. It is the **next** card.

Thirteenth card: 10 of diamonds. Spell T-E-N O-F D-I-A-M-O-N-D-S. It is the last card spelt.

Fourteenth card: King of clubs. Spell, colour, B-L-A-C-K, suit, C-L-U-B, value, K-I-N-G. Next card. (Note you leave the 'S' off clubs or, if included, it will be the last card of the spelling.)

Fifteenth card: 3 of hearts. Spell colour, R-E-D, suit, H-E-A-R-T-S, value, T-H-R-E-E. Next.

Sixteenth card: 4 of spades. Spell colour, B-L-A-C-K, suit, S-P-A-D-E-S, value, F-O-U-R. Next card.

Seventeenth card: 7 of diamonds. Spell colour, R-E-D, suit, D-I-A-M-O-N-D-S, value, S-E-V-E-N. Next card.

Thus you can spell any card from the tenth to the seventeenth, both numbers included. Except for the thirteenth card (the proverbial 'unlucky number') the card spelt is always the card **following** the spelling.

108. Call a Card. Members of the audience name various cards, and you proceed to state their positions in the pack, each time counting down to that position and exhibiting the card.

The method of doing this has already been fully dealt with, but here again is a summary:

> **Sequence** number deducted from **suit** number gives **group** number.

> **Sequence** number in **that group** gives the **card** number. (Example: 4 of spades, first sequence, deducted from fourth suit, gives third group. Therefore, $3 \times 5 + 1 = 16$. For fifth card of sequence just multiply by group number.)

109. Name a Number. Audience call numbers (up to fifty-two) and you give the names of the cards at these positions, again counting down to prove your statements. This has also been already dealt with in detail. But here is the summary of process:

Combine sequence numbers with suit number. (Example: forty-second card is second sequence, second suit. Second sequence is 12 (Queen), second suit is clubs. Therefore, Queen of clubs. Group numbers are **not** of interest in this connection.

'Call a Card' and 'Name a Number' are perhaps the finest examples of card magic possible with the Identity Pack, although speedy presentation is essential to impressive performance.

110. One After Another. This follows naturally on the heels of either of the last two effects.

A number of cards are named in quick succession as they are removed, singly, from the top of the pack, and exhibited to audience for verification.

This is where your short-corner card is useful. You riffle, locate the card, cut (lifting off the first twenty cards and placing them under the rest), and you can go through a fair number of cards without fear, for the first ten cards are all different. You can safely name any number up to thirteen, which is quite sufficient for any audience to accept the belief that you could name every card in the pack, and they have no reason to suspect pre-arrangement.

111. Card from Pocket. A chosen card is returned to the pack —actually back in its original position—and a break maintains location. The pack is then cut at this point and the cut completed. Putting the pack in the pocket request audience to name a low number (up to ten is sufficient). Suppose 'Seven' is called. Remove six cards singly from the **bottom** of the pack, counting each as brought out; the seventh card take from the **top** of the pack. Hold this card face-down, look intently at the person who chose it, then name the card, and hold it up for all to inspect.

112. Three-handed Nap. This is a very good finale when using the Identity Pack, and, although the respective hands are far from impressive, they are fairly representative of what one might expect if dealing in the ordinary way.

Request the assistance of three members of your audience and, if possible, seat them at a table. If that is not possible, bring them to the front and stand, or seat, them, a little apart from each other, **facing** the audience. Deal out the three hands from the top of the pack. It is, of course, necessary that you do that yourself, or at least, that anybody handling the pack does not shuffle it.

Should anyone insist on cutting the pack (and some card-players may) this need not cause you any concern. You simply cut again at your 'short', and proceed to deal. It is advisable to patter a little as you deal, so that no one thinks of the fact that you retain the deal or that the cards haven't been shuffled. (You can give them a good false shuffle if you wish.)

Patter something after this style may be of assistance: 'Of course, you know how to play Nap? If not, I'll help you. I shan't go away, so you needn't be afraid.'

Each player sorts his own hand while you stand at a distance— too far away to be able to see the cards.

The hands will result like this:

	Diamonds	Clubs	Hearts	Spades
1st Hand	6, 10	3	7	6
2nd Hand	Jack	Jack, King	4	10
3rd Hand	King	4	Ace, 3	7

Addressing the first player, proceed: 'Now, sir, don't tell me or anyone else what cards you hold as you're playing for a very high stake—my prestige.' Appear to concentrate. 'It's an awful hand, isn't it? I don't think you can make any call with that hand, do you?' This advice is certain of acceptance. Concentrate on the second player, then suggest he has a good two tricks, but a most unlikely three. Again advise passing. When you 'consider' the last hand, suggest there is a possible three call and that the holder bids it.

Proceed: 'Now, as caller leads and first card is trumps, you'd better play the Ace of hearts. You sir [to first-hand player], play your . . . 7. It is a 7, isn't it? And you [to holder of the second hand] the er—er . . . 4 of hearts. That's one trick in the bag. If we get the other two we shall have a hat-trick. Now, I should play the King of diamonds, you follow with the . . . the 6, and you the Jack. Two tricks. How the tension grows! Better try another trump if we've got it. Yes, we have: the 3. You play the 3 of clubs I should think, wouldn't you? And you, sir, which would you suggest, the Jack of clubs or the 10 of spades!' Many players will discard the spade, although the club is the right one to throw. If the spade is discarded the caller has an extra trick. As you know, it is usual in Nap to 'throw in' once a call has been secured, but it is here suggested that, if the fourth trick can be made, it should be mentioned, and give the play of that round.

The play of a Nap hand is always extremely well received, and its inclusion in any card programme is well worth the initial trouble of memorizing the fifteen cards.

If you are working with two packs of cards you can, prior to performance, remove fifteen cards from the first pack (when you are doing tricks with that pack no one will realize the discrepancy), and after having the Identity Pack shuffled and cut by the first-hand player-to-be, you remark that you want him to enjoy the game, and offer him a cigarette.

Unknown to your audience the fifteen stacked cards were hidden under the cigarette packet. (If the packet is nearly half-open and projecting over the table or chair-edge the cards are completely concealed by the packet, and are easily picked up with the cigarette packet. The flap of the packet should be turned back, thereby

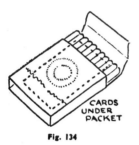

masking the cards. The packet is held somewhat tilted until the cards have been disposed of.) The full pack of cards is all this while in the right hand, the cigarette packet in the left. (Fig. 134)

When the cigarette has been taken by your assistant, tap your pocket with the right hand, as though to find if you have any matches there, then, recollecting (?), place the cigarette

Fig. 134

CARDS
UNDER
PACKET

packet with its hidden cards, on top of the pack, and dive your left hand into the trousers pocket and bring out the wanted box of matches!

This is a perfect method of loading your pack and **cannot** create even the slightest suspicion.

Should your assistant prove to be a non-smoker, or pipe-smoker, say: 'Well, have a match: they're always useful.' This gets an amused laugh and serves your purpose.

If you adopt this method (the extra fifteen cards) you can arrange the hands to give the first player a three call; the second a four; and the last a Nap hand.

113. Double Divination. Here is an original and most baffling trick—never before put in print. The effect is that the pack of cards is in full view on a chair or table. A hat (bowler or trilby) is shown empty and is also placed in full view, crown downwards. Performer asks a person to think of a number without uttering it, say a number between ten and twenty. Looking intently at the person, the conjurer writes something on a slip of paper, folds it up and tosses it into the hat. The number thought of is now requested and, drawing attention to the fact that no indication was given before writing, also that the cards have not been touched by him since the trick was begun, the performer picks up the hat, and walks over to another member of the audience, who takes out the slip and reads from it the identical number and the name of the card at that position in the pack. Another person counts down in the pack to the number given and finds the double prediction correct.

Now the method. First the choice of number is limited to nine, because you state 'between ten and twenty', that is, any number from eleven to nineteen. Curiously enough, the majority of people think of seventeen. Why, is difficult to know, but it is a recognized and indisputable fact. A slip of paper has to be prepared for eight of the numbers. Thus you write on one: 'The eleventh card will be the 4 of hearts'. On the next write: 'The twelfth card will be the 7 of spades', and so on up to the nineteenth, except the seventeenth, which you omit. The slips of paper are just about half the size of a 10s. note (about 3 in. by 2¾ in.). Numbers twelve to eighteen are folded in four and inserted under the sweat band inside hat, at regular intervals. Imagine the hat to be on the head and the slips placed as follows: 12 over centre of forehead, 13 over right temple, 14 over right ear, etc. Or you can think of them being placed clockwise, at two-hourly intervals. (Fig. 135.) No. 11 is folded in the left trousers pocket, No. 19 in the right. That is all the preparation necessary. When performing, do the necessary concentration and write on the slip 'The seventeenth card will be the 7 of diamonds', fold it and toss it into the hat. When the

SLIPS UNDER BAND

Fig. 135

number is stated, if it is seventeen, you're in clover and you need not even approach the hat. Let someone take the slip out and read it. For numbers 12 to 18 dip the hand in the hat and as you pick up the '17' slip suddenly look over at audience and say: 'Perhaps you would rather remove the slip of paper yourself.' Whilst saying this, the thumb draws the slip down to the base of the fingers and apparently drops the slip back into the hat—in reality you merely lower the hand into the hat—then grip the hat over the appropriate number with the fingers inside— effectively concealing the '17' slip; the sweat-band is lifted (by the fingertips of the second and third fingers, which press the edge of the sweat-band against the first and little fingers), and the desired slip falls into the hat. The unsuspecting person who removes this is often the most perplexed of all—so convinced is he that nothing could have been pre-arranged.

If No. 11 or 19 is chosen that is picked up in the fingers and concealed, as already described (this is known as finger-palming) and the hand put in the hat. The palmed slip is dropped, the '17' slip finger-palmed and—the trick goes on to its happy conclusion.

CHAPTER 8

CONTRIBUTIONS BY MASTER MAGICIANS

♥ ♣ ♦ ♣ ♥ ♣ ♦ ♣ ♥ ♣ ♦ ♣ ♥ ♣ ♦ ♣ ♥ ♣ ♦ ♣

In this chapter is a fine array of good quality magic with cards, as practised in these times. Each item, specially written for this book by the particular magician under whose name it appears, is mostly in the wording of the contributor himself.

The various conjurers who have so kindly given their secrets were especially chosen as proved members of great ability in the magical profession.

GEORGE BRAUND, M.I.M.C.

Tall and very fully proportioned, Mr. Braund was billed as 'The Biggest Thing in Magic'.

Often attired as a cleric he sped through his show with **boundless energy and abundant good humour, infusing his audience with his jovial spirit, until, by the end of his act, all** were in hilarious mood.

For more than thirty years a member of the Magic Circle, he performed before the Royal Family at Windsor Castle, and in his travels through twenty-three countries, entertained Royalty abroad, as well as having been consistently popular with the Royal Family here. Specializing in close-up magic, he was an active cabaret artist.

Off stage he was still the good-natured enthusiast, radiating a keen sense of cheerful companionship.

Here is one of his original effects; a fine example of non-sleight-of-hand card-work at its best.

THE 'FLY-OVER' CARDS. No. 114

George Braund

Effect. Three red-suit cards are counted separately and held up in a fan. This fan is then closed and put in a clip-stand, or otherwise left in full view. Six other cards, three red and three black suits, are now fanned, then closed up. They are fanned out again, and one of the black cards has vanished.

Upon fanning the three reds again, the missing black card is discovered among them. These four are closed up and put back. (Fig. 136)

Again displaying the five cards, they are once more closed up, flicked, and opened out yet again. A second black card has gone—only to reappear in the other packet.

Fig. 136

The same procedure is gone through again, and the third black card passed from its original packet to the other.

Requirements. Two sets of cards, each consisting of three red cards, and three black cards. The black cards in each set are duplicates of those in the other. All the black cards are treated **on their faces** with roughing fluid. All the red cards are roughed **on their backs.**

Method. First of all arrange one set, which we will call A, so that no two roughened sides come together (*see* **Note**). Show as six cards. Close the packet and see that one black card is brought behind a red card (**Note**). Upon opening the fan again, this black card will stick to the back of its adjacent red card, and only five cards will be apparent. This concealment of a black card is repeated for the other two.

The second packet (B) starts with each black card hidden behind a red. When next displaying, the rear card is easily separated from its red counterpart, and four cards are shown. Count these cards singly into the right hand, reversing their order, and bringing the exposed black card to the front, and another double card to the back.

When these are next shown, again separate the back two cards, and now there is a black card at the front and another at the back, with the three reds between.

At the final fanning of B, hold the cards, backs towards audience, and spread them slowly, separating all six.

Note. The best method of interleaving the reds and blacks of A, is to begin with the reds at the back, blacks in front. Count the six singly, bringing the blacks behind. The first black will now adhere to the last red card when next fanned.

Show the five and again count singly (the adhering cards counting as one). The two black cards are now at the front. Openly remove these and place behind the reds, leaving the face (red) card showing.

Fan as before, and only one black is visible behind the three red cards. Count again, bringing the lone black to the front. Fan these 'four' and say: 'We'll hide this last black card among the red,' and slip it behind the middle red card. At the final fanning, only the three reds are visible.

COL LING SOO

Past President of the Magic Circle

The late Herbert J. Collings, under the professional name of Col Ling Soo, presented a Chinese magical act, which any audience was calculated to remember long after the rice was dry.

His magic was impressive, yet often effected by the simplest means at his disposal. His contribution below is a classic example of the use of a Forcing Pack. I do not think I have ever come across a finer example of how to get the most out of such a simple expedient.

As an entertainer, Col Ling Soo was brilliant. His wit was tremendous, his repertoire of fun inexhaustible. He crammed a whole lifetime of humour into every performance.

Much liked and admired by all his friends, he was a genius in his style, and his genial bearing was always apparent on or off the stage.

A CHEEKY TRICK. No. 115

Col Ling Soo

Some years ago a party of Chinese engineers were dining at the Savoy Hotel and I was engaged to entertain them.

The following cheeky experiment completely baffled them, and left them guessing.

Effect. A card is selected and replaced in the pack which is shuffled. About ten cards are then placed face downwards on the table in a large circle.

A dinner knife is borrowed and one of the guests is invited to place it within the circle, and rotate it. When it stops, the card opposite the point of the knife is turned over, and proves to be the one chosen. (Fig. 137)

Fig. 137

Explanation. A Forcing Pack is used. In the circle nine are the same, say, 10 of clubs, and one red, say, the Ace of hearts. When the knife stops spinning turn over the card and show it is correct. In picking up the remainder see that the Ace of hearts is at the bottom and draw attention to it, remarking that the knife **might** have stopped at that one. Should the knife stop at the Ace of hearts, ask your helper to spin it again to prove it does not always stop at the same card.

Note. If using a Single-Forcing Pack have the indifferent card at the top. False-shuffle after the return of the chosen card, then deal your circle from the top. The odd card will thus be the first laid down.

With a Triple-Forcing Pack have both end cards of the middle run crimped, short, or otherwise easily located. Force from this section and have the card returned. Cut the pack at **one card from** the top crimp, false-shuffle if you wish, then deal out the circle.

DOUGLAS CRAGGS, O.B.E., M.I.M.C.

Hon. Vice-President of The Magic Circle

Regarded by many of the most experienced performers in the profession as the finest ventriloquist in Great Britain, Mr. Craggs is just as faultless with his magic.

In whatever he undertakes he shows a clear understanding of every angle of his subject, and applies himself with such vigour, and a calm thoroughness seldom encountered, that he achieves the utmost.

Strong in personality, popular with all, an organizer of the first calibre, kindly and helpful—a friend to treasure—he is also a most entertaining raconteur with a keen wit. These qualities singled him out particularly for the position of Secretary to The Magic Circle, a post he held for a number of years, until pressure of other work prevented his continuing in that strenuous task. His recent retirement from active performance is an undoubted loss to the whole entertainment world.

A Royal Command ventriloquist, he wrote *The A.B.C. of Ventriloquism*, a classic, and the greatest work on the subject today. His *Masterpieces of Magic* is another book, with a golden store of magic for the experienced performer.

Here is an appropriate example of his high standard of card magic.

'YOUR LUCKY NUMBER'. No. 116

Douglas Craggs

This is an entertaining card effect based on a four-ace routine shown me some years ago by my good friend, Wilfrid Jonson, and I believe Victor Farelli has since used the principle in two of his ingenious card problems. The routine and presentation I am about to describe is of special value in intimate conditions, where several members of the audience are known to each other. It has the advantage that it demands from the performer a minimum of skill while achieving a maximum of effect. For one member of the audience, at least, its impact is electrifying, provided its presentation has been well done.

Effect. The conjurer explains that there is a school of thought which today believes in the science of numbers, they call it Numerology because it is founded on a supposed law of periodicity which assumes that everyone has a fate, or fadic, number which recurs during his lifetime on important occasions. During this discourse the performer has been mixing a pack of cards, and he now turns to a spectator and asks him if he will take part in an experiment in this ancient branch of knowledge. The spectator assenting, the performer hands him the pack, and asks him to deal six cards face downwards in a row. When this has been done, the conjurer recovers the pack and asks his assistant to touch one of the cards in the row. When the spectator has indicated his choice the magician tells him to push the card to one side and reminds him that he had a free selection of six cards.

The performer then shuffles the remaining five cards into the pack and begins to deal the cards face downwards in a heap. After he has dealt one or two cards, he turns to the spectator and asks him to call 'stop' whenever he likes. As soon as the spectator calls 'stop', the performer starts dealing another heap and the procedure is repeated until there are three heaps on the table. The balance of the cards in the performer's hands are then placed aside, and he proceeds to take up the thread of his story.

He says that if there is anything in Numerology there must be some importance attaching to the first card chosen by the spectator. He then asks the spectator on what date he was born, i.e. the date of the month. Supposing the reply is 24th the conjurer explains that the figures must be added together to produce a single figure. Therefore the spectator's fadic number should be 6.

He remarks it would be a wonderful thing if the first card chosen by the spectator were a six. Turning over the card, it is seen to be, say, the 6 of hearts. The magician says: 'You remember you said stop as I was dealing each of these heaps.' He then turns the three heaps over one by one impressively and says quickly: 'Six, another Six; and the last Six in the pack. So it looks as if there is something in the science of numbers after all.' It is seen that the bottom card of each heap is, in fact, another six, and the spectators are left to draw their own conclusions which cannot fail to be favourable to the performer.

Method. The performer must first of all ascertain the birth-date of one of the company. He should do this secretly, if possible, as the effect is greatly heightened if it appears unlikely that the information is within the performer's knowledge. Whatever the date —in our example we have taken 24—it must be reduced to a single digit by addition. Where the performer knows the person's date of birth he refrains from asking the question openly until all his preparations have been completed. If he cannot ascertain this information secretly he must inquire openly of his assistant and then proceed; but quite obviously something of the miracle is lost in this case.

The only preparation necessary, and it is so simple that it can be done without notice under the eyes of the audience in glancing through the pack 'to see if there are the full fifty-two cards present', is to place four cards of like value under the top card of the pack. These four cards must correspond in value to the assistant's birth number.

While the performer makes his introductory announcement he gives the pack any form of false-shuffle he favours, which will leave the top stack of five cards undisturbed. The spectator is then allowed to deal the top six cards face downwards in a row, which places the four cards to be forced between the two indifferent cards at the ends of the row. It is long odds on the spectator choosing one of the four centre cards and if he does, all is well. If he does not, the conjurer says that for this experiment the cards must end up in heaps, so will the spectator push another card aside and push it underneath the first card. There is thus a force card at the bottom of this heap when it is ultimately turned over. If by some chance the spectator chooses another end card for his second choice, a third card must also be pushed under the heap.

The performer then gathers up the remaining cards and apparently shuffles them into the pack. What he really does is to bring one force card on top of the pack and the other two on the bottom, then false-shuffle.

As the performer deals from the top of the pack it does not matter when the spectator calls stop, since the bottom card of the heap is bound to be a force card. After the spectator has called 'stop' for the first time, the performer shuffles the pack to bring one force card to the top and retain the other force card at the bottom.

The rest of the working should now be clear. The last force card also is brought to the top of the pack and so becomes the bottom card of the last heap. If the performer can now innocently ask the assistant his date of birth for the first time, he is in a fair way to scoring a real bull's-eye. In any event, even if the conjurer has already asked the question at the beginning of the trick, he can now affect to have forgotten and say: 'What did you say was your date of birth?' before turning over the heaps.

I hope the reader who tries this excellent though simple trick will have as much fun with it as I have done. Patter, should, of course, take a pseudo-scientific form to enhance the effect when the 'four of a kind' are revealed. A little astrological jargon may not be out of place in some company, although it should not be overdone, as some people are very impressionable. On one occasion I performed the effect when I was staying at the Queen's Hotel, Brighton, with William H. Lane, the vaudeville magician, and selected a gentleman whose wife had previously supplied me with her husband's date of birth. He was so affected by the result that he went to Brighton Races the following day and backed all runners carrying his birth number. Fortunately the results were not unfavourable, but it was a lesson to me not to overdo the 'atmosphere'.

Note. The get the one force card to the top and the other two to the bottom when picking up the five, start at each end of the row simultaneously with the two hands, the pack in left hand.

Each card is taken separately, and added to the pack, the left-hand cards to the **bottom**. The right-hand to the **top**. Two are taken by right hand, three by the left.

After the first deal, bring the next force card to the top by giving the pack an overhand shuffle, drawing one card off the bottom with left fingers when making the first 'drop'.

For the last heap, overhand shuffle, bringing the final 6 to the top.

LIONEL KING

A professional performer of great ability, he specialized in card work. His forcing of cards by the customary procedure was delightful; a lesson in nerve and perfection. A most uncommon force was behind the back. In Mr. King's hands this was achieved with immaculate precision. His Nap hand was entrancing, while his charm and manner of presentation, stamped him as one of the foremost card conjurers of the century. You could not be in his company many minutes before becoming alive to his drive and personality; qualities which helped him to reach the heights.

He had that invaluable flair for making immediate friends with his audience. A seasoned entertainer, he had nearly a dozen Royal performances to his credit, in addition to showing before the Kings of Norway, Spain and Portugal. A showman of the highest order, he left some wonderful memories behind him.

THE MISSING CARDS. No. 117

Lionel King

Effect. One or more cards may be taken from the pack and, without any previous knowledge of the cards taken, they can be named by running through the remaining cards, which are placed in rows on the table.

Method. This can be made into a very useful drawing-room trick, which will leave your audience guessing.

Apart from the application of this effect as a trick it is extremely useful in checking a pack of cards, or in case a card is missing after giving a performance.

The method of checking the pack is as follows:

Place the cards out in rows of six, seven or eight cards to a row, faces uppermost, on the table. As the cards are put down, look for any two of **the same suit** whose combined values come to eleven (i.e. a 6 and a 5; 7 and 4; 8 and 3; 9 and 2; 10 and Ace). For the purposes of this effect, Jack, Queen, and King (always of the one suit) **together** equal eleven.

Each pair of 'eleven' is eliminated by being covered with a further card in the process of continuing to deal out the rows. Thus, if you see an Ace of hearts in the first row and, as you deal the second row, you lay the 10 of hearts, you **shortly** afterwards cover each of these with a card from the pack in the hand. Do **not** cover the cards immediately for, with a little practice, you can note two pairs of 'elevens' and cover three of these cards, leaving the fourth till you have dealt a few more cards, or until you spot another 'eleven' when you cover the remaining card from the previous sets and the newly exposed 'eleven'. This makes the effect absolutely bewildering, even to conjurers (who will be on the look-out for a mathematical formula).

Again, suppose you have two 'elevens' in sight, such as the 6 and 5 of one suit and the 8 and 3 of another. Only cover, say, the 6 of the one eleven and the 8 of the other. Then lay out a couple more cards, and go back and cover the 5. Lay one more, and go back and cover the 3.

When all the cards are laid out you will have some covered once, twice, three, or possibly four, times. Look at the first card in the top row and quickly look for its companion card. If you see it, then glance at the second card and seek the fellow for that one. When your search is unsuccessful, you know the card you cannot see has been retained.

Any number of cards up to four can be retained from the pack, provided they are of different suits.

Tell your audience that you must concentrate on all the cards.

Continue talking (you can do this, provided your patter has been rehearsed and does not need much thought), telling audience that the only way to remember the cards is by **not** talking—but you see to it that you **do**. This talking starts as soon as the first card is placed on the table, and continues until you can name the missing cards.

JACK KINSON

Jack Kinson's untimely death in 1955 robbed the world of magic of a delightful personality, a performance of unique originality, and a fine, friendly man. His trick with live white mice used to cause quite a stir. Fortunately his charming wife, Mary, still carries on the act in which she so ably assisted during his lifetime. Her neat exhibition of card fanning and flourishes is worthy of close attention and high praise.

The effect below is based on two existing subtleties, but it is the combination of these, and the presentation, which results in a new effect—points already brought out in the opening remarks of this book.

A MATTER OF TOUCH. No. 118

Jack Kinson

Briefly, the effect as seen by the audience is as follows: A card is chosen from the pack and placed face-up on the table. The conjurer's pocket is examined by a spectator, who shuffles the pack and places it therein, satisfying himself that the pocket contains nothing but the cards he has just shuffled.

Let us suppose that the chosen card is a king. The conjurer, after showing his hand to be empty, brings out of his pocket, one by one, the other three kings, thus proving the acuteness of his sense of touch.

Method. Before commencing the trick, three Kings are removed from the pack and placed in the top right-hand waistcoat pocket.

The faces should be towards the body. The other King is on top of the pack.

Ask the audience for any small number and explain that you will count down to that number in the pack and use the last card, thus ensuring that the card is chosen purely by chance. On being told the number, count down to it quickly, removing the cards one by one, from the top of the pack, immediately turning over the small packet of counted cards on to the table, and exposing the King. This was, of course, the top card, and the others were counted on to it. This sounds the last word in cheek, but I have never had it questioned.

Place the King on the table and ask someone to satisfy himself that your inside breast pocket is empty. Give him the pack to shuffle and ask him to place it inside.

Show your hand empty, and put it in your breast pocket, apparently trying to distinguish a King from the rest of the pack by touch. As you remove your hand from the pocket, take one of the Kings from the waistcoat pocket. This is easy and is perfectly deceptive, as, when the coat is close to the body, the two pocket openings almost coincide. Bring out the other two Kings with appropriate hesitation, and, if you wish, the pack can be searched for the Kings just removed, this proving that you really found and removed them by touch alone. (Fig. 138)

Fig. 138

VICTOR PEACOCK, M.I.M.C.

Hon. Vice-President of The Magic Circle

Over forty years' continuous membership of The Magic Circle is tribute to any person's lasting enthusiasm for magic. Add to this enthusiasm, capacity for achievement, plus new ideas, and performing ability—and you have a rare combination of desirable talents in the world of magic.

Mr. Peacock has a particular turn for thoughtful, or mental magic, to which field he has added many gems of his own.

Clean, convincing presentation make his magic thoroughly baffling to the layman—and often to the conjurer too!

In his long association with The Magic Circle he has done great work in the furtherance of magic, both behind the scenes and before the footlights.

He has expressed the conviction that the future of magic depends less on the invention of new effects than on the discovery of new ideas for presentation and on thorough production: a thought for all to ponder.

MARRIAGE BY PROXY. No. 119

Victor Peacock

Here is something which I have used occasionally. I have been told that it has been well received and caused not a little fun, but unfortunately, as I have never been present, I have never really known whether the results have been worth while or not; but I pass it on with pleasure.

I have used the idea when I have been asked to do a show at a dinner, or other intimate gathering where I have performed before, and where I am personally known, but cannot this time attend. The offer is made to do a trick by proxy. All that is necessary, is for the Chairman to nominate who is to be the conjurer from among those present. All the rest is provided—cards—patter— even a certain number of clichés beloved of conjurers.

The effect is of the spelling-bee type, and is more of a puzzle than a card trick: in fact it is really just the vehicle for the entertainment. Nevertheless, the combination is one which to my knowledge has not been published before, and may have a certain interest in its own right!

The following will therefore explain itself.

1. Covering Letter

In the covering letter to the Secretary or whoever it was who had asked me to perform, the idea is explained, but not the effect.

It is pointed out that three sealed envelopes are enclosed, which should be taken along to the show—one marked 'CONJURER', another 'ASSISTANT', and the third 'EMERGENCY'. (Fig. 138A.) The 'Emergency' envelope should be put in a pocket somewhere out of the way. It is really a duplicate of the 'Assistant' envelope, and is only to be used in case something goes wrong —the cards are dropped, or something

Fig. 138 A

like that; a safety-first precaution. All that is necessary is for the two envelopes to be passed to the Chairman, together with a typewritten sheet as follows:

2. Suggested Introduction by Chairman

(*Do not read aloud what is in brackets*)

'Ladies and Gentlemen,

'I had hoped at this stage to have been able to call on our old friend Victor Peacock, but unfortunately he cannot come. He wishes to be remembered to you and he suggests that he might be able to do a trick by proxy. I'll read what he says.

' "All you have to do is to select someone to be the conjurer, and someone to be his assistant. You will then hand to the conjurer the envelope marked 'CONJURER' and the other envelope will be handed to his assistant. [Show the two envelopes.]

' "So will you please select the conjurer. He should be a man of mature age, strict morals, a sense of humour, a good voice, and a certain low cunning."

'[Make selection now. There should be a certain amount of fun over the selection. Make the most of it! When the conjurer has been selected, continue.] "Now we must select his assistant. He should be sensible, do what he is told, and not argue about it. He should be 'easy'. Who do you think, Mr. Conjurer?"

'[After the selection has been made.] I now pass the arrangements over entirely to you, Mr. Conjurer. Here is your envelope. [Pass to him.] You will read what you have to do in the envelope.

[To assistant.] All **you** have to do is what you are told. Here is **your** envelope.

'All set? Right.'

3. Contents of Conjurer's Envelope

In order to make most economical use of available space the following is not spread out as it would be when typewritten. Double-spacing should be used and whenever there is to be a question, comment, or pause, **start a fresh line**—even if there are only one or two words in the line. It will make for clarity; it will make it easier to read, and the reader will not have to look for his place.

All directions should be bracketed, and indented—for still greater contrast. The matter is as follows:

[Read aloud what is not bracketed only. What is in brackets is for your own information—to help **you**.]

[MAKE THEM LAUGH RIGHT AWAY. LOOK AT AUDIENCE AND **shout**.] 'EXCUSE ME—Shan't keep you a moment.'

[KEEP SMILING AS THOUGH YOU ARE ENJOYING THE JOKE.]

[Now talk in the way you think Conjurers do.]

'I want you to notice that I have nothing up my sleeve—except my arm. [Pause.] And notice that my hands never for one moment leave the end of my arm! [Explaining.] I have to talk like that so that you will know I'm a real conjurer.

'[Turn to Assistant.] Have you examined your envelope, sir? No secret springs or trap doors? No rabbits? Now inside that envelope you will find some playing cards. These cards are arranged in a certain order. I want you to take them from the envelope [emphasize this] **without disturbing the order**. [Instructions must now be carried out exactly as requested by you.] Now hold the packet face downwards. [See that he does this.] Now do you know whether the top card is a black card or a red one? [Wait for reply.] No! Neither do I. Transfer that card from the top of the pack to the bottom. [When he has done that.] Ah—the next card I **do** know. It is a **red** card. Show it please; now place it **face upwards** on the table. [Wait for this to be done.]

'Again place the top card to the bottom of the pack. The next card will be a black one. Show it please. Now place it **face upwards** on the card already on the table. Now again. Top card to the bottom. The next card will be a red one. Show it. Add it to the others. Now keep on doing the same thing. Top card to bottom and the next card will be black. [See he shows it and adds it to the others.] Top card to bottom. Next card red. [Continue in this way until all cards are exhausted, having been shown alternately red and black.] [WHEN THIS HAS BEEN FINISHED, TAKE HANDKER-CHIEF FROM POCKET AND MOP BROW.] [IF YOU KNOW ASSISTANT WELL, MOP HIS BROW TOO.] Say: "Well, we're all right so far!" [To assistant again.] Now pick up the cards from the table **without disturbing the order**. [See that he does this.] Hold them face downwards. Good. Now I want you to SPELL them in this way. For each letter as you spell, you place one card from the top to the bottom of the pack, and the **next** card will be the card you spelt. Let's try. First the Ace.

'A—Top card to bottom; C—Next card to bottom; E—Next card underneath; spells ACE. Turn up the next card. [The fourth card.]

'There you are. ACE. Throw the Ace on the table. Now the same with TWO. T—top card to bottom; W—top to bottom; O—top to bottom—spells TWO! Show it. Throw it on the Ace. Now carry on. THREE. Can you spell? [See that he does it properly.] T-H-R-E-E spells THREE. [See that he adds this card to the others on the table.]

'[Repeat now with four, five, and so on, right up to Jack and Queen. The King will be left in his hand.]

'[Clap him! ! The audience will, too.]

'[Turn to audience and say.]

' "Now that problem is one that will while away many an hour. All you have to do is to rearrange the cards so that you can start all over again. You will find it a fascinating puzzle. Remember what you have to do. One underneath—red; one underneath—black—and so on. Then pick up the cards right away and spell out—putting one card to the bottom for each letter spelt. For a small consideration I will be pleased to let you know the order—when I know it myself." [Thank assistant; thank Chairman, and, after bowing, return to seat.]'

4. Contents of Assistant's Envelope

Order of cards in envelope is as follows:

Bottom card when cards are face upwards: Red 4, then Red 3, Black 9, Black 8, Black 2, Red 7, Red 10, Black Ace, Red Jack, Red Queen, Red 5, Black 6, and the last card a Black King.

STANLEY STEPHENSON, I.B.M.

More popularly known among his friends as 'Steve', he is one of the slickest card workers in the North of England, excelling in close-up work. I have seen very few performers make such frequent and excellent use of 'the slip'. His usual approach is to fan the cards as he unerringly forces a card which a moment earlier was at the top of the pack.

THE MAGIC MIRROR. No. 120

Stanley Stephenson

Effect. A spectator shuffles an ordinary pack of cards, which he fans. The performer selects a card, or the spectator can point to one for the conjurer to take. This card is placed in the magician's pocket without anybody seeing its face. A clear glass monocle or magnifying glass is then introduced and the assistant who fanned the cards is asked to look into the glass. Slowly the card appears to the spectator, who names what he sees. When the card is taken out of the pocket it is found to be the one just named. The performer can take out the card before the spectator names it—it can be done with a complete stranger, and using any pack.

INDEX CONCEALED BY THUMB

Method. The requirements are: one pack of cards, a small circular piece of clear glass and one index corner. Paste the index which we will presume is the 6 of diamonds, near the edge of the glass. (Fig. 139.) The 6 of diamonds from the pack is placed in the right-hand pocket of your coat. The procedure will now be evident.

Fig. 139

It doesn't matter what card you take from the fan, for you simply put this in the pocket, along with the previously stolen card, taking care, of course, that you know which is which. You then produce your 'magic mirror', concealing the stuck-on index with the thumb. Ask your assistant to concentrate on the glass and **read what he sees**. Naturally he can see nothing. Suggest that he is not concentrating sufficiently, 'or perhaps the materialization has not yet become apparent'. You then hold the glass to the mouth, breathe on it, then rub it on the sleeve, and as you hold it for the assistant to look once more, move the thumb back, exposing the index through the glass (but allowing only your assistant to see) and again ask him to read what he sees. The answer, of course, will be 'the 6 of diamonds'; you remove the secreted card from the pocket and the miracle is complete.

Note. If the glass is held between the thumb and first finger, and the index stuck, by means of wax, to the tip of the forefinger, the materializing effect is easily obtained by resting the forefinger behind the middle of the glass on the second showing. Also, when you breathe on the glass, instead of rubbing it immediately afterwards, if you hold it up for the spectator to have another look, the card will appear as though through a mist (the condensation of the breath on the glass).

Another idea would be to have the index gripped in the crook of the thumb and then, at the appropriate moment, slip the first fingertip down on to the back of the index and proceed as just suggested. In this last method the glass can be held by the opposite edges, between the second finger and thumb. As soon as the card has been named, rub the glass on the sleeve, at the same time bending the first fingertip into the crook of the thumb, and leaving the index there. (Back of index should be waxed, or fingertip damped.)

The most suitable index for these latter versions is one taken from the miniature cards sold in most toyshops. If the index is not attached to the glass you have the added advantage that you can pass it for examination at the close of the experiment.

EDWARD VICTOR, M.I.M.C.

Hon. Vice-President of The Magic Circle

A sleight-of-hand performer, *par excellence*, Mr. Victor had much professional experience yet, like most magicians, was always ready to talk, and show, more magic.

Author of three fine works, *Magic of the Hands*, *More Magic of the Hands* and *Further Magic of the Hands*, in each of which he revealed some original masterpieces, he was also constantly advancing sleights to that nearer perfection which is always the dream of the sleight-of-hand worker.

In addition, an expert, without rival, in that too-little-seen entertainment, 'Hand-shadows', Mr. Victor's performance in either magic or shadows was polished and refined—a true delight to witness, as those who witnessed his fine TV performances will readily agree.

Apart from his undoubted skill, he was also a great companion, held in the highest esteem by all who knew him well.

THE 'DO-IT-YOURSELF' CARD TRICK. No. 121

Edward Victor

I have been asked to contribute an easy and non-sleight-of-hand card trick to this book.

Perhaps I cannot do better than describe the first one I learned, giving it a twist or two of my own. The effect is as follows: A pack of cards is on the table and the performer states that he will perform a card trick without once handling the cards himself.

An assistant from the audience is asked to cut the pack (which lies face downwards) into three heaps and to then remove a card from the inside of any heap and to note and remember its name and value. He is then told to replace his card on the top of any one of the three heaps, and finally to reassemble the pack.

The cards are now cut several times by the assistant and he is then asked to deal the cards from the pack faces upwards on to the table.

The performer suddenly cries 'stop' and it is seen to be the selected card.

The secret is simplicity itself but it should be remembered that in any trick it is not so much WHAT you do as the WAY you do it; good presentation is always essential.

During the performance of a few card tricks the pack is left face downwards on the table, the performer having previously secretly noted and memorized the bottom card. He then states that he will perform a card trick without once handling the pack himself, and calls for any assistant from the audience.

The helper is told to cut the pack into three heaps and to select any card from any heap.

As the cards are cut the performer must note under which heap is the bottom card he has previously memorized.

The selected card is noted by the assistant and he is then told to place it face downwards on the top of any heap.

The three heaps must now be reassembled as follows (the instructions being given by the performer to the assistant).

1. Should the chosen card be placed on the heap containing the memorized card at the bottom, the performer says: 'Maybe you would like to cut that heap once yourself and lose your card in the middle.'

This cut brings the memorized card above the one selected.

2. Should the chosen card be placed on either of the other two heaps the performer would say: 'Now place this heap [indicating with his finger the heap containing the memorized card at the bottom] on top of the heap where you placed your card; pick up the remaining heap and place it as you wish either at the top or the bottom of the pack.'

This move will still bring the memorized card above the one selected.

It only remains now to have the pack cut once or twice by anyone and to ask the assistant to deal the cards faces upwards from the top of the pack onto the table.

As soon as the performer spots his memorized card he is ready to cry 'stop' as soon as the next card is dealt.

As I have stated above, 'it isn't so much WHAT you do as the WAY you do it'.

PETER WARLOCK, M.I.M.C.

Hon. Vice-President of the Magic Circle

Has one of the most fertile and inventive brains in the world of magic today.

A constantly increasing number of highly ingenious effects stand to Mr. Warlock's credit. He is a magician who will leave a lasting mark in the art to which he has so helpfully applied himself.

Apart from the numerous tricks of his which have been marketed, he is the author of a number of first-class books on conjuring, in addition to being the editor of the *Pentagram*, a very prominent monthly periodical on magic.

THE COUNT OF CALIGULA. No. 122

Peter Warlock

Effect. The operator requests a member of his audience to think of a number between seven and seventeen—as seven is the mystic number. Another spectator is requested to draw a card from a pack but **not look at its face**. This card is now sandwiched between two other cards and an elastic band placed round all three; the latter are now placed in a prominent position. The operator **turns his back** and asks the person who thought of the number, to take the pack and count out three heaps of cards **each containing the thought-of number**. In counting, he is requested to do it as silently as possible so that, by hearing, the operator can obtain no clue.

'Tell me when you have finished,' says the operator. The spectator does so. 'Now,' says the operator, 'I want you to follow my instructions. First of all, take five cards from the right-hand heap and place them on the centre heap.' This being done, the operator continues. 'Now from the **left-hand** heap take **three** cards and place them on the centre heap. . . . Will you now count the left-hand heap? From the centre heap remove a similar number of cards.

Now please place the remaining cards of the centre heap in your pocket. When you have done this I will turn round.'

The operator turns round, and recapitulates what has happened . . . free choice of number . . . free choice of card. He takes the three elastic-encircled cards and, removing the elastic band, shows the centre card for the first time. It is a Jack. 'Ladies and Gentlemen,' says the operator. 'Numerically a Jack equals eleven. Would you mind [to the spectator who placed the cards in his pocket] counting your cards.' The spectator removes them, counts them. There are . . . eleven.

This effect may, with its counting, seem rather complicated, but in actual practice it is quite straightforward. The calculation part is very old but also very neglected. It will be found in *More Magic*, but Hoffman could have incorporated a wrinkle which I have introduced and which helps to throw any astute person off the scent.

There are two actual phases to the effect. The first is the method whereby the operator finds out the denomination of the chosen card. To the expert there are many ways, but as this is for a book where skill is nullified I have had to make use of a special method.

The second phase is the calculation whereby the centre heap finally contains the number of cards which equal the numerical value of the chosen card.

Preparation. One card of the pack has an oval portion cut out of that part normally occupied by the index pip and number (Fig.

140.) Consequently, any card placed face-down directly above it, can be identified instantly. This card is placed at the bottom of the pack. With an elastic band in his pocket the operator is ready for the presentation.

The operator talks of mathematical laws and how, under certain conditions, certain effects can be obtained. He offers to demonstrate with a pack of cards. As already outlined, spectator A is asked to think of a number

Fig. 140

between seven and seventeen. The operator now holds the pack up, with the faces showing to the audience. (Care, of course, is taken to cover the cut-out portion of the bottom card.) Turning the cards down, another member of the audience is asked to withdraw a card, but not to look at its face. Withdrawing the two bottom cards of the pack with his left-hand fingers (this is easily accomplished, as the tip of the left-hand second finger presses through the cut-out, on to the card second from the bottom), the right hand gives the rest of the pack to spectator A. The right hand now fans the two cards in the left hand, the lower left-hand corner of top card (together with the left thumb) covering the cut-out. Spectator B is asked to push his card in between these two. Squaring the cards the right hand dips into the pocket, removes the elastic band, and places it round the three cards. From the audience's point of view the selected card is completely boxed in.

In placing the cards in a prominent position it is the easiest thing in the world for the operator to glimpse the index of the selected card through the oval cut-out. He thus knows the number that must be arrived at in the centre heap.

The operator turns his back to the table, and spectator A is asked to count three heaps of cards on to the table. The procedure from this point is purely mathematical, but to make it impressive the operator must not give the idea it is easy. Five cards are removed from the right-hand heap to the centre and three from the left hand to the centre. The left-hand heap is counted, and a similar number removed from the centre heap. If the reader likes to do this with cards in his hands he will find that whatever the number of cards in the heaps to start with, the number now in the centre will be eleven. Hoffman said remove three from each of the side heaps, and then, from the centre heap, take the same number as that in the left-hand heap. This left nine cards in the centre heap.

With the knowledge of the chosen card it is for the operator to adjust the counting according to the particular value before the cards are placed in spectator A's pocket. For example, if the chosen card is a Queen, six cards would be directed from the right-hand heap. In the case of a King, seven, and so on. With the desired

254 CONTRIBUTIONS BY MASTER MAGICIANS

number in the centre heap the spectator is requested to pick it up and place it in his pocket.

The operator now turns round and picks up the packet of cards. Very deliberately he removes the elastic band. He fans the three cards face-down and then removing the centre and selected card shows its face for the first time. Spectator A is asked to remove the heap of cards from his pocket and count them. Their number agrees with the value of the card.

CHAPTER 9

THE LAST WORD

♥ ♣ ♦ ♠ ♥ ♣ ♦ ♠ ♥ ♣ ♦ ♠ ♥ ♣ ♦ ♠ ♥ ♣ ♦ ♠

This work does not purport to be exhaustive in non-sleight-of-hand card magic (the *Encyclopaedia of Card Tricks*, referred to later, makes this unnecessary). My object has been, in addition to setting the beginner on the right road—as already indicated—to offer as diverse a collection of quality material as possible. When the reader finds one particular principle appeals to him, the ideas put forward here will give him ample scope for originating other effects based on this same principle. This development will, of course, only come with the acquisition of experience and knowledge.

Throughout, I have given credit to the originators of the effects, where I have succeeded in tracing them. In a number of cases I have altered the original ideas somewhat to please my own taste, but have still given credit to the minds that supplied the foundation, for, to such, greater credit is due. I wish I were able to thank all concerned personally, but in the absence of such a possibility I record my sincere thanks here. To any others whose names have been omitted, my truest apologies are tendered for the omission, occasioned through inability to link the originators with the effect.

To the contributors of Chapter 8 especial thanks are due. Their willing co-operation, together with the quality of the material supplied, indeed makes their chapter conspicuous.

If it is desired to proceed further with card tricks of the non-sleight-of-hand type I cannot do better than recommend *The Encyclopaedia of Card Tricks*, edited by Jean Hugard and John J. Crimmins, Jr. and published by Faber & Faber at 30s. net (Faber Paper Covered Editions 13s. 6d. net). It is a truly wonderful book of over 400 pages and with nearly 650 tricks and now includes *Nikola's Card System* in full. Originally it was put out by Glenn Gravatt, under the title of *The Encyclopaedia of Self-working Card Tricks*. It was an instant success.

A number of the effects in this book of mine have been founded on material from Glenn Gravatt's great work, although I have, in most instances, put in certain twists of my own.

I can recommend only one substantial book of non-sleight-of-hand card magic, in the American field. To the beginner at least, the prices of most of the books would seem somewhat exorbitant and often the quality of the material does not, judged by English standards, justify the cost. The one exception is:

Effective Card Magic by Bill Simon. Almost all non-sleight-of-hand card effects, containing many good originalities, *plus* a chapter on new, original sleights. 181 pp., L. Tannen, $6.50.

To those interested in good books of sleight-of-hand with cards, or Card Fanning, and Card Flourishes, the following are all well recommended. Those priced in dollars are published in America, but are obtainable from the bigger magical dealers in Britain, at approximately the current rate of exchange. Prices quoted in sterling are for works published in England.

Card Mastery, by Michael MacDougall. Deals not so much with actual tricks as with Stacking, Bottom-stealing, Gambling Exposures, new Sleights; and includes Erdnase's *Expert at the Card Table*. 286 pp., Circle Magic Shop, $2.50.

Card Fantasies, by E. G. Love. Not magical effects, but for those interested in Card Flourishes—Fans, Double-Fans, Spectacular Cuts and Shuffles—this is a very informative and well-illustrated 50-page book. L. Davenport & Co., 15s.

The Royal Road to Card Magic, by Jean Hugard and F. Braue. Excellent for the beginner in sleights. Painstakingly detailed. 302 pp., Faber & Faber, 18s.

Deck-Sterity, by Harry Lorayne. Contains a host of excellent card mysteries—and a few telling effects without cards. Mostly original, and mainly involving sleights, it is a very useful book for the professional and the eager magician. 154 pp., Tannen, $7.50.

The Cardician, by Ed Marlo. Advanced sleights, and some appropriate effects. 190 pp., $7.50.

Cy Endfield's Entertaining Card Magic, by Lewis Ganson. Good sleights and effects. In three small volumes, each about 60 pp., distributed by L. Davenport & Co., each 25s.

202 Methods of Forcing, by Theo Annemann, as its title tells us, is not a collection of magical effects, but rather a great variety of ingenious dodges and methods for forcing a card or cards. Written by the late Theo Annemann it is not, of course, a new work, but Annemann had one of the most inventive minds ever applied to magic. This is the one *small* book I have recommended in this list. 48 pp., L. Davenport & Co., 5s.

Expert Card Technique, by Jean Hugard and F. Braue. 474 pp., Faber & Faber, 42s.

Card Manipulations, by Jean Hugard, published in four volumes, L. Davenport & Co., 5s. 6d. each.

More Card Manipulations, by Jean Hugard, published in four volumes, L. Davenport & Co., 5s. 6d. each.

Miracles of Card Magic by Annemann, edited by John J. Crimmins, Jr. and George Armstrong. Nothing by Annemann should be by-passed. 158 pp., Faber & Faber, 21s.

A most excellent method of improving one's knowledge and views on conjuring is to see the actual performances of the men who earn their living by 'doing tricks'. The style, patter, speed, misdirection, applause—these are just a few of the important points to note and, having noted, ponder.

As interest grows in the doing of magic, many are anxious to meet other conjurers—to join a Magical Society. Magical societies do not accept beginners for membership, as these societies are essentially for magicians, and it is customary not to accept a new member unless at least two established members can vouch for the sincere interest and professional conduct of the applicant. This is a wise and very necessary procedure, for magical secrets are not to be divulged to anyone but a fellow-magician: this is a strictly observed rule. Anyone who breaks it is immediately out of favour with other magicians, and loses caste. There is, on the other hand, a great *camaraderie* among conjurers. It is a natural freemasonry, the endless scope of the subject also making it a source of eternal interest and pleasure to its real adherents. The premier Society of Conjurers in England is The Magic Circle. With headquarters in London, its membership extends throughout the world, embracing practically every nationality. The Inner Magic Circle is, as its name implies, the Inner Sanctum of The Magic Circle.

The International Brotherhood of Magicians, founded in the U.S.A., where it flourishes with undiminished vigour, has a large following in its branch in this country. Various other societies are functioning, some with impressive membership, others with but a score or so on their books. Finally, it should be borne in mind that an applicant who is unknown to anyone in a Society is usually requested to perform before the Society's committee before the question of his inclusion can be settled.

Throughout this book (with the exception of Chapter 8, where the titles were given by the contributors) I have endeavoured to couple the *name* of the trick with the *method* employed (for example, 'Drawn from the Spread', No. 94). This, I feel, makes it easier for the reader when he wishes to refer to some particular effect in the book.

My very last comments are both a message, and an appeal.

Please—and I repeat, *please*—do *not*, at *any time*, tell, or show, *any* person, unless an *established* magician, the working of *any* trick.

In this book are some very fine, and so far well-guarded, secrets. The purchase of the book does not give anyone the right to expose any part of the contents. Quite a few magicians have complained to me (and some in strong terms) that I have given too much, and of too high a quality, in this book, for the price charged. My reply has been simply and frankly that I wanted to supply *good* magic, *easy* to do, at an *encouraging price*. I want to see *more*, and *better*, magicians. If I have succeeded in stimulating beginners to further interest, I am happy to do this, and I feel the true interests of magic are well served in this way.

It is natural, and all too easy, to wish to impress others with one's own knowledge. But I can firmly promise you—and I mean *promise*—that if, after you have done a 'trick', you satisfy the curious inquirer who asks: 'How's it done?' he, and all those with him, will think *far less of your abilities than they did before*. This may seem obvious as you read, but do remember that it is an invariable rule. For it is a very definite fact that a puzzled spectator *must* hold you in *some* esteem: a disillusioned person has a sense of 'let-down' at being so easily fooled, once the secret is explained. Instead of proving yourself clever, you have proved your audience simple . . . and no one likes to be labelled simple, gullible. So keep your secrets intact.

Good luck, and may you enjoy Good Magic, always.

INDEX

♥ ♣ ♦ ♠ ♥ ♣ ♦ ♠ ♥ ♣ ♦ ♠ ♥ ♣ ♦ ♠ ♥ ♣ ♦ ♠

Chapter 1. Conjurers' Terms and Artifices

Chapter 2. Beginners' Tricks

Chapter 3. Impromptu Mysteries

Chapter 6. Pre-arrangement

Chapter 7. Identity Pack

Chapter 8. Contributions by Master Magicians

Chapter 9. The Last Word: with Bibliography and General Recommendations